MW00940660

Tide
of
Change

Hossca Harrison

Order this book online at www.trafford.com/06-2968
or email orders@trafford.com

Most Trafford titles are also available at major online book retailers.

© Copyright 2007 Hossca Harrison.
All rights reserved. No part of this publication may be reproduced, stored in a retrieval system, or transmitted, in any form or by any means, electronic, mechanical, photocopying, recording, or otherwise, without the written prior permission of the author.

United States Copyright Office TX 6-564-492

Note for Librarians: A cataloguing record for this book is available from Library and Archives Canada at www.collectionscanada.ca/amicus/index-e.html

Printed in Victoria, BC, Canada.

ISBN: 978-1-4251-1209-7

We at Trafford believe that it is the responsibility of us all, as both individuals and corporations, to make choices that are environmentally and socially sound. You, in turn, are supporting this responsible conduct each time you purchase a Trafford book, or make use of our publishing services. To find out how you are helping, please visit www.trafford.com/responsiblepublishing.html

Our mission is to efficiently provide the world's finest, most comprehensive book publishing service, enabling every author to experience success. To find out how to publish your book, your way, and have it available worldwide, visit us online at www.trafford.com/10510

www.trafford.com

North America & international
toll-free: 1 888 232 4444 (USA & Canada)
phone: 250 383 6864 • fax: 250 383 6804
email: info@trafford.com

The United Kingdom & Europe
phone: +44 (0)1865 722 113 • local rate: 0845 230 9601
facsimile: +44 (0)1865 722 868 • email: info.uk@trafford.com

10 9 8 7 6 5

Front Cover

The picture on the front cover of this book was taken by Daryl Harrison, 24 hours prior to being pulled under the water by a rip tide where the rainbow ends.

******

Some names in this book have been changed to protect their privacy.

Tide of Change
is
Dedicated To

Rebecca Harrison, the most powerful woman in my life. For 35 years, she has stood beside me facing each and every challenge that life has given us. Without her this story would not have been experienced, and this book would not have been written.

PREFACE
By
Tina Herring

It was a great pleasure to edit this book for my brother. I enjoyed reading and rereading each and every chapter. When I told Hossca that I would edit his autobiography, I had no idea the profound impact that it would have on me as a person, and my relationship with Hossca and his wife Rebecca. As a child, I remember hearing most of these stories, but I could not truly comprehend the significance of the events. Due to the 22- year gap in our ages, I did not know my brother like most siblings who have the benefit of growing up together. It has only been in the last few years that I truly got to know my brother as a friend. However, this past year, after working on his life story I feel closer to Hossca than I ever have in the past 34 years we've been in each other's lives.

I vividly remember the day that my brother made the transition from Daryl to Hossca. I was ten at the time. My parents, with a look of deep sadness and concern, took me aside and told me that Daryl had an accident while on vacation in Hawaii. I was devastated and started screaming and crying before they even finished telling me what had happened. A few weeks later we went to visit Daryl and Wanda at their house in Olympia. I was warned that Daryl would not remember me. I walked into his bedroom following closely behind my parents. I saw him laying in the middle of his king size bed looking dazed. My parents introduced me as his sister. Looking at him, even in the condition that he was in, I knew everything would be all right. And it was.

When I realized the content of the book, I became worried about editing this story for publication. I am protective of my brother and his privacy.

Over the years, I've seen him slandered by the media and idolized by people. I didn't want to give the world another reason to judge or slander him or even idolize him. But to not share this story would be tragic. There is so much to learn from the events of my brother's life. This book is more than an autobiography of a medium, it is a book about the potential we all have to create joy and happiness and to find our inner strength and our God essence. This story reminds us that we are a part of something much greater, much more powerful than our human minds are capable of comprehending.

ACKNOWLEDGEMENTS

I have been blessed with great teachers in this life. Teachers come in many different relationships all of the heart, all with a purpose of love.

Rebecca, my wife of 35 years, has been my constant support, my constant inspiration, my grounding rod to assist me in remaining focused while I walk in two different worlds.

My children, Jason Harrison and Tami Urbanek, are two of my teachers. We have a bond that transcends time and space. It is with their assistance and persistence that helped this book become a reality.

My sister, Tina Herring has offered immense assistance with the editing of this book. Her insight into presenting my history in a concise orderly fashion was invaluable.

Without her assistance, this manuscript would still be sitting on a shelf gathering dust.

My very dear, long time friend of 40 plus years, Franklin Slavensky, has made this book possible. Franklin has always been there with his unconditional love and support. It is with Franklin's love and support we were able to continue our work with the Universal Education Foundation, and it is with his love and support this book has made it into print. Franklin gives true meaning to the phrase from Jonah. A friend of the heart will never depart.

Tom and Bonnie Harrison, the parents of Daryl, have always shown their support even when they did not know what they were supporting. Their love has always been there, their love has always been felt and accepted.

CONTENTS

Introduction

This book is not about phenomena, although phenomena are part of the story. This book tells about an emotional journey between life and death that begins in Central America and ends in England. It encompasses my journey through two near-death experiences over an eleven-year period. This book is not about death, although death is part of the story. Nor is this book about healing, although healing is a part of the story.

My life may seem full of pain and suffering. Quite the contrary, it has been filled with experiences beyond the conscious conception of many. I have had the opportunity to experience life beyond the dreams many people hold. My life's story is not for the casual reader. This story is for those who know there is much more to life than meets the eye. My journey involves experiencing life beyond traditional beliefs — beyond traditional ways of thinking, creating, and healing.

If someone had come to me in December of 1981, and forewarned me that before December ended, my life would end and begin again, that I would give up everything I thought to be true, including my business, my home, and my way of life, I would not have believed it possible. I could not believe it. My mind was very much entrenched in the illusions we make for ourselves in this reality. My mind could not have dealt with the future I was about to embark upon. Thankfully, no one told me what my future held. If someone had and I had believed it, I would have hidden under the biggest rock I could find.

Before December 1981, I was a contractor, successfully building apartment complexes and developing land. I had just moved into my dream home on the shore of Long Lake outside Olympia, Washington. Months earlier, I had bought a new Lincoln Mark IV. My wife and children loved being on the lake and living the easy life. The bankers in town knew me by name and often took me to lunch. I had friends who respected the work I did. My plan was to retire by the age of forty. This was due more to necessity than desire. At twenty-four, I had injured my spine, and since that time I had lived in constant pain.

During my early twenties, I drove a truck to deliver stainless steel tanks filled with a resin for softening water. One day part of the truck bed broke, sending a 170-pound tank on top of me. After nine months of examinations, the doctors determined that I had ruptured two discs in my lower back. The doctor performed surgery, but the damage was so extensive that even after surgery I was not able to walk for months.

It wasn't until a year later that the doctor who preformed the surgery took me aside and told me they had removed a large tumor surrounding my spine as well as the two ruptured disks. He had not spoken of the tumor before because he was concerned the State Compensation Insurance would not pay for the surgery to remove the tumor. He told me only when he was preparing to release me as a patient; he knew the difficulties that lay ahead for me. At the very least, I would need a walker and braces to get around.

Each subsequent year demanded that I take more and more pain medication to get through the day. I thought if I could retire by forty, I could take it easy and spend my days fishing from the pier I was planning to build in my backyard. I thought of different ways I could invest my money and take care of my family and me for the rest of my life.

What is often said about the best-laid plans couldn't be truer. My plans to spend endless days fishing never materialized. I did not retire at forty; instead, I was led on a new journey with new pathways. I was propelled into a field where retirement does not exist. However, through this field I traveled the globe, met thousands of people, and made friends from all walks of life.

One of the many things I have learned from my experiences since December of 1981, is that we are all guided, but we do not always allow ourselves to see or hear the guidance. We do not always allow ourselves to trust what is happening to us. We do not always understand why we are drawn to do some of the things we do. I have learned one thing well: Whatever you do, do it in the Light, and the Light will be your guiding pathway.

Chapter 1
Jungle Fever

My best friend Don, also my realtor and business partner, handled the apartment complexes I was building. He was always looking for ways to invest our money. One day in September 1981, he called and his voice was filled with excitement. "I know where we can invest our money, Daryl. It will blow your mind. Let's talk about it at lunch."

We met that Thursday at the Governor's House Restaurant in downtown Olympia. We always enjoyed our time there, often running into people with whom we had conducted business or were going to at some point in the future. Don, a young energetic man with deep blue eyes and dark hair, was about to propose an adventure I would later wish to forget.

"You will never guess who I had breakfast with this morning!" He exclaimed as soon as I sat down. "This guy is a friend of the President of Costa Rica. He has a lot of contacts for us to invest our money."

"Invest our money where?" I asked.

"In the hard wood forest of southwestern Costa Rica," he answered with a smile. "We can buy this forest and ship the hard woods back to the United States. He is going to handle all of the details and permits for us. He is even going to arrange our flight and travel arrangements in Costa Rica. In fact, Daryl, why don't we invite my friend Rick and your brother Tim to join us on this investment? We can each spend three months out of the year taking care of business down there."

I was always ready for an adventure, and Don had never led me wrong when it came to making money. Within a matter of days, Don, Tim, and I were flying off to Costa Rica. Rick stayed behind to take care of his new pizza restaurant he had recently opened on September 7.

We arrived in San Jose, Costa Rica September 9. We were met at the airport, quickly taken through customs, and driven to our hotel in down town San Jose. The next morning, we boarded a small chartered plane that would take us to a remote village next to the Panamanian border on the Pacific coast.

When we arrived, my first glance at the Central American village took me by surprise. Scattered along the shore of the bay were rough wooden shacks with slanted roofs made of rusted metal. As we entered the village, we got a closer look at the makeshift walls of these buildings and their dirt floors. The walls were made of old wooden planks. Smaller planks were placed around small square openings to create spaces for windows. There were no screens or glass for the windows and no wood for the doors. The village reeked of poverty and despair. I was beginning to feel uncomfortable about our prospects but was hesitant to say anything, perhaps hoping that not all was what it seemed on the surface and the situation would improve.

We decided the bay looked inviting, so we went out for a swim. We soon found ourselves immersed in raw sewage. The village evidently dumped their sewage into the bay. I should have recognized this situation as a sign of things to come. But instead, we cleaned up and got ready to travel again.

"So where is this place?" I asked Don.

"We need to take a couple of small boats up the coast. Then we follow a river inland deep into the jungle. We will be spending the night at a small guest house on the property," he explained.

We loaded our suitcases into the two small motorboats and began our adventure. I climbed into the boat with the driver, a young muscular man I believed to be of Guayami Indian heritage whose home was the rain forest. Don and Tim climbed into the larger boat whose driver was the owner of the property.

As we started I asked my driver who knew very little English, "How long will it take to arrive at the property?"

He held up four fingers and said, "Hours."

Instantly my heart sank. Four hours in a small boat? I had no idea it would take that long. My back was killing me, and I was not feeling well. Already, I wanted to be back on my deck at home enjoying the secluded waters of Long Lake.

About an hour into the trip it started to rain, and not just rain but a constant downpour. We had not brought any rain gear; therefore, we soon became soaked. Everything got drenched, including the suitcases. As the waves in the ocean grew stronger, my stomach became queasy. I had taken some pain pills just before we left, which always upset my stomach; now the waves were making the boat rock in every direction, adding to my discomfort

An hour and a half later, the rain stopped. The sun came out, which made the heat and humidity almost unbearable. We had reached the mouth of the river and now began our journey through the jungle.

Another hour passed while we slowly cruised up the river. Snakes large and small were hanging from the vine-covered trees growing out of the mud-caked banks of the river. A six-foot gray snake was swimming in the water next to our small boat. They were everywhere, some black and yellow with bright bands of red, some with brown.

I could not envision myself spending three months a year in this jungle with raw sewage, multicolored snakes, and drenching rain. Just as I was thinking how much I didn't want to be here, the motor on the boat quit. The young Indian man jumped into the river. He motioned for me to jump out and help him pull the boat. Even if I had wanted to, I could not physically get out of the boat and into the water. I was not able to pull anything, especially while walking through the swift river currents. My back pain was too intense.

The Indian kept motioning me to jump into the river. I just sat there saying, "No, no, no. I can't get out of this boat." Then he started pulling on my arm, trying to get me into the water. "No!" I said. "You pull the boat."

With an expression on his face that transcended our language barrier, he gave up and started pulling the boat up river by a rope attached to the bow. I hoped a snake didn't pull him under. I imagined being stranded here for days. The driver struggled with the weight of the boat, mustering all his strength. I wondered how long it would take to pull the boat to our destination since I couldn't help in any way. As we entered deeper into the jungle, vegetation began filtering out the daylight. The sounds of the jungle became louder.

Don and Tim didn't realize our motor had quit; they continued up the river and arrived three hours ahead of us. We arrived as the sun was setting. The air was so thick with bugs it was hard to breathe without swallowing a few of them.

We met the owners of the property and asked to go with them to the main building for dinner. It was a one-room shack that had a few wooden chairs and a rustic stove made of concrete blocks in the corner. There did not appear to be any electricity or plumbing on the property. We ate a dinner made of something that was not of any culinary knowledge I had, but it looked like stew. I never did learn what kind of "meat" it was.

Now we were to be introduced to the Indian workers who came with the property. As we entered into the next building, I noticed a young man sitting in the corner. He was the Indian who had pulled our boat. It was not a warm greeting. Since we did not speak Spanish and they knew very little English, our meeting was quite short.

We were then taken to our sleeping quarters. The small "guesthouse" was about 15' by 15', with no glass or screens in the window openings. The only furniture I noticed looked like old rusted army bunk beds. Someone had placed a thin sheet of cardboard on the springs to make them more comfortable for our sleeping pleasure after a very long, exhausting day. There were no mattresses. There were no sheets. I noticed one small, soiled blanket on my cot. It was more the size of a scarf than a blanket. No wonder they wanted to sell this place.

As the evening wore on, I became more and more ill. I was very tired but somehow fell into a deep sleep, only to be awakened a few hours later by the jabbing pain in my back. As I tried to sit up, I felt my left arm stinging. I reached with my right hand to rub my arm and found it covered in blood. Insects covered my arm, sucking every ounce of blood they could bring to the surface. The scrap of a blanket offered no protection.

I sat up on the side of the bed and realized how much pain I was in. I could feel a fever raging, and I began shaking. I leaned over and pushed on Don's shoulder to awaken him.

"What is it?"

"I think I'm dying," I told him.

"We'll talk about it in the morning. Go back to sleep."

When the sun came up, I could see my arm was covered with dried blood and swollen from hundreds of bites. My back was still racked with pain, and my body ached with fever. I wondered how Don and Tim could have slept through the night.

"Damn, look at that arm!" shouted Don. "You really were dying last night."

"I am not into this," I said. "Let's just go back home."

Thankfully, they were not impressed with the land either.

"We'll take a flight back to San Jose and get you to a doctor. Maybe there's another piece of land we can look at while we are in Costa Rica." Don never was one to miss an opportunity.

"Whatever. Let's just get the hell out of here!" I said. For the first time I began to doubt Don's wisdom.

Someone had fixed the small motorboat, and we were able to take both boats back to the village. Not surprisingly, I had a new driver.

Four hours later, we arrived at the airfield just outside the small village. I could hardly walk, and now I had a small four-seater plane to look forward to with my back stiff and swollen. I kept assuring myself that when I could get to a doctor, I would feel better. I repeated this over and over.

We had been flying for about an hour when we encountered a severe thunderstorm. The sky turned black and lightning striking from cloud to cloud. The plane started diving down, pulling up, and tilting left and right.

I held on to the seat with all of my strength.

I glanced at the pilot and saw him cross himself. I could see the look of fear on his face. I turned around to look at Don and Tim in the back seat. They were watching the pilot, and their faces were filled with fear. I wondered how many pain pills I had left. Without even counting them, I took some more. Eventually, the clouds parted and we landed a short time later in San Jose. As soon as the plane stopped, I crawled out and laid flat on the ground, my arms and legs spread out. "Don't touch me," I said. "Don't talk to me. I just want to lay here on ground for awhile."

Don kneeled beside me, resting his hand on my shoulder. "Come on, let's get a taxi and get you to a doctor."

When the taxi arrived, I pulled myself up and saw a small four-door car. "You want me to fit into this?"

"Sit in the front seat. Tim and I will sit in the back."

My back was still throbbing with pain as I slowly climbed into the car.

"Doctor! Doctor! Go to Doctor!" Don shouted to the driver as he leaned over the front seat and grabbed my arm. "See arm? Doctor, Doctor!" By this time, my arm looked like it was full of buckshot.

"Si," said the taxi driver. "Doctor."

The taxi took off, not slowing down for anything. When we approached a stop sign, the driver blew his horn and continued driving. Again, I wondered how many pain pills I had left.

Twenty minutes later, we drove up to a building. Everything seemed a blur because I had been taking double doses of pain pills. The taxi driver pointed to the building saying, "Doctor inside. See?" My back hurt so much that both Don and Tim had to pull me out of the car. The doctor's office was in the back of a drug store. Suddenly the "Doctor" was in front of me. He wasn't my original image of a doctor, but I was in so much pain I couldn't care less. The doctor did not speak English, so Don again held up my arm and said, "See arm, medicine!"

The man examined my arm and went into a back room. He returned with a small sealed glass vial of clear fluid. I couldn't see a lid or opening. I asked him how to take it. He gestured for me to break the glass and drink. At this point, I was so filled with pain I did not care if I swallowed slivers of glass. I just wanted to feel better. I broke the vile against the counter, and I drank the smooth sweet fluid as Don paid the doctor. I was glad that my mouth and throat felt intact.

Don found another taxi to take us back to our hotel room. I lay down and immediately went into a deep sleep. I slept the reminder of that day and through the night.

The following morning, a loud pounding on my door awakened me. "We found another piece of land to look at!" Don shouted. "This one isn't in the jungle. It's on the eastern side of Costa Rica." I sighed with the thought of remaining in this nightmare.

We rested for two days. I started feeling better emotionally but felt bruised from head to toe. I wasn't sure I wanted to continue, but I agreed to check out this new deal since the pain in my back had become more manageable.

We drove to the eastern side of Costa Rica to look at the land. The ranch had a dairy farm, pepper farm, hardwood forest, wood mill, and a protected tribe of Indians who lived on the corner of the property. What the hell, I thought. It has everything we wanted and more. Let's just buy it and go home. We can work out the details later. The owners wanted $5,000 earnest money and the rest in thirty days. We met the realtor in a small office in down town San Jose, signed the papers, and handed over $5,000 cash. As we paid the money, we heard gunfire from a machine gun out on the street, just in front of the building. As soon as the gunfire started, the realtor quickly slid the money into the desk drawer. "Thank you very much," he said. "You can wire the rest of the money to me." As it turned out, the gunfire was just part of a celebration.

The next day we flew back to Olympia. On the flight, I became ill again, and my back continually throbbed with pain. I told Don and Tim that I didn't want to buy the land. I told them I was sick of Costa Rica and did not want to return. Since I backed out of the deal, the project fell through and we lost our $5,000. I know if I had not become so ill, we would have bought the land. As it turned out, Spirit must have had another plan for me, and it did not include Costa Rica.

Back home, I continued to sleep most of the time. My fever continued and my back was still very painful. "Go to Dr. Armentrout," suggested my wife Wanda. "You pay enough for your insurance; use it."

* * * * *

"So Daryl, what seems to be the problem?" asked Dr. Armentrout.

I held out my scab-covered arm, which was healing from the insect bites.

"Good Lord! What got hold of you?" he exclaimed.

I told him about the night in the jungle and how ill I had become. In addition, I told him that since my trip, without warning, I could suddenly break out into a deep sweat and start shaking. He thought I might have malaria and ran a test.

The following day Dr. Armentrout called and said I didn't have malaria. He asked me to come in for more tests. Weeks went on with one test after another showing negative.

"I just don't know what to do," said Dr. Armentrout. "Every test shows you are healthy except for your back."

As Dr. Armentrout spoke those words, I turned white as a sheet. Sweat began pouring out of my pores, and my eyes glassed over. He grabbed me just as I was about to collapse and helped me lie down on the couch. After about ten minutes, the symptoms ceased; I returned to my normal self.

"How long has this been going on?" he asked. I reminded him it had been occurring since the trip to Costa Rica in September seven weeks ago.

"Go home and relax, Daryl," he suggested. "I'll do some more research on this. I'm sure we can find out what's going on with your system. I'll call you in a couple of days and let you know what I find."

That night I decided to go upstairs to our recreation room. The room had large windows overlooking the lake. Wanda and I had installed a wet bar and were planning to install a wood burning stove later. At the other end of the room, we had planned to put in a pool table. These were finishing touches we wanted to put in our dream house.

We had two bright orange barrel chairs in the room. We bought them on sale some years ago. They stood out boldly, and they were the most comfortable chairs we had. Wanda had told me one day when we finished working on the house, the chairs would go up in the attic, out of sight, or to the dump. In the meantime, I enjoyed them. When I was tired, I would sit in one of them and watch the seagulls dive into the lake.

I had been sitting in my chair that evening for about ten minutes, thinking about Costa Rica, when suddenly I could feel someone staring at me. Had Wanda come into the room without me hearing her? I could still hear the television commercials downstairs, and she usually turned off the television when she wasn't watching it.

I looked up, and straight in front of me just a few feet away stood three figures, each about six feet tall wearing brown robes with hoods covering their heads. The hoods had openings to reveal their faces, but there were no faces or heads—just blank space. I shook my head and rubbed my eyes, thinking this hallucination was yet another symptom of my declining health. But, alas, they were still standing there, in front of me, without faces. "What is going on?" Just as I got my breath back to say something, they disappeared.

My first thought was I must have fallen asleep. But I could still see the birds flying across the view in the window. I continued to hear the television down stairs. I was completely awake. Maybe I had another spell, and the fever created a vision. No. My body was not wet from sweating.

The figures had appeared solid; when they stood in front of me, they had blocked the wall behind them. I had never seen or heard of any such experience. In fact, I didn't believe in such nonsense.

I grew up with a very religious mother. But I had since given up any belief in religion, God, heaven, or hell. I believed in the here and now, the solid physical. That was it. I knew what I saw, but I didn't have a clue how to understand what it was.

I went downstairs to the kitchen and found Wanda cleaning up the dishes. I told her what I had just experienced. "You must have fallen asleep, Daryl, and had a dream," she responded warily.

I didn't feel like getting into a discussion about something I didn't understand. I simply replied, "Maybe. I think I'll go to bed. I'm really tired."

I crawled under the covers. In what seemed like seconds, I awoke with the sensation of a firecracker going off in the center of my brain. I quickly sat up in bed. It was daylight. Wanda had gone to school where she taught in an elementary resource room. Our children, Jason and Tami, were also at school.

I looked at the clock and realized I had been sleeping for fourteen hours. For the first time in a long time I felt rested and hungry. I stood up, felt the room spinning in circles, and quickly sat down again. I remembered seeing the brown-robed people the night before. Then I thought about the loud noise that seemed to come from the center of my brain. I wondered if these two events are connected. I got up again, this time without the dizzy spell, and made my way into the kitchen to cook myself some eggs and bacon.

I decided to work in my home office for the first time in a couple of weeks; perhaps it would help me refocus. Then Don called.

"Let's have lunch, Daryl. It's been a while. We need to catch up on the plans for our next project. Let's meet at the Governor's House Restaurant."

We met for a few hours, going over the plans and financing to build seventy-two four-unit apartment complexes on the land we had bought in Tumwater, south of Olympia.

Following lunch, I came down with a headache and fever again. I felt like I had not slept in days. I went back to our house and found Wanda and our children already home. I didn't have the energy to say anything. I just went into the bedroom and fell asleep. A couple of hours later Wanda woke me for dinner. I felt as if I had been drugged.

After dinner Wanda said, "Why don't you get in the hot tub, Daryl? It will help you to relax."

That's it. I'm tired and up tight. I just need to relax and everything will get back to normal. After Wanda and the kids went to bed, I turned on the hot tub in the room just off our master bedroom. Adjacent to the tub were two glass walls that looked out over the lake. I stepped down into the warm water and rested my exhausted body against the strong jets. I looked out over the lake. The night was totally black, except for the house lights in the distance reflecting off the water. Between the hot tub and the view, I was in utter contentment and reminded myself that I needed to do this more often.

A few moments later, I saw a ball of bright light across the lake. I thought someone must be out in boat fishing with a floodlight. However, the ball started to move toward me. I sat straight up in the hot tub and watched as it crossed the lake. The ball of light came through the glass wall and hit me in the forehead. I could feel my head being pushed backward and hitting the edge of the tub.

The next second, I saw myself standing on a walkway winding through lush flower gardens and green lawns. People were walking around carrying books and talking with each other. No one seemed to notice me. Who are these people and where am I? I could feel the back of my head pounding. I reached up to rub the back of my head; suddenly I was back in the hot tub again. The light was gone and everything was quiet.

What is this? The vision of the people and the gardens flashed clearly in my mind. I rubbed the back of my head, remembering that I'd hit it against the back of the tub when the light came through the glass wall. I must have slipped and knocked myself out. Thank God I didn't drown. As I sat there, I noticed the timer had shut off and the water was cool. I must have been in the tub for a couple of hours.

The following morning I shared the experience with Wanda. When I saw the reaction on her face, I knew I couldn't tell anyone else. "Give Dr. Armentrout a call, Daryl. You need to get some help."

That afternoon Dr. Armentrout was able to fit me in. I decided to just tell him I had been having some strange dreams, although I knew they were not dreams.

"I've researched your symptoms, Daryl, and I can't find anything wrong with you. You know, what you need to do is get away. Go someplace warm and just relax. Get away from your phone. You need to take a break; when you come back, I'm sure you will be over whatever it is," Dr. Armentrout stated kindly.

That evening my brother called and told me about a great deal he saw advertised in the local paper. "What deal is this?" I asked, recalling the last "deal."

"A seven-day trip to Hawaii. The price includes airfare, hotel, and car," said Tim. I immediately thought about Dr. Armentrout's advice for a vacation.

"I'll talk with Wanda about it tonight and let you know tomorrow."

"I think Dr. Armentrout is right," said Wanda. "We need to get away. Let's do it. We've never been to Hawaii. This can be an adventure for us. Your parents can watch Jason and Tami. Call Tim and tell him we would love to go."

Chapter 2
The Death

On December 10, 1981, we were set to go to Hawaii. My wife and I had just celebrated our thirty-first birthdays.

I awakened that morning with a throbbing pain in my right foot. At first I thought my back was going out again. Great, I take my doctor's advice and before I even get on the plane, my body starts to fall apart. I pulled the covers off my foot and noticed it was bright red. I had never seen my foot like this before. When I stood up, I fell back down, unable to put the slightest pressure on my foot.

I called out to Wanda in the living room, packing the suitcases, "Get my pain pills. I can't stand on my foot."

She rushed into the bedroom and asked, "What?"

"I can't stand on my foot. Look at it. It's bright red."

"Daryl, we are leaving in a couple of hours. What is going on with you? I'll get your pain pills. I already packed them in the suitcase. Take your pills and I'll be back after I take Jason and Tami to school. Maybe your foot will be better when I get back." My wife, ever the optimist. Looking at my foot, I didn't think it would get better anytime soon.

I swallowed an extra dose of pain pills and hopped into the bathroom to take my shower, wondering why today, of all days. Enough is enough.

After I took my shower, my foot started to feel better. I had just finished dressing when Wanda came home.

"Well, at least you can walk around," said Wanda. "I'll carry the suit cases out to the car."

"I think you need to drive. I can't use my foot."

We were off for a well-deserved trip. I couldn't remember the last time we had taken a vacation just to relax. As we drove to the airport in Seattle, I thought, once I float in the warm water and get the weight off of my foot, I'll be just fine.

Wanda pulled up to the entrance of Sea Tac Airport to let me out and check our baggage. "I'll go park the car and meet you at the gate. Can you make it?" she asked.

When I stood on the sidewalk, I felt pain racing through my foot, up my leg, and into every cell of my body. I hobbled toward the gate, thinking that my old walker I used when I hurt my back would be handy right about now, or perhaps a nice wheelchair. Wanda arrived right behind me at the gate. "Sit down and rest. We have about an hour before the plane takes off," she suggested.

In the seating area, we found Tim and his wife Judy waiting for us. "What happened to you, Daryl?" asked Tim.

"I don't know; I think it's my back," I replied.

"This is supposed to be a trip for you to recover from Costa Rica," he said, shaking his head.

"Don't tell me about it, Tim. Just find me a seat before I fall down."

On the flight to Hawaii, my foot continued to swell and the pain continued to throb deeper and deeper. I popped pain pills like candy, with no effect on the pain, except for the new pain developing in my stomach. Maybe this is what the doctors were telling me about when I was 24. Maybe this is it; from now on I will need a walker or a wheelchair. I didn't dare say anything to Wanda about my thoughts. She needed this trip as much as I did, and we didn't need to discuss the possibility of spending the rest of my life in a wheelchair.

Despite my pain, the time passed quickly. While we were landing in Honolulu, I looked down at the beaches. They were beautiful, the blue-turquoise water joining with the white sand. I thought to myself, "I just need to lie in the water and relax. When I get all the weight off my foot, surely the pain will go away."

We walked out into the airport and were met by two young people, who each put plumeria leis around our necks. Wow, I thought, I'm beginning to feel better already.

At the hotel I said to Wanda, "I think we need to get some food. I took too many pain pills, and I need something for my stomach."

"How many did you take?"

"I lost count. They're not working as well as they usually do. Maybe I need a stronger medication. Let's get lunch and go to the beach," I said.

I had always heard about Hawaii and the clear warm water but it surpassed my expectation. I walked out in the hot sand, put my swollen foot into the warm water and lay down. It felt like the weight of the world was lifted off my body. After what seemed to be a few minutes, I could hear Wanda shouting.

"Daryl, you never put any lotion on. You're red as a beet!" My thoughts flashed back to when I was seventeen and had just moved to Southern California. I had gone out into the ocean body surfing for hours without suntan lotion and received a second-degree burn. Treatment involved being covered in a substance that looked and smelled like lard. Then they wrapped gauze around my body from the top of my neck to my ankles. I looked like a mummy and was bedridden for two weeks. Since then I have had to be very careful about being in the sun for a prolonged time. I thought, "Oh, God, don't tell me I've overdone it again," recalling my symptoms of malaria, which continued, along with the pain in my foot and back, and now my sunburn.

Wanda arrived with the lotion and said, "Here, put this on. I don't want to have to cart you back to Olympia worse than you came. Let's go back to the hotel and rest."

"Yes," I said, "let's go and just sit where it's cool. I need a drink."

"You need a drink?" said Wanda. "I think I'm the one who needs the drink. Besides, with all the pain medication you've taken, I don't think you should drink any alcohol for a while. Let's go plan out our week."

We sat in the open area shaded by beautiful green trees. A pleasant breeze blew, surrounding us with the most wonderful fragrance of flowers.

I decided I had waited long enough. It was time to drink, eat, and play. I was feeling better. The cream I put on my skin had taken the sting out. We ordered food and drinks. I propped my red, swollen foot on a chair and enjoyed the moment.

We spent the next couple of days lying on the beach, going to the falls, eating coconut shrimp, and drinking Mai Tais. My foot continued to increase with pain and swelling. I had to buy a pair of leather thongs because my foot wouldn't fit in any of my shoes.

Tim had made reservations for a luau one evening. He described what we would experience: long tables filled with wonderful food and drink and beautiful women dancing in their grass skirts and coconut bras. I could hardly wait. We arrived with empty stomachs and great excitement, though my foot was still very painful. The tables were low to the ground, and we would have to sit on the sand. How could I do that with my sore foot?

Wanda said, "Just sit here. Tim, Judy, and I will get the food. Sit down, don't move, and relax."

I leaned over and supported myself on the table as I lowered my body onto the sand. I kept moving in different positions, trying to make myself comfortable. I folded my left leg under my right leg and stuck my right leg out in the walkway between the tables. When I finally became comfortable, I noticed a man sitting behind me. He had his left leg under his right leg. His foot was big, swollen, and as bright red as mine. I tapped him on the shoulder and asked him, "What is wrong with your foot?"

"I have gout," he said.

"Gout? What is that?"

He looked down at my foot and said, "My God, man, you have a case of gout worse than mine."

"I don't know what I have."

"You have gout," he said. He explained that it is one of the most painful forms of arthritis a person can have.

I replied, "You have that right."

"Is your medicine working for you?"

"I have pain pills for my back, but they aren't working."

"No, no, you need medicine for the gout. Don't you have any?" He seemed amazed.

"No," I said. "I didn't even know it was gout."

"Go see your doctor. He can fix you up," he assured me.

I wondered why the medicine wasn't working for him.

I must have been thinking out loud because he said, "I just came down with this gout attack this morning. It takes a day or two for the medicine to work."

"Great; I should see my doctor a few thousand miles away. No problem," I mumbled to myself. I turned back to the table just as Wanda, Tim, and Judy arrived with the food.

I said to Wanda, "Look at that guy's foot. He has gout."

"Gout? What is gout?" she asked.

"I don't know, but it must be what I have," I replied.

We enjoyed eating and drinking and then some more drinking. I was starting to feel good. At the end of dinner, the show was about to begin. Because of all the drinking, I needed a restroom and knew I couldn't wait until the end of the show.

Lamenting the pain, trouble, and agony that emptying my bladder would create, I pulled myself up with Wanda's help. I stood there for a few minutes, took one step, and fell over. I fell right on top of the man's gout-swollen, red foot. The scream he let out silenced everyone. I rolled off his foot and looked up at him. He was in shock and his eyes filled with tears as he crawled away into the bushes. I knew the pain he was in. Gout is so painful you can't even lay a sheet across the foot without intense pain, let alone a 250-pound body. By the time I stood up, the man was gone. I hopped on my good foot to the rest room. I decided to remain there for a while for fear of encountering the man when he returned. Thankfully, I never saw him again.

The next day was the second part of our trip. We planned to pick up our rental car and go to the north shore of the Island. My foot continued swelling, taking on the appearance of a shiny red ball. I knew I was not going to be able to drive, so Wanda drove, following Tim and Judy.

We decided to stop at the Polynesian Cultural Center on our drive north. When I opened the door and started to stand up, I fell back into the car. "I can't walk," I said to Wanda. "Maybe we should just go and check into the hotel."

"No, maybe we can find a wheelchair to rent. Wait here." Wanda was determined to enjoy our time in Hawaii.

About twenty minutes later, she returned with a wheelchair. Seeing the wheelchair brought back the memories of my back injury five years earlier and my doctors' premonition that I would be unable to walk by age 40. I thought angrily, "I have nine years to go!"

We enjoyed seeing the Polynesian Cultural Center, but I was ready to get to the hotel and lie down. Pain pulsated through my entire body with the same intensity I had felt the day after my back surgery, when the nurses decided to sit me up. The shot of morphine they gave me barely took the pain away.

At last we arrived at our hotel on the north shore. Tim, Judy, and Wanda helped me hop up to our room. I went to the bed, lay down, and went into a deep sleep. It seemed like a few minutes later when I awoke from the firecracker sound I had been hearing, coming from the center of my brain. I sat up just as Wanda came into the room. "Let's go eat dinner," she said.

"Eat dinner? What time is it?"

"It is almost seven o'clock. You've been sleeping for three hours. We're all hungry."

I stood up and realized the pain had decreased some. "Look," I said to Wanda, "I can walk on my heel."

"Great, let's go eat. Tim and Judy are waiting for us."

Tim and Judy were already seated at a perfect table next to a large open window overlooking the private lagoon next to the hotel. While I ate, the lagoon kept drawing my attention. Maybe if I put on my snorkeling gear and just floated for a while, my foot would feel better.

After dinner, my foot again swelled into a large red ball. The pain pulsated through my entire body. Wanda and I decided to go back up to our room while Tim and Judy went for a walk on the beach.

The next morning I awoke with the firecracker sound again. I looked over at Wanda as she lay sleeping. I wondered about the strange firecracker sound. Was it the beginnings of a brain tumor, or just my own imagination? It had started when I returned from Costa Rica. I wondered if it had anything to do with the bug bites.

I went to the bathroom. My foot still looked like a bright red ball. As I hopped back across the room, I hit my swollen foot directly on the metal leg of the bed. It was as if all the breath was drawn out of my body. As soon as the breath came back into my lungs, I let out a loud scream as I fell onto the bed. Wanda jumped up out of a dead sleep with her eyes wide open. She saw me on the bed curled up into a ball, moaning and holding my foot. "My God, I cannot believe this pain."

Then Wanda said calmly, "You look just like the man you fell on at the Luau."

I crawled under the blankets and laid there for about an hour before I could move. Later we dressed and met Tim and Judy for breakfast. I suggested we spend the rest of our time lying on the beach and floating in the lagoon. I was not up to sightseeing. We all agreed this would be best. After breakfast, Wanda and I changed into our swimming suits. Leaving the room, we walked out on the deck overlooking the lagoon, and I could not believe what I saw. The most brilliant rainbow I had ever seen looked like it ended in the middle of the lagoon. I asked Wanda to go back to the room and get our camera so I could take a picture. I remember saying, as a joke, "I wonder if there is a pot of gold in the lagoon?"

We spent our last full day in Hawaii lying on the beach or floating and snorkeling. It was wonderful not having any weight on my foot. The next day we would need to leave at eleven o'clock to catch our afternoon flight. We had a delicious dinner, enjoying each other's company and talking about all the sights we had seen.

The next morning I awoke with the sound of the firecracker again. I thought I'd put this on the list for Dr. Armentrout to check out when I got home. When Wanda finished packing, we went down to meet Tim and Judy for breakfast. As soon as we sat down, Tim said, "Let's go snorkeling one more time, Daryl. I checked the flight, and we don't need to leave the hotel until noon."

"Wanda has already packed the suit cases and snorkeling gear."

"Just go get your swimming suit. We don't know when we will ever come back here. This could be our last time."

"I don't know, Tim; my foot is still killing me."

"Come on, Daryl, one more time. We have enough time left."

I looked at Wanda and she said, "Why not? We have a few hours before we need to go. Maybe it will help your foot for the trip home. It sure helped yesterday. Let's go put on our swimming suits." I would later find out that one decision on December 17, 1981, would affect us the rest of our lives.

I hopped up to the room and dug out my trunks and snorkeling gear. As soon as I put on my swimming trunks, everything seemed to move in slow motion. I sat on the edge of the bed thinking, if only I could feel like I did before I went to Costa Rica. My body seemed to be falling apart. My thoughts were interrupted when Wanda came out of the bathroom already in her swimming suit. I hopped down the steps, using Wanda as a balance. Tim and Judy were already at the lagoon.

I put on my snorkeling gear except for the fins, which wouldn't fit on my foot. I walked out into the water while Wanda lay down on the sandy beach next to Judy. As I floated into the water, I could feel the pressure being released from my foot. I just allowed myself to float freely, looking at the sandy bottom through my mask. I could feel myself gently being pulled back and forth by the current. At that moment everything felt so peaceful.

Suddenly, I felt a crushing blow hit my back. My body was pushed down to the bottom. I felt myself being pulled and twisted every which way. I tried swimming back, but the pain in my foot was so great I couldn't use it. Suddenly, I was pushed back up out of the water for a few seconds. I saw a large Hawaiian man walking up to the shore. I cried out for help as he looked in my direction. Then just as suddenly, I was pulled back under the water. I was trying to get my breath when I went back under and sucked water into my lungs.

Again everything was in slow motion. I was pushed up out of the water again, and I saw Tim next to me; we were both being pulled out by the strong current. In panic I grabbed him, and we both went down. He panicked and tried to push himself away from me, not realizing that he had pushed me further into the current. I went under again. I could feel water pouring into my body. Every second lasted a lifetime as I felt my lungs fill up with seawater. I did not know what was up or down, which way was out to sea or back to the beach.

Just as I was losing consciousness, I felt a hand grab my arm and another arm wrap around my body. I felt limp. I had no strength left in my body. It felt like I was in a dream or being pulled out of a dream. I remember being placed on the beach and looking up at the large Hawaiian man standing over me. By that time, Tim had pulled himself free from the current and swam back to the beach. Wanda and Judy watched in horror as the man pulled me out of the water and laid my limp body on the sand. The Hawaiian man looked at my very shaken wife and said, "Not to worry; he will be all right."

Wanda looked down at me and then looked back up to thank the Hawaiian man. He had vanished. The beach was a wide-open area. He could not have walked away within a few seconds. Wanda then looked back at me as I was heaving up salt water.

Tim said, "We need to get him back up to your room."

Both Tim and Wanda helped stand me up; I leaned on them as we walked back to the hotel room. Every few minutes, we had to stop as I continued to heave up salt water into the bushes lining the path. We finally made it up to our room where Tim and Wanda sat me on the edge of the bed. A few seconds later my eyes rolled backward, and I fell back onto the bed. Tim realized I was not breathing; frightened, he immediately called the front desk.

The hotel called the paramedics. It seemed to Tim and Wanda only a few minutes before the hotel doctor, security, police, and paramedics arrived. They pushed on my chest and put an oxygen mask on me. While they were putting me on a gurney, the police and hotel security asked Tim and Wanda questions for their report.

They were describing the large Hawaiian man when the security people interrupted and asked, "Are you saying this Hawaiian man was not wearing a uniform?"

"Yes!" Both Tim and Wanda replied.

"That is impossible. The only Hawaiians at this resort are wearing uniforms. You did not see a Hawaiian man."

Both Tim and Wanda insisted they had indeed seen him and that he pulled me out of the water. "And how did he do this?" asked a security man.

"He walked onto the coral reef with his bare feet and pulled him out."

"I don't think so," said the man.

"He was not wearing a uniform. He was bare foot and walked on the coral," insisted Wanda.

The paramedics were ready to transport me to the clinic a few miles away, so the conversation ended. Judy had gone back to her room to pack, unaware of my condition. Looking for Tim, she opened her door and saw the paramedics wheel me down the hall. "What is happening?" she asked.

"Daryl stopped breathing. I'll call you from the clinic."

The ambulance arrived at the emergency door of the clinic followed by the police. The doctor immediately tried to revive me but to no avail. The police came into the hospital and continued to talk with Wanda to complete their report. The doctors asked Tim if I had taken any water in. Tim, still in a state of shock from almost drowning himself, didn't comprehend the question and said, "No, he did not take on any water." He had already forgotten about all the water I had heaved on the beach and along the path to the hotel room.

The doctors used electric shock paddles to revive me in addition to putting an ammonia stick up my nose to awaken me. Nothing worked.

As I lay on the gurney in the emergency room, I felt myself float up to the ceiling. I rolled over in mid air and looked down at my body, watching the doctors shock me. With each shock my body would jerk. I thought about how much that must hurt. As soon as I had that thought, I felt myself being pulled backward into what seemed like a tunnel. I was slowly moving backward until I heard a loud roaring sound. Suddenly, I was moving at a very rapid rate of speed. My thoughts went blank. I forgot I was in a hospital having electric currents surging through me. I forgot I was floating above my body watching it all occur. I forgot I was in a tunnel being pulled backward away from the events in the hospital. I forgot it all, but there before me stood this magnificent being.

He was tall with deep blue eyes and bright golden hair braided in a circle on top of his head. When I looked into his eyes, they changed to different shades of blue. He wore a long white robe with gold symbols across his chest. I had never seen such symbols before. He did not say anything. He just looked at me. I looked around him and saw many different people dressed in regular clothes in the distance. I was curious about them. I tried to walk around him toward the group of people. I couldn't make out who they were or what they looked like. As soon as I took a step forward, the being reached out and put his hand on my shoulder to stop me.

"Now the work shall begin," he said with a full deep voice I felt throughout my body. "Ye must return now."

Work? Return? Those words did not register in my mind. I took another step, but he put his hand on my chest. As soon as his hand touched me, I fell backward into the emergency room, into my body. I could feel pain from head to toe. I felt unusual and strange. I opened my eyes and saw several people bending over me looking at me. I didn't know any of them.

I didn't know where I was or who I was.

I heard a male voice ask, "Daryl, are you all right?"

I looked at him but nothing connected. "Daryl, do you know who I am?" he asked.

I couldn't find words to speak. I just looked at him perplexed. Who was this man speaking to me? I felt lost and detached, like I was in a stranger's body.

I heard another man say, "Tim, go get his wife. Let's see if he remembers her."

Tim went out into the waiting area and told Wanda that I was going to live. Wanda felt all the energy drain from her body. "What do you mean, he's going to live? I thought he was all right; they were just observing him. Why didn't anyone tell me what was going on in there?" She couldn't believe there was a chance that I wouldn't live. To this day she does not know if she was in shock or simply in total denial of the seriousness of the situation.

"The doctors were so busy working on him, they wanted to wait until they knew what was happening first. They think he has amnesia. He doesn't recognize me. They want you to come back with me and see if he recognizes you. They are trying to decide if they need to fly Daryl in a helicopter to Honolulu."

Wanda was furious. She felt betrayed. All along she thought I was being watched and nothing serious was occurring. If something serious were to occur she assumed they would tell her. I was observing all the confusion occurring in the room from above my body.

I thought, "Tim, wife? What is happening to me?"

Wanda came into the room. She walked toward me and said, "Daryl, how are you feeling?"

My thoughts were only questions: who is this woman, who is this Tim, where am I, and why am I in this body?

Someone said, "Let's cancel the helicopter. We can take him to Honolulu in an ambulance. He's stable. Wanda, did you handle all the insurance paperwork? I don't think Daryl can leave until it's all handled."

"Yes, Tim! Judy is dealing with the airline. I called work and told them I won't be there as planned. I called Mom and told her Daryl had an accident, and we won't be home as soon as we thought. She asked one of us to call her as soon as we know more." Wanda barely finished speaking when tears started flowing as she allowed the severity of the event to sink in.

As I kept moving in and out of consciousness, I could feel myself being moved into an ambulance. Throughout the drive I knew someone was holding my hand. I thought, I do not want to be touched and I do not want to be moved. I do not want to be in this body.

My next memory was awakening the following day in a Honolulu hospital. I began realizing how much pain my body was in. My foot was too tender even for a sheet. A doctor came in with some younger adults following him. "Well now, let's see what's going on with you."

He looked into my eyes while moving a light around my head. Glancing at Wanda, he said, "I understand they did an EEG at the clinic."

"I don't know what they did. They wouldn't let me in the room. How come he doesn't remember anyone?"

"Apparently the EEG showed some abnormalities. We will have to keep him here for a few days under observation. I see he has gout; how long has he had this?"

"Since the day we arrived. He woke up with it," Wanda replied.

"How many years has he had gout attacks?"

"Never. We didn't even know it was gout until a few days ago."

"Well, we can give him some medication for the gout. It should be gone in a few days. According to his chart, he has the highest level of uric acid in the blood I have ever seen in a man. All his vital signs are normal for now. We just need to wait and see how he progresses."

The next morning the doctor came in with the same students following him. Again he leaned over and shined a light in my eyes. "Good God Almighty, I can't believe this."

Wanda jumped up and ran over to the bed. "What?"

"I just scratched my Rolex on the bed frame. Damn!" He turned around and left the room with all his young adults in tow.

"That's it. I am checking you out of here."

"Where are we going?"

"Home. Don't you remember anything about our home? Tami, Jason, anyone?"

I lay there thinking, who are Tami and Jason? Where is home? I was too tired and full of pain to try to remember.

Wanda left to arrange my discharge from the hospital. When she came back, she told me that Tim and Judy were able to change our tickets.

"They should be here in a few minutes. I am going to finish checking you out of here. You can see your doctor in Olympia when we get home," she explained. I listened, but I was not fully aware of what was going on.

Tim came in behind Wanda. "Hi, Daryl. Do you remember me?"

I looked at him and could only think of the time a couple days ago when he stared into my face. I didn't answer; I didn't want to talk to anyone.

An hour later a nurse showed up with a wheelchair, followed by Wanda.

"Well, Mr. Harrison, it is time for you go."

Wanda helped me get dressed. My foot was already beginning to heal. When I settled into my wheelchair, I realized that I was being wheeled out of the hospital by a woman I didn't know, going to a place I had never heard of, and furthermore, I didn't want anything to do with any of it.

Chapter 3
The Amnesia Factor

I slept on the flight back to Seattle. Wanda woke me up as we were preparing to land. After we pulled up to the terminal, I tried to stand and fell back into my seat. The pain and swelling had returned to my foot during the flight, and I was having dizzy spells.

"Let's just wait until everyone gets off, Daryl," suggested Wanda.

I tried to stand up and again fell back into my seat. "What's the problem?" asked the stewardess.

"I don't know. He was in the hospital for a few days, and he's still dizzy," replied Wanda.

"Wait here; I'll get him a wheelchair."

Wanda looked around; Tim and Judy had already left the plane. I was wheeled to the baggage area and sat there looking at all the people. I noticed everyone had different colors around them. Some people had a muddy red color; some had a bright yellow or pink color. My vision and my mind were drawn into their color. I could feel what they were feeling.

"What are you looking at?" asked Wanda.

"Just the colors," I replied calmly.

"Colors? What colors?"

"People colors."

Wanda shook her head in confusion and said. "The bags are here. Will you sit with them while I go get the car?"

"Sure," I replied, as if I could actually go anywhere in my condition. I continued looking at the magnificent colors.

While I was sitting there a little boy about five with dark curly hair and big brown eyes came up to me and asked, "Mister, what are you looking at?"

"All the colors."

"Oh, I see them. I like the colors around you."

What a strange statement, I thought. Just as I was about to ask the little boy what he saw, his mother came up and said, "Peter, don't talk to strangers. Let's go!"

Perfect timing. Sigh.

I looked at his mother and saw a muddy red color around her. As she took his hand and pulled him toward the door, he turned around, smiled, and waved good-bye.

A few minutes later Wanda returned. "Sit here while I put these suitcases in the trunk. I'll come back and get you; don't leave." Obviously, Wanda was not grasping the concept that I didn't have the physical or mental ability to go anywhere.

On the drive home, Wanda kept asking me questions about Tami, Jason, and my parents, Tom and Bonnie. She asked about our new dream house we had just moved into six months earlier. She talked about my best friend Don and our business together. Everything was blank. The more questions she asked, the more uncomfortable I felt. I told her I didn't wish to answer any more of her questions. She fell silent, disappointed.

I looked out the window, watching the scenery go by. The thick green trees looming over the highway were very different than Hawaii.

We drove up to a large wrought iron gate, sheltering what looked like a wealthy neighborhood. Wanda pushed a button to open the gates, and we drove through. A few houses down, she drove into a curved driveway leading to a large house. "This is it. Do you remember?"

"No."

I could feel Wanda becoming desperate but wanting to sound calm. I didn't say anything. I stood up and felt lightheaded, but I was able to regain my balance. I watched as she pressed buttons on a panel. I saw a large oak door with stained glass in the center and on both sides. "What a beautiful door," I commented.

"Yes, you picked it out."

Nothing seemed familiar. Wanda opened the door, and we walked into a large formal living room with a marble fireplace. Next to the living room, one step higher, was the formal dining room with a twelve-foot table. "A big table," I said.

"You like to have friends over. So you remember the table?"

I just shook my head no.

"Let's go into the kitchen," Wanda suggested.

I followed her through a short hallway into a large room. The kitchen had an island in the center with an adjoining eating area. The room continued into the family room with an entire wall filled with windows overlooking the lake.

Wanda opened the sliding glass door out onto a deck. "Let's go outside."

I looked at the water and felt very uncomfortable. "No thanks. Show me the rest of the house." It was just my luck we live next to a body of water. After drowning, I no longer felt kinship with large bodies of water or variations thereof.

We walked back into the kitchen and down another hallway. At the end were two doors, which opened from the center. Wanda opened them into a huge bedroom with a stained glass window, king size bed, and light blue satin wallpaper. Across the room was another door. "What's in there?"

"The bathroom that leads into the spa room. I'll show you." She opened the door to a large bathroom with a full mirror above the sinks.

I looked in and was shocked. All the blood rushed from my head. A spa tub almost the size of the entire room was full of water. "What is all this water doing in here?"

I turned around and went back through the bathroom and lay down on the bed. "I'm going to lie here for a while." The next thing I remembered was Wanda waking me up in a dark room.

"Daryl, Tami and Jason are here. Don't let them know you don't remember them. We're getting ready to eat. Can you walk to the kitchen?"

"I think so. What do I say to them?"

"Nothing. Just give them a hug, tell them you missed them, and you're happy to see them. Then we'll eat and watch TV."

I walked into the kitchen. There standing before me were two children, apparently belonging to me. As directed, I hugged each one and said that I missed them, but I didn't make eye contact. How can I miss someone that I have no memory of?

I felt hollow and strange. I stood in a house that was mine but couldn't remember building it; I talked to a wife that I couldn't remember marrying and hugged children that I couldn't remember ever being born. I didn't know how to speak what I was feeling, so I remained quiet.

Tami and Jason, though they were only seven and eight, knew I was not feeling well. They assumed it was my foot, so they didn't think anything of my quiet behavior as we ate dinner and watched TV.

The next morning, Wanda called Dr. Armentrout and set up an appointment. She described what had occurred, and he said he could see me that afternoon. She made a map with directions to the doctor's office for me, explained her work schedule, and gave me her number to call if I happened to get lost.

After I arrived at Dr. Armentrout's office, I sat in the car for a few minutes thinking, what am I doing here? My foot is much better. I am no longer dizzy; in fact I was beginning to feel much better.

I walked into the office and saw a man standing there dressed in a white jacket. "Well, Daryl, what have you done to yourself now?"

I just looked at him blankly. I could see his energy and feel his concern. I wondered why he was so concerned. He came over and put his arm on my shoulder.

"Come in, Daryl. Let's see if we can find out what is going on with you."

I sat down and looked at him. "Do you remember me?" he asked.

"No, I don't remember anyone."

"So tell me, what do you know?" the doctor asked.

"Wanda told me I drowned and was unconscious for six hours."

"Do you remember any of this?"

"No."

"I understand you came down with a good case of gout?"

"Yes, but my foot is doing much better."

"Well Daryl, I think you just need some rest. Why don't you go home and rest for a week or two? We'll see if your memory comes back. If Wanda has any questions, have her give me a call."

As I stood up to leave, he said, "You know, I sent you two to have a fun vacation and recover from your jungle attack."

"Jungle attack?"

"Yes, don't you remember? You were quite ill when you returned."

"Did I have gout?"

"No, Daryl. Why don't you come back next week, and we'll see how you're doing."

The next week, my parents, Tom and Bonnie, and my aunt Lillian collected all the pictures they could find of my childhood. They even found old black and white soundless movies of family reunions made at my grandparents' house in Fort Bragg, California. We would sit for hours looking at the pictures. It was as if I was looking at someone else's life, someone else's body, and someone else's family. I had no feelings or emotions for anyone. I still felt confined in a strange body with no memory.

Wanda thought it might help to drive to Southern California and visit with her stepmother, sister, and family. "Why don't we drive through Fort Bragg on the way home? Maybe this trip will help jog your memory," she suggested. Somehow I doubted this, but was reluctant to disagree because Wanda seemed desperate to restore my memory.

Throughout the week, Don kept calling and asking Wanda if I was all right or if my memory had come back. Finally he said, "I want to come over and give Daryl his Christmas present. I think he will remember me after all we've been through."

At last Wanda gave in and told Don he could come over that

afternoon.

When he knocked on the front door I walked over and opened it. I was looking at a stranger. The blank look in my eyes was reflected by the shock in his eyes. "Daryl, I'm Don. You must remember me."

I invited him in. We sat on the couch in the living room. "Here, this is for you." He had in his hand a small box wrapped in bright red Christmas paper.

"What is it?"

"Open it." Inside was a beautiful gold and silver watch.

The only thing I could think to say was, "Don, we must have been good friends for you to give me such an expensive watch."

Tears started rolling down his cheeks. "Don't you remember me at all, Daryl? How could you forget all we've done together? How could you forget about our plans of developing apartment complexes? How could you forget our plans of becoming millionaires by the time we're forty?"

I just looked at him; I didn't have answers to his questions. He soon got up and left. Wanda came into the living room and asked, "How did it go?"

Just as she asked the question, she heard Don spinning his tires on the road in front of the house. "He must be very upset, or he would never drive his new Mercedes like that."

I held up the watch. "Look what he gave me. I sure hope this trip to California will bring back my memory."

"Dr. Armentrout called while you were visiting with Don. He wants you to come in tomorrow. I told him about our planned trip to California; he thought it was a good idea."

The next day I drove across town to see the doctor. "Well, Daryl, does anything feel familiar to you? I see you're walking normally; the gout has dissipated."

"Yes, but I feel strange."

"Come into my office and let's talk about it."

As I sat down across from him, I described how strange I felt in my body.

He looked perplexed. "What do you mean?"

"I don't know. The only way I can describe it is, this is not my body."

"Daryl, Wanda told me yesterday about your strange experience in the hot tub before you left for Hawaii. Do you remember any of it?"

"No, what strange experience?"

"Wanda hasn't told you about it?"

"No."

"Daryl, you're leaving for California. All of your vital signs seem normal. Why don't you go on your trip? When you come back, if you still have amnesia, I want you to go over to the hospital and have some tests done. Will you do that for me?"

"Why not? I have just as many questions as you do."

* * * * *

We packed the Lincoln and the four of us headed to Southern California in early January. It was a wonderful time to get to know Tami and Jason as we spent hours driving. I learned all about McDonald's Big Macs and French fries, their favorite meal.

Wanda told me about her parents who had died a few years earlier. They had divorced when Wanda was 12 and living in Pennsylvania. Her father married Betty and moved to Southern California. Her mother moved a year later to the same area and later remarried. Without warning, her father Joe died from a massive heart attack suffered at work. He was 48. The next year, her mother Phyllis had a heart attack that put her in a permanent coma. She died a few months later at the age of 49, almost to the day Wanda's father died.

We arrived in Huntington Beach, California, two days later. We drove into the driveway of Terri, Wanda's sister. She ran to the car. I watched as Wanda and Terri hugged and whispered to each other. I got out of the car and looked at Terri, drawing another blank. She ran to me and gave me a big bear hug. "Daryl, it is so good to see you again."

From the back seat Jason shouted, "Can we go to McDonald's for dinner?"

It broke the tension I was feeling of knowing I was supposed to remember Terri.

We spent the next day visiting and seeing some of the sights in the area. The following day we decided to drive an hour away and see Betty, Wanda's stepmother.

"She is really upset," said Terri. "She can't understand why you don't remember her."

We parked in front of her house and walked to the front door. As I reached for the doorbell, Betty opened the door. My first thought was to hold out my hand and shake hers. As soon as I did, tears started pouring down her cheeks.

"Daryl, this is Betty," she said. "Don't shake my hand; give me a hug!"

Again we pulled out all the pictures; again, nothing. I could not feel anything about these people who loved me so dearly. They were strangers, just as the body I was in felt so strange.

On the way home, we drove up the coast through San Francisco and north to Fort Bragg. We arrived early in the evening and decided to get a motel and sightsee the next day. The following morning, I awoke with a loud popping sound coming from the center of my brain. I told Wanda about it at breakfast. Her eyes grew wide and said, "You were having that before you drowned. Maybe your memory is going to come back." I looked at her, confused. I had no memory of this strange sound.

After breakfast we drove around town, and I felt this urge to drive on a narrow road heading east up the hill. "Where are you going, Daryl?"

"I don't know. I just have a feeling to drive this way."

I had not been to Fort Bragg since my grandfather died in 1964, yet I drove into the driveway of where he had lived so many years ago.

"How can you remember where he lives when you don't even remember him?" Wanda asked, confused.

"I don't know," I said. "But I'm feeling very strange. I want to leave and go home."

We returned to the motel, collected our luggage, and headed back home to Olympia. During our drive home, Wanda and I had time to talk about our life together, before my drowning. She told me our history. We were married in June of 1972. We both had worked at Ambassador College and attended the World Wide Church of God in Pasadena, California. I worked as an artist for **Plain Truth** magazine, and Wanda had worked at the library.

We met at a beach party in Huntington Beach planned by a childhood friend of mine, Jim, who was now living in Pasadena. Wanda was a cousin of Jim's wife, Patty. Soon after we met, we started dating and married ten months later. Several months after we married, we quit our jobs at the college and moved to Marysville, California. I had lived there as a child. My father and I started a short-lived construction company in Marysville. In April of 1973, our son Jason was born and we decided to move back to Southern California, where I joined the carpenters' union. Thirteen months later, our daughter Tami was born. Both our children were born at home; I helped to deliver them.

During a slow period in construction, I took a job driving a truck delivering stainless steel tanks filled with a resin for softening water. One day while delivering tanks, one of the restraints broke, sending a 170-pound tank on top of me. I heard a loud pop in my lower back. I lay there for a few minutes in a daze. Pain began shooting down my legs. I was able to drive the truck back to the plant; however, when I climbed out of the truck I could hardly walk.

After being examined for nine months, it was decided I had ruptured two disks in my back. I went into surgery for an expected hour and a half of surgery. Six hours later, the operation was complete. The damage was so extensive, I was not able to walk for months. I began with the aid of a walker. The doctors told me at best I would be able to walk until I reached age 40. I was told there was much more occurring in my spine than ruptured disks, including a tumor. Since State Comp was paying for the operation, they could not do much for me. For nearly three years, I was on disability income.

The day I was released from the doctors' care, we decided to move to the Northwest. I received a nice settlement from the insurance company the day before we loaded up the U-Haul and left California. It was during that three-year time that Wanda's parents died. She was ready to leave the state and start a new life out of the big city.

We made our first choice Coos Bay, Oregon, and our second Olympia, Washington. We called realtors in both cities to prepare a list of houses to show us. The day we arrived in Coos Bay, our realtor had become ill and was taken to the hospital an hour before we arrived. No one else knew we were coming, and the list was at the hospital with the realtor. We stayed long enough to have lunch and continued driving to Olympia.

Soon after we arrived in Olympia, we found our first house to purchase. I started a construction company called D&H Investment Builders. Business was booming, and soon we found ourselves with enough money to do whatever we wanted. We bought and sold several houses until we decided to build our dream home on the shore of Long Lake.

As Wanda was telling me our history together, I kept feeling she was talking about a life that did not exist. I had no sense of connection to this history except for the pain I experienced in my back.

When we returned home, we had a message from Dr. Armentrout's office. He wanted to know if my memory had returned; if not, he had set up an appointment at the hospital in Olympia for some tests. He said he wanted to see me first and to call as soon as we returned.

The next morning I drove over to Dr. Armentrout's office. Again I sat down across from his desk. "Well Daryl, how did the trip go?" I told him about the experience in Fort Bragg.

He seemed pleased. "Maybe your memory is beginning to come back. Do you remember anything else, or anyone?"

"No, I hear all these people talking about my past but it doesn't feel like my past. In fact, this doesn't feel like my body."

"You mentioned that before. Elaborate on what you mean."

"I don't know. I just feel like I don't belong here."

"Daryl, I have set up a series of tests for you at the hospital. You will be an outpatient. You need to arrive at one o'clock tomorrow afternoon. The first test will be a blood gas test. When I get the results, I will know what other tests to run. Don't worry; your memory will come back. We just need to give it some time."

I wished I could share Dr. Armentrout's confidence.

The next day I arrived a few minutes early at the hospital to fill out the insurance forms. A nurse came and asked me to go with her to a small room with an equally small bed.

"Lie here for twenty minutes. I'll be back to draw some blood," directed the nurse.

The next thing I knew, Wanda was leaning over me asking, "Are you all right?"

I was in a different room; a man who looked like a doctor was standing over in the corner.

"Where am I? How did I get into this room? Who is he?"

"I don't know what happened. The doctors don't know, either. You were lying on a bed waiting for a blood gas test when the nurse heard a loud banging on the wall. She came rushing in and you were having a seizure. They gave you a shot of something."

"I'm not clear what happened next. Someone rolled you into the emergency room and pulled a curtain around you. Apparently the nurses and doctors had a shift change at the same time, and they forgot you were there. I called your father when you didn't show up at home. He called the hospital, and they told him you had your test and left at two o'clock that afternoon. Your father drove around town hunting for you. He decided to check the hospital parking lot and found your car. That was at eight last night. He confronted the nurses again, and they told him you left at two in the afternoon. He told them your car was still in the parking lot, so you had to be in the hospital. Your father raised quite a ruckus; you know how he gets."

"I do?"

"Well, you used to. Anyway your father, two nurses, and two doctors began hunting throughout the hospital. They found you unconscious, stuck in a corner behind a white curtain. The hospital was full last night, so some doctor put you into a waiting room. The nurses on duty were quite angry with the doctor for doing that. No one knew what was wrong with you, and they couldn't wake you up." Wanda went on to explain that she had arrived soon after the hospital staff found me. She sat with me all night.

"This morning the doctor came in and asked me to leave," Wanda continued. "He told me he was going to inflict you with pain to try and wake you up. I said no, I was going to stay here. First he stuck you with a pin. Then he lifted your arm up over your head and let it drop. He expected you to hit yourself in the face, but you didn't. The doctor turned to me and said, 'He is making this happen. There is no reason he should be unconscious.'"

Wanda showed me some torn clothing. "This is what's left of your shirt and pants," she said. "They cut them off of you."

I didn't know what to say, but Wanda had more news. "Dr. Armentrout called this morning and said he wants you to see this psychiatrist who works in the hospital. He thinks maybe he can find out why you did this."

"Did what?" I asked.

"Go unconscious."

"You think I made a choice to go unconscious?"

"No, but the doctor does. I just want to find out what's happening to you." She sighed. "I'm going back to the house and get you some clothes. You have an appointment with the psychiatrist in two hours. Just lie here and get some rest," Wanda stated in a very concerned tone.

When Wanda returned, I got dressed just in time for the new doctor. "So why do you think you went unconscious?" asked Dr. Jones.

"You think I'm supposed to know that?"

He continued asking Wanda and me questions about what occurred in

Hawaii. About an hour later he gave me a slip of paper with a prescription and stated, "Daryl, I want you to take this medication and come back and see me in a couple of weeks."

As we were leaving the hospital I said, "You know, I don't think I like hospitals. I lost my memory in one, and they lost me in the other."

"Let's pick up these pills on the way home, Daryl. Maybe you'll feel better."

"I feel so sore and stiff."

"This morning the doctor said you would be sore for a couple of days from the seizure."

"Yes, the seizure I wanted to have, sure."

Twenty minutes after I took the first pill, I was fast asleep. I slept for fourteen hours. When I awoke, I took another pill and slept for twelve hours. When I woke up the next morning, Wanda told me Dr. Armentrout had called and asked me to return his call and come see him that afternoon.

"Daryl," said Dr. Armentrout, "what are we going to do with you? Are those pills helping?"

"All I do is sleep when I take them."

"Did Dr. Jones help you any?"

"No," I said. "He thinks I made this happen. All he said was to take these pills."

"Well, I didn't think he could help you, but he was the only one available to see you at the time. I met a man in Seattle last week, and I talked to him about your case. He is willing to see you. He thinks he can help you regain your memory. His name is David Calof. He is a well-regarded therapist who uses hypnotherapy."

"He uses what?"

"Hypnotherapy. He thinks hypnotherapy will help bring back your memory. Look Daryl, I don't know what else to do, but I think this man can help you."

"Well, I'll think about it. I haven't been too impressed with the ones I've met so far."

"Don't take too long, Daryl. I want you to see this man."

The next afternoon Don called and asked if I would meet him for lunch. Apparently he had recovered from the initial shock of me not remembering him or our friendship. I had stopped taking the pills and felt much better. We met at the Governor's House Restaurant for lunch.

"Daryl, do you remember me at all?" said Don, sounding hopeful.

"No," I said.

Don changed the subject. "I heard about what happened to you in the hospital."

"Yeah, I guess the whole town has heard about it by now."

"You know, Daryl, the banks are getting worried about you. This is not good for business. Can't you just pretend your memory came back?"

"Pretend? How can I pretend what I don't know?" I felt frustrated. "Dr. Armentrout wants me to go see a man in Seattle who does hypnosis. He thinks he can help my memory return."

"Hypnosis!" shouted Don. "That's only good for stage tricks, barking like a dog, jumping around like a chicken, that nonsense."

"Don, I'm really tired of not being able to remember. I just want to go home, but I don't know where it is."

"You live on Long Lake, Daryl; you should remember that. You've been driving around town for nearly six weeks."

"No," I said, "not that home."

"What in the hell are you talking about, Daryl?" Don's voice was tinted with worry.

"I don't know. I feel like I left home, my real home. The place where I am from, but I don't know where that is."

"On Long Lake, Daryl."

"Not that home, another home."

"I can just see you now, Daryl, jumping around like a chicken saying, 'Home . . . home.'"

"Don't worry, Don. I don't think I'll be seeing this man in Seattle."

"Don't worry? I have bankers calling me every day asking about you. Yes,

I am worried. We need these bankers; we have a lot or work to do."

The next morning Dr. Armentrout called and asked if I was willing to see David.

"No. I had lunch with Don yesterday and he told me about hypnotherapy."

"What? Don doesn't know anything about hypnotherapy. What did he tell you?"

"He told me about chickens running around."

Before I could explain, I heard him shout, "Good God, Don told you that? The next time Don comes in for his physical, I know just what to do. No, Daryl, David does not do any such thing. This is not a stage act. This is a valid treatment. I think he is your best hope of getting your memory back."

"Let me think about it."

The next morning Dr. Armentrout called and said, "I just talked with David and set up an appointment for you."

"Why do you want me to see this David guy?"

"He is your only hope, Daryl. You have a lot of people worried about you. You need to go see him."

"OK! OK! I'll go, but that chicken story better not be true."

"Good God, Daryl, just go. Your appointment is in two days." Dr. Armentrout gave me the number to call for directions to the office in Seattle. I wondered whether it would be yet another dead-end.

Chapter 4
Awakening the Spirit

By the time the appointment day arrived in February 1982, I had changed my mind several times. Don's words about clucking like a chicken echoed in my head. In the end, however, the thought of my family and friends propelled me to go. It was the look on Wanda's face as she shared precious memories of our life together that I could not remember; it was the two young children sleeping in the bedroom next to us, whom I did not know; it was the family and friends who shared a lifetime of memories of me while I held no memories of them.

During the one-hour drive to Seattle, I considered turning around at each exit. Yet something inside of me said, "Keep going." I knew I couldn't live off my savings forever. My insurance company was paying all the medical bills and a disability payment to me, but in time it would run out. I couldn't remember what I had done for a living. I couldn't remember how to build apartment buildings. I didn't even know if I liked it or not. Thousands of thoughts passed through my mind.

I drove into the parking lot of David Calof's office and sat there for about ten minutes thinking about all the people I couldn't remember. What if my memory comes back and I find out I don't like them? What if everything I had been told was a lie? What if they were not my family? I started getting a headache.

I walked up the stairs to David Calof's office and was greeted by his young receptionist. She handed me a clipboard with several pages. As I read the questions, I realized I couldn't answer most of them. What is the date of my birth? I had to look on my driver's license. What were the birth dates of my wife and children? What were my favorite hobbies? The list went on. I looked over at the receptionist and said, "I can't answer these questions. I don't remember the answers."

"Just do the best you can. David will be with you in a couple of minutes."

A few moments later a door opened next to me and a man walked out.

"Hi, I'm David Calof. You must be Daryl Harrison."

He was very professional and courteous. I felt relieved. I walked into his office and looked around. His large desk was covered with papers and folders. He had a couch next to the wall with a coffee table. In the corner, a recliner faced his desk and a large window.

He noticed a pack of cigarettes in my pocket. "I see you're a smoker; so am I. How long have you been smoking?"

"I've been told I started smoking a few months before I went on vacation to Hawaii."

He just looked at me. "I see you're 31. You never smoked before?"

"I guess."

"Daryl, I have talked with Dr. Armentrout about your case. I think I can help you. I don't plan on putting you under hypnosis today. I think it would be good for us to just talk and help you understand what hypnosis is and how it works. Have you heard anything about hypnosis?"

"No," I lied, as visions of clucking chickens raced through my head.

For the next hour I described to him what I had been told about my family history and what I had done for a living. I also described to him the experience in Fort Bragg when I drove directly to my grandfather's house.

"Did the area look familiar to you?" he asked.

"No. I don't even know how I got there. But I knew it was his house from all the pictures I had seen. I felt very uncomfortable as I was driving up to the house. I just wanted to turn around and leave, which we did."

"Why do you think you felt uncomfortable?"

"How should I know? I just wanted to leave."

David looked at his watch and said, "Well, our hour is just about up. I want to give you some information to read. Can you come back next week?"

"Yes."

"We'll try hypnosis then. I think you will be more relaxed."

Driving back to Olympia, I realized I felt good about seeing David. For the first time, I began to feel that someone could help me put the pieces of my mind back together. That evening Wanda and I talked about my meeting with David. She read all the material David had given me. For the first time, I saw her excited and filled with hope. Jason overheard us and asked, "Is he going to make you jump around like a chicken?"

My mouth fell open. Wanda said, "Jason heard us talking about your lunch with Don. No, honey, Daddy is not going to jump around like a chicken."

"Oh! Ok. "He went back to watching TV.

The next day Don called up and asked me out to lunch. While we were eating, I told him I had shared his comments about the chicken and hypnosis with Dr. Armentrout.

"You what? God, Daryl, you used to keep everything between us private. "Why did you tell the doctor about that?"

"I didn't know we kept everything private. By the way, Dr. Armentrout said he knew what to do with you when you go in for your next physical."

"Shit! Listen, Daryl; let's keep our talks just between us, OK? So do you like this Calof guy? Is he going to help you?"

"I hope so."

"You hope so? Half the banks in this town hope so, too. We have a lot riding on your getting well. By the way Daryl, when you get better, don't go on any more vacations. I can't handle any more of this."

Although I still did not remember Don, I was beginning to like him. He always said what was on his mind and always wanted to help in his own way. He seemed like a good friend to have.

"I haven't seen you taking pain pills for your back lately, Daryl. Are you still taking them?"

"I don't remember taking pills. My back feels great. Wanda asked me the same question the other day. I guess I had a pretty bad back."

"Ha, drowning cured your back?" he asked, laughing.

"Who knows? I'm not sure what it was like before."

The next week, I spent most of my time sitting on the deck behind the house looking at the lake and trying to get over the uneasiness of the large body of water. I watched the life around the lake evolve: fishermen in their boats, children skipping rocks, dogs plunging into the water to retrieve a stick. Hours would pass while I sat silently observing the activity around me.

After one afternoon of exploring the property, I discovered a riding lawn mower parked in a small building behind the house. I read the instruction manual on how to use it. Even though the lawn did not need to be mowed in February, it gave me something to do.

When I was not on the deck or mowing the lawn, I watched movies at the theater. The stories fascinated me. I could follow and understand the plots and characters of the movie even though I couldn't understand the plots and characters within my own life. Movies became a great escape for me. Since Wanda was at work and Jason and Tami were at school, I saw a lot of movies. Roger Ebert would have been jealous.

The next week arrived, and it was time to see David Calof. I was curious about what it would be like to remember. Would the memories come flooding back like a tsunami or slowly resurface as I interacted with the people and places I once knew? Most importantly, would I remember anything at all? Or were my memories gone forever, lying on the bottom of the Pacific Ocean, where my life should have ended?

I drove into the same parking lot at David Calof's office, but this time I could feel excitement about knowing myself and understanding a conversation about my past. As I walked into David's reception area, he was talking with someone who was just leaving. "Daryl, it's good to see you. Come in. Did you have a chance to read the material I gave you?"

"Yes, I did."

"And are you ready?" he asked, inviting me into his office.

"Well, I guess I am. How do we get started?"

"Sit in the recliner and just relax."

I sat down. David asked me to relax and breathe deeply. He started counting down from ten to one while giving me suggestions on relaxing. He asked me to go to the place where I was pulled underwater. I could feel my lungs filling with water and the sensation of being pulled into a whirlpool. As I looked up, I could see a bright golden light through the water. My body reacted as if I were drowning. David pulled me out of the hypnotic trance. I was completely exhausted.

"You started re-experiencing your drowning, so I needed to bring you out. The purpose of hypnotherapy is to not create distress, but to transcend it," David said. "At least we know you can be hypnotized. You spoke of someone pushing you into the rip tide; do you remember that? Were you in the water with anyone when you drowned?"

"Yes, I was swimming with my brother."

"Did he push you down?"

"I'm not sure what happened. He said I grabbed him and he started going down, so he pushed me away. Then I went under."

"Well, why don't we try again next week? Maybe you can recall the event without experiencing the trauma."

I looked at the clock and saw that an hour had already passed. While driving home I kept thinking of the bright golden light I could see when I was being pulled under. David had suggested that perhaps I had seen the sun through the water as I was being pulled down. I felt a sense of excitement about the hypnosis working. If it worked, I could remember my life and get back to work. I knew that would make Don happy, and Wanda would not be worrying so much.

During the next week, I awoke on two different mornings with the loud popping sound in the center of my brain. Wanda wanted me to share this with David during my next appointment. I said I would think about it.

The next week, I told David about the popping sound in the center of my brain, although I wasn't sure I trusted him completely.

"Does Wanda remember if this occurred before the drowning?" he asked.

"Yes. It began after I became ill in Costa Rica."

"Well," he said, scratching his head. "Last week you told me about your experience going to your grandfather's house. You said you had not been there since 1964, but you were able to drive straight to his house."

I nodded. "I got a very strange feeling after that and wanted to leave and go home."

"Daryl, why don't we try to help you remember your childhood first and work toward the present? Since you remembered your grandfather's place, maybe it will be easier for you to remember your childhood first. Sit back, relax, and start breathing deeply."

I heard him counting backward from ten, but this time before he got to one, I was already in a deep trance. David assisted me back to my early childhood. I began seeing pictures of myself at an early age. It was like watching a movie. I could see and hear Daryl talking and playing. I followed this movie up to the age of thirteen. In what seemed like minutes, an hour had passed. I woke up out of the trance to David smiling.

"We are making progress, Daryl. Do you remember what just occurred?"

"Yes, I can remember up to the age of 13." What I did not say was that it felt like someone else's life.

As I drove home, I kept thinking about the experience. Why couldn't I feel anything about my life? I could remember the events, but I couldn't remember how I felt or thought as a child. I still couldn't remember my own children, my wedding, or my work. Maybe when my entire memory comes back, my emotions would come back as well. Then I will know how I felt about people and events in my life.

The following week I would wake up, yet again, with the loud popping sound. I had thought when my memory began to return, the popping

64

sound would stop, but it became louder than before. At my next appointment with David, I described the sound. He didn't know what caused it, but he hoped that when my memory returned completely, the popping sound would stop.

Under hypnosis again, I saw a movie of the rest of my life, up to and including my drowning. Yet I had no emotions, just a movie of events in the life of a man named Daryl, much like the movies I saw in the theaters. After the session, David was happy for me because my memory came back. He didn't understand that I still felt disconnected from the memories. "Wanda wants me to share my experience in the coma," I mentioned, thinking that if I have been told to do it by someone else, then it would be easier to tell David.

"Experience? What do you mean?"

"When they were working on me, I floated up above my body and was watching them. Then I felt as if I was sucked backward down this long tunnel. I found myself standing in front of this person. He was in a white robe with gold hair braided in a circle on top of his head. In the distance I could see other people standing, wearing regular clothes. When I tried to walk around him to see who they were, this person in the robe stopped me. He put his hand on my shoulder and said, 'Now the work shall begin. Ye must return now.' That's when I remember waking up in the hospital."

David said nothing. I looked up to find him staring at me. He seemed shocked.

Confused, I asked, "Have you ever heard of any such thing happening to anyone?"

David then shared his experience with me. "Back in 1967, I remember I became incredibly tired and went to lie down. Almost immediately, I found myself floating up out of my body and traveling at a high rate of speed. I looked down and saw I was over the Middle East watching a war. The war between Israel and Egypt had just started. It had not been announced on the news in the States yet, but I was there, watching it happen. I do not pretend to know about these things or how they happen, but I do know they happen. Would you like to come back again, Daryl, and explore this experience of yours under hypnosis? Maybe you can remember more of the event and the people."

"Yes, I haven't been able to get that experience out of my mind. It's the only thing I can remember."

"Come back next week and we'll see what we can uncover."

Knowing I wasn't the only person who had had such an experience gave me a sense of peace. Wanda would be happy to know David has had an out of body experience as well. She would also be very happy that my memory had returned. But I still couldn't understand why I had no feelings about my life. I decided not to tell Wanda about my lack of emotional attachment to the memories. I hadn't shared this information with David, either, but I thought I would discuss it next week.

The next week passed quickly. I was feeling a different apprehension this time. Since my memory had returned, I knew I didn't believe in life after death, and I had dismissed from my mind anything related to religion. Yet I knew what I had experienced during the coma. I was able to describe the emergency room, the bed I was on, and what they were doing to my body. I had not regained my original consciousness in that room. I knew it was real, and I knew it was against what I believed in.

During the week, I thought about different events in my life and wondered what I felt about particular events. The more I tried to think about it, the more perplexed I became about who I was.

I visited with my parents, my brother, and his wife; we talked about the past, and I realized not all of my memory had returned. In addition to the absence of emotional experiences, there were large gaps in my life. At the risk of being overly dramatic, I couldn't help wondering who I was and what I was doing here, in this reality, in this life. The age-old rhetorical question was very relevant to my situation. Perhaps when I saw David again I would re-experience the being with the golden hair, and then I would have some answers. I couldn't imagine what those answers would be, but I needed relief from the mounting tension and confusion in my mind.

Chapter 5
The Voice

I went to my next appointment with David. When I walked into his office, he greeted me with his usual compassionate smile and asked me to sit in the recliner. I felt very tired. I could hear David starting to count backward from ten. Before he reached the count of one, I woke up, wondering why I hadn't fallen into a trance. I opened my eyes and saw David sitting on the couch. His eyes were wide open and far away. His face was pallid. He looked at me and asked in a voice masked with great confusion, "Do you remember anything?"

"No, what happened?"

David took a deep breath and stared at the floor, seemingly looking for the strength to recount what happened. Possibilities flooded my mind, but given that I was still alive and breathing, I wasn't too worried.

"You started talking and all of a sudden I saw this cloud-like apparition come through the door. It moved across the room and entered into your body." He shook his head, as if he didn't believe what he had seen. "I mean, I have never experienced anything like it before. It was like I was talking to someone else. You, or it, or whatever it was, started talking about psychology. Have you ever studied psychology?" David had a hint of condemnation in his voice.

"No, I don't know anything about psychology. What does this mean?" I felt uneasy and confused about who was the therapist and who was the patient.

"Look, I think we should explore this experience further if you are willing," David suggested.

"I guess I am. I still have not re-experienced what occurred in the coma.

What do you think that cloud was?"

"I don't know, but I would like to find out."

He followed me as I walked out of his office, then immediately shut the door behind me.

On my drive back to Olympia, my mind was filled with thoughts going from one extreme to the other. Had I lost my mind, or had David lost his mind? Did I want to explore this further or just get back to business? Speaking of business, it just occurred to me that although I could remember my personal experiences, I still could not remember my business or how I conducted it. And that seemed to be the biggest issue for both my wife and Don, especially since our entire livelihood depended on my memory about how to make money.

Then I thought of another question: What am I going to tell Wanda? She wanted me to find out what happened during the coma. Should I tell her a cloud walked into David's office? Somehow, I didn't think that information would go over well, yet I continued to brainstorm different ways to tell Wanda that an apparition walked through the office, entered my body, and scared the hell out of my hypnotherapist. Also, I'm going back next week so that we can "explore" the whole twisted experience.

I figured after that little tidbit of information, maybe I could add that, by the way, I don't have any emotions whatsoever surrounding my memories of the past, including our wedding day and the birth of our children. And finally, so as to not leave anything out, I would tell her that I still don't know how to run my business, so we don't have any means to support ourselves after our savings and insurance run out.

I drove up the driveway and stopped the car. My hands had been gripping the steering wheel so hard that my knuckles were white and my fingers were numb. I took a deep breath and slowly pried my fingers off the wheel. Perhaps I am overreacting, perhaps she will take the information about today's office visit much better than I imagined. I don't really know her that well yet. I should give her the benefit of a doubt.

I walked into the house and realized she was not home from work yet. "Good," I said to myself. I have more time to think how I am going to explain this experience.

About half hour later, Wanda drove up with Jason and Tami. As soon as she walked into the house, out came the question I had dreaded, "Well, how did it go?"

"Ahh, fine. Yes, just fine. Nothing much happened today. David wants me to come back next week to continue with the therapy." I couldn't believe what just came out of my mouth. I looked at her straight on, just daring her to confront me, but she didn't. She started talking about upcoming school events for the kids, and I breathed a sigh of relief.

However, during dinner she asked again, "What do you mean nothing happened? How come nothing happened? I thought David was going to hypnotize you again so you could remember what occurred during the coma?"

"I don't know," I said, wishing she would drop the subject. "Maybe next week it will work."

That night as I was about to fall asleep, I felt my body start to vibrate. I seemed to be floating. The next thing I remembered was the loud popping sound coming from the center of my brain. It was morning; Wanda and the kids were already gone. What was that popping sound? I envisioned a tumor enveloping my brain. But David was the one who saw the cloud and I know we couldn't both have brain damage, so what is going on? I looked up at the ceiling and asked myself, who in the world can I tell this to? Then the answer came back to me: no one.

I got up, put on my robe, went out to the deck overlooking the lake, and just sat there trying to calm myself. I watched different boats go by with older men enjoying themselves fishing. What a simple life. Then I remembered my plan to buy a fishing boat and build a dock off my back yard. Maybe I should just cancel my meeting with David next week and get back to work and put all of this behind me. As soon as I had that thought, my back and head started hurting. I made myself breakfast and took one of my pain pills.

I decided I would go back and see David one more time, just to find out what was occurring and to see if that cloud returned. I had to know so I could put this entire experience behind me and get on with my life. It still bothered me not feeling any emotions and still having large gaps of memory missing. Maybe my memory had not returned at all. Maybe I was just remembering what everyone was telling me had occurred in my life. Maybe my life's memory was a collection of everyone's perception of my life. My mind would not let it alone. Besides, I still didn't know the cause of the popping sound in the center of my brain. I had to know.

When I walked into David's office, he seemed recovered from last week's event.

"Daryl, I have been talking to a psychologist who works in the office upstairs. She recommended I try automatic writing with you."

My mind immediately thought of a machine I would put my arm in and would move my hand. I asked, "What is automatic writing?"

David explained how he would put me under hypnosis and give me a pen and tablet to write on while I was in a trance state. "Do you think the cloud will return?" I asked.

"I don't know, maybe we can find out more by trying this technique."

David pulled up another chair for me to sit in close to his desk. He handed me a pen and tablet and started counting down from ten. In what seemed a few seconds, I woke up. I saw David holding the tablet.

"What happened?"

"I asked what the cloud was and you wrote the word Kitesa. Do you know anyone named Kitesa?"

"No, I never heard the name before."

"Do you know the name Phyllis?"

"That was my mother-in-law. Did I write that name, too?"

I looked up at David standing next to me; he was turning the tablet around and upside down. "What are you looking at?"

"You wrote something else but I can't make sense of it. It looks like it is written upside down or backwards. I need a mirror. There is one in the restroom down the hall."

I followed him into the restroom. He put the writing up to the mirror and turned the paper upside down.

"Look at that! It says, 'I have come to teach love between the mind and the heart. I have come to teach true healing.'"

We looked at each other and returned to his office. He sat at his desk and I sat in the chair facing him. "Look Daryl, I feel it is important we continue to study what is happening here. If you are willing, why don't you come once a week on Saturday, on my day off? I don't think I should charge you for exploring this experience together. What do you think?"

I stood there, staring at David, trying to process what he was saying. How had all these things come to be? How did it progress from me drowning in Hawaii and losing all my memory to having an apparition walk through walls and me transcribing messages from beyond the grave? With that thought, I remembered David mentioning Phyllis.

"What about Phyllis? What—I mean—where—ah—how?" My ability to form complete sentences seemed to go the way of my memory, but David understood and responded.

"Well, the writing says Phyllis is giving a message to Wanda. She is saying how much she loved Wanda and that she is around watching over her. When did you say she died?"

"In 1977."

"We really need to explore this further. Are you willing to meet next Saturday?"

All I could think about was my mother-in-law, who has been dead for over four years, was leaving a message for her daughter. How would I tell Wanda about that?

"Daryl. Daryl! Are you ok? Are you listening to me?"

I responded weakly, "Yes," though I really hadn't heard what he said.

"Yes, you will come Saturdays and let me work with you?" David asked eagerly.

"Yes, yes. Ok, I'll come." I couldn't believe what I was agreeing to. Then

I remembered something. "You know, when you started counting I felt this pressure on my lap."

"Pressure? What was it like?"

"It felt like a large beach ball pressing on my lap and into my stomach and chest."

"And when did you feel this?"

"As soon as you started counting." Apparently, I wasn't the only one in shock and awe.

"Can you make it here at one in the afternoon this Saturday?" David asked me.

"Yes." I answered. "Do you have any idea what the pressure was on my lap?"

"No, but I think we can find out the answers as we explore this further. Here, take these pages with you and show them to Wanda."

Wanda, I thought. I have to tell her what is going on. I have to tell her everything.

On the drive home I kept playing in my mind how I was going to tell Wanda about the last two visits with David. I wasn't sure how she would react when I told her about Phyllis. I tried to imagine going up to her and saying, "By the way sweetheart, your dead mother has a message for you." That should make for a nice conversation.

Should I tell her at dinner? No, the kids would be there. I should tell her as soon as the kids go to bed, but she would probably ask me as soon as I get home. If I tell her to wait until after the kids go to bed, she would worry. I played it out in my mind over and over driving home. Where are the simple days when I was just a carpenter? Then I realized that I had absolutely no idea if my days as a carpenter had been simple.

Wanda and the kids were already home. As soon as I opened the door, Wanda asked, "How did it go?"

"I'm tired. I'll tell you about it tonight."

"Tonight? Tell me about it now. I've been waiting all day to hear about it. Did you remember your experience during the coma?"

"No, but something else happened."

"What? What do you mean, something else happened?"

"Well, this cloud came into the room, and I did automatic writing." I flinched as the words flew out of my mouth. Shit! I thought. That could have come out a lot better.

"What?" Shock and dismay painted her face. "What are you saying, Daryl? What are you talking about? I want you to tell me everything." Her voice was reaching a higher pitch with each word.

I saw Jason and Tami watching TV. They gave us a quick glance to make sure nothing was wrong and then went back to watching cartoons. TV is an invaluable tool, I thought. I looked at Wanda and motioned for us to go upstairs.

We sat in the orange barrel chairs and faced each other. Wanda just stared at me, waiting for me to explain. I stared back, wondering how to explain what I didn't understand myself. I took a deep breath, closed my eyes, and started from the beginning.

I talked for an hour about what had occurred last week and today. I was surprised at how calm she was. "Tell me again what my mother said?"

I showed her the paper; she touched it as if Phyllis had written the note with her own hand.

"David said he wants me to come in every Saturday for a while to explore what is going on."

Wanda was still reading the note, engrossed in the meaning.

"What do you think?" I said, a little louder, trying to draw her attention back.

"I think you need to. Yes, certainly. I don't understand about the cloud. Was that this Kitesa person?"

"I don't know what it was."

"We need to understand what's going on. At least your memory has come back; that's all that really matters."

I looked down, hoping she wouldn't notice my expression. I really didn't want to think or talk about my memory or lack thereof. Besides, she had enough to digest right now. When the next Saturday arrived, I was just as confused as ever. I kept thinking of the name Kitesa. Somewhere deep inside me I knew it sounded familiar, but I couldn't figure out why. When I walked into David's office we talked a little about the cloud, the automatic writing, and the name Kitesa. David was just as confused as I was. The recent events were new experiences for both of us. I sat in the recliner and David started counting. As soon as he counted to one, I felt the pressure of a large beach ball sitting on my lap, moving into my body from my chest to my knees. And then everything went black. A voice speaking through me, said, "I am here."

"Are you Kitesa?" David asked.

"Yes, I am the Kitesa."

"Where do you come from?"

"From beyond physical matter. I have come to awaken Daryl to remember. I have come to teach healing of the mind, body, and spirit."

"Do you have a message for me?"

"Yes," said Kitesa. "There is a woman. She has gray hair that changes to blond. You must heal with this one. She is to depart the physical within a year's time."

"Who is this woman?"

"This is your mother. You must heal with this one. I must leave now. I must not tire the vehicle."

I was now awake and remembered nothing. David was sitting on the couch with a dazed look on his face. He looked at me and said, "Kitesa described my mother to me and said I must heal with her because she is going to die within a year."

"What? You never talked about your mother to me."

"Yes, I know," said David. "Kitesa said she has gray hair which changes to blond. She does have gray hair and has it dyed every month. We have been having problems for some time, but as far as I know, she is not ill. I think I'll call her this afternoon. That's all we can handle today. Are you up for next Saturday?"

"Yes, I am. Will you let me know how your mother is doing? I don't understand any of this. If this is a part of me speaking, how could I speak about a person I don't know?"

"I don't know. But I do know the cloud that appeared was not you. I will see you next Saturday."

That statement was unsettling to me. How could it not be me? Am I possessed? On the drive home I kept running through my mind the events of the afternoon. Why would this voice talk about his mother and her dying within a year?

When I arrived home, Wanda was waiting to hear what happened. I filled her in on David's mother.

"I don't know, Daryl; this is getting really strange." In her next breath she said, "You must continue with David. You have to find out what this is all about."

The next week Don called and asked to have lunch and go over our plans to build the apartment buildings. The Tumwater City Counsel had approved them. We decided to meet Tuesday afternoon. I wondered what I should tell him about my sessions with David. Don knew that my memory had returned, and he thought that was the end of it. He felt it was now time to get back to business. Something did not seem right about returning to building apartment buildings and developing land. I just didn't know what it was.

At the restaurant, Don was already sitting at a table in the corner. He was dressed in a new business suit with a new, bright red tie. I knew he was ready for things to get back to normal. "Daryl, it's good to see you. Sit down; we have a lot to talk about."

"Yes, we do," I said. "You know I'm still seeing David."

Don looked surprised and asked, "Why? I thought your memory had come back." "I want to talk to you about something."

His face turned pale. "I know, he said this whole thing was a put on, wasn't it?"

"No, Don, what happened to me was real."

"Then what is it?"

"When my memory came back, something else returned as well."

Just then, the waitress brought us our soup. I could tell Don was getting quite nervous. He started eating his soup and tried to change the subject by commenting on how excellent the soup was. "Maybe I could get some to take home with me," he said.

I ignored his soup comments and continued. "Don, when my memory came back, something else came with it—a spirit."

Soup dropped from his spoon and made a nice brown trail down his new tie. He was so shocked, he didn't notice at first. He smiled and said, "A joke, right?" He then realized what he had done to his new tie and said a few choice words as he was wiping up the mess.

"No, it's not a joke."

"Shit! Daryl, you can't tell anyone this. They'll think you have lost your mind. The banks will pull our line of credit. You will be ruined. What do you mean 'spirit'? What is this?"

I recounted the entire experience with the cloud appearing in the room and the discussion about David's mother. "Hell, Daryl, I thought this guy would make you jump around like a chicken, not any of this spirit shit. I thought you didn't believe in that crap anyway."

"I don't, I mean I didn't, but I can't explain any of this, Don."

"Now look, Daryl, you said you didn't see the cloud. You said you didn't remember saying anything to David about his mother. Maybe David is making all this up to get your insurance money; have you thought about this?"

"He stopped charging me when the cloud first occurred. He's not after my money. I don't think he's making any of this up. He wasn't acting when I saw him sitting on the couch after the cloud appeared. I can't tell you why, but I think this is for real. Besides, I am the one who felt the large beach ball on my lap."

"This is too strange, Daryl. We have apartments to build and you are off to Seattle talking to spirits. Hell, Daryl, you need to get with it. Drop this shit and let's get back to work and don't tell anyone about this."

"You are the only one who knows, Don, except for Wanda."

"And what does she think about all of this?" asked Don hopefully.

"She thinks I need to continue seeing David."

"Shit! Look, Daryl, if anyone asks why you are still seeing this David guy, just tell them you're seeing him for weight control. Let's keep this between ourselves." We finished the rest of our lunch in silence.

That evening, Don called. "Daryl, did you tell this Kitesa person to do anything to me?"

"What do you mean?"

"I was driving home and I said, 'If you are a real, whatever you are, Kitesa, get out of Daryl's life. We have business to do!' As soon as I said that the transformer at the traffic signal we were stopped at blew up and threw out sparks on the hood of my Mercedes. Did you make that happen? Did he make that happen?"

"I thought you didn't believe in Kitesa."

"Hell! I was just talking to myself because I was upset about how you're changing. I don't believe in any of this shit. So did you make Kitesa do that?"

"No, I didn't ask Kitesa to do anything. Did it damage your car?"

"No. It was strange. The hot pieces of metal landed on my hood, but they didn't damage the paint. I guess it was just a coincidence. Remember, don't tell anyone about this Kitesa fellow."

The next Saturday arrived and it was time to drive to Seattle.

When I arrived at David's office, he was sitting at his desk going through books.

"What are you doing?" I asked.

"I'm doing some research on what's occurring here."

"What have you found out?"

"Nothing. I guess I need to ask Kitesa. I don't know where else to turn."

I sat in the recliner. As David began to count, I felt the beach ball on my lap. The next thing I remembered was waking up. I looked at David and asked what was said.

"Kitesa said there would be a healing demonstration soon and that I would be feeling his presence."

"What does that mean?"

"I don't know. I asked him if I could feel his presence and he said, 'Yes, soon'. He then went on to tell me there would be a healing demonstration."

"Could that be your mother?"

"I talked to my mother, and she's feeling quite well. I don't know what that was about her dying in a year."

We talked for a little longer and then it was time to drive back to Olympia. After two Saturday sessions with David, I was feeling more confused than ever. His mother was not ill, yet she would die in a year? There would be a healing demonstration? It was too much for me to think about. Maybe Don was right; I just need to get back to building apartment complexes. But I honestly had no idea how I did my previous work. I needed to talk to David about the fact that my emotions and my knowledge of work had not come back.

I arrived home and told Wanda the news of the day and how confused I felt. "I still think you need to continue seeing David. We must find out what this is about."

That night I fell into a deep sleep and awoke with the popping sound. The house was empty. I looked at the clock and realized I had been asleep for twelve hours. I found a note in the kitchen; Wanda had taken the kids shopping.

I made a cup of coffee and went out on the deck to watch the fishing boats. As I was sitting there, everything disappeared and I saw myself standing in front of the being with the white robe and golden hair. This time I saw a picture being shown to me with a message. I could feel myself walking closer to the picture. I saw a group of children and teen-agers walking in and out of a building. I heard a voice say, "This you shall create."

"What is it?"

"A healing place for children."

The vision disappeared; I was looking out at the lake, still holding my cup of coffee. "What was that about?" I asked myself out loud. I then felt and heard the popping sound coming from the center of my brain. This was the first time it had occurred while I was fully awake. Maybe I have a brain tumor. Maybe this whole thing is the result of a brain tumor. Maybe I should go back and see Dr. Armentrout. Before I could continue that thought process, I heard Wanda and the kids coming into the house. They had a bag full of hamburgers and I was hungry. The thought of the brain tumor faded away.

Chapter 6
The Healing

"Daryl!" David shouted into the phone. "I just received a phone call from the parents of a client I had a couple of years ago. They told me their son is in the hospital and not expected to live. Can you come to Seattle tomorrow? I want to ask Kitesa if this is the healing demonstration he talked about last Saturday."

"I guess I can, but I don't know how this will help that boy. How old is he?"

"He's 14, but I haven't seen him for a couple of years. We became close when I was working with him during his parents' divorce. We have since lost contact. I feel it's very important we talk to Kitesa. Can you come up?"

"Yes, I'll come up tomorrow," I said, although I didn't want to. I didn't want to participate in a "healing demonstration," whatever that was. I didn't have any idea how I could help a dying child, and I had not had any positive experiences in hospitals. What am I getting myself into? I walked to the kitchen window, sat down, and stared out at the lake. Everything has changed so fast. I went to David to regain my memory; now an entity named Kitesa is speaking through me.

Despite my concerns, I went to David's the next day as promised.

"Daryl, sit down. I just received another call from Michael's parents. They told me the doctors give him about two weeks."

"What's wrong with him?"

"He has a rare blood disorder. His blood pressure is 300 over 200. He's in the intensive care unit. Let's talk to Kitesa and see if Michael is the one he was talking about."

Just as David started counting, Kitesa appeared and said, "I am here."

81

"Kitesa, is Michael the one you talked about last Saturday?"

"Yes, this is the one."

"Do you know this one?"

"We see this one. He is lying in a bed with many wires and tubes coming from his body. He has whiskers on his face and is very pale. You and the Daryl go to this one now. Daryl will be guided as to what to do."

Then Kitesa left. As soon as I awakened, David said, "This is the one. He even described what he looked like. Except I don't think he has whiskers on his face."

"What?"

"Kitesa said he has whiskers on his face. I don't think he does; he's only fourteen. Kitesa said you would be guided what to do when we arrive."

"He did? And what is that?"

"I don't know. Let's go. I talked to Michael's parents a little about you."

"What did they say?"

"They said they don't care who you are. They are willing to try anything to save their son. Are you ready?"

I couldn't believe what I was hearing. I'll be guided? To do what? I don't know how to heal anyone. Despite my doubts, I followed David out the door.

"Let's go in my car," David said. "I know how to get to the hospital."

A light drizzle was coming down from the gray sky. I watched the wipers move back and forth as if they were putting me into a trance. "What am I doing here?" I muttered myself. "I don't know anything about healing and I hate hospitals. The last one I was in, they lost me." If I had been in my own car, I think I would have made a dash for the freeway.

We arrived at Seattle Community Hospital just as the drizzle ended. The sun peeked through the clouds. We walked into the hospital; the directory listed the intensive care unit on the fourth floor.

In the elevator, David pushed the fourth floor button and we started moving up, but we went up to the sixth floor without stopping. David and I looked at each other. The button for the fourth floor was lit up, but the elevator did not stop. The doors opened at the sixth floor and before us stood a woman. She looked straight at us and said, "Children do need our help, don't they?"

Before we could answer, the elevator doors closed and the elevator moved down to the fourth floor. "What was that about?" David asked.

"You think I know anything about this?"

The doors opened. Michael's parents were sitting on a couch in the open area closest to the elevator. The woman was sobbing. When she saw David, she ran over and held onto him. "The doctors just saw him and told us they have given up hope."

Holding tightly onto her hand, David introduced me. "This is Daryl, the one I told you about over the phone."

"What is he going to do?"

"We don't know," David replied. "Daryl, this is Margie and Joe."

Joe stood up to shake my hand and Margie grabbed me and said, "Please do what ever you can. Michael is the only one I have left. Please help my son."

Joe led Margie back to the couch and told her to sit down. "I'm sure he will do whatever he can. Michael is in here." He pointed to the room across from him.

David looked at me and asked, "Are you ready?"

A calm feeling came over me. "Yes, let's go in."

Michael was lying on the bed with wires and tubes coming out of his body. The room had an odor I had never smelled before. We walked up to Michael and I heard David whisper, "He does have whiskers."

Michael opened his eyes and looked at us. "Hi, Michael, this is my friend Daryl. He came to help you."

He was too weak to answer, but his eyes gave an approving sign to us. I heard the popping sound followed by a voice that said, "Pull the sheet down to his waist. Place your left hand on his chest and your right hand on his stomach."

God, now I'm hearing voices, I thought. What the hell. I'm here; I might as well do it. I don't have any other ideas. I leaned over Michael and pulled down the sheet. I placed my left hand on his chest and right hand on his stomach. I began to feel heat moving through my body, down my arms, and out my hands.

"Keep your hands there. Do not remove them until the heat ceases to be," directed the voice.

Heat continued to increase. I moved my head over to the side to allow sweat to fall from my head. I didn't want the wires to get wet, thinking it might shock both of us. David was leaning over to look at me, watching the sweat now pouring from my head. I could feel his thoughts, but he remained silent. After about ten minutes, the heat stopped and I removed my hands. The heat left a bright red imprint of my palms on his chest and stomach. The palms of my hands were bright red as if they had been scorched. Michael looked up at me and just smiled. "That is all I can do," I said.

"Let's go talk to the Margie and Joe," David said.

We walked out of the room and sat down on the couch next to them.

"What did you do in there?" Margie asked.

"I put my hands on his chest and stomach." I didn't want to tell her or David I heard a voice saying to do that, so I answered, "I think it will help him."

"Oh," she said. "Did it help him?" Her voice trembled.

"I don't know. Let me know tomorrow how he's doing."

Margie and Joe started talking about their divorce and how it had affected Michael. At first, I felt like I was taking a back seat; then I heard myself telling them they needed to heal their relationship for the sake of Michael. I talked about their patterns of anger and fear. Out the corner of my eye, I noticed David staring at me with wide eyes. Finally he said, "I think we need to get back to the office, Daryl."

We all stood up and Margie thanked me for seeing her son as she and

Joe went into Michael's room.

"Where did you come up with that speech?" David asked.

"I don't know; it just came to me."

"Well, what you said was totally correct, and they needed to hear it. I knew they wouldn't listen to me." David shook his head. I just wanted to go home and relax in the spa. I'd had enough strangeness for one day.

The palms of my hands remained bright red for three days. I shared with Wanda the events that occurred at the hospital. Wanda kept repeating, "Daryl, helping that boy must mean that all this has to be good. Only words of love and healing are coming through you."

"What about David's mother? Kitesa told David she was going to die."

"Yes, but Kitesa also told David he needed to heal with his mother before that occurred. What if she dies before he has a chance to heal with her?"

"I've been thinking the same thing."

A couple of days later, David called. "Daryl, Michael has taken a turn for the worse. Can you come up here today and work on him again?"

Before I could answer, I heard the voice in my head, "Yes, go." I told David that I would leave immediately and meet him at the hospital. As I hung up the phone, I felt myself leave my body and enter Michael's hospital room. I saw him surrounded by nurses; his skin was pale and his eyes were closed. I snapped back into my body and sat down.

"What is it?" Wanda asked.

"I just saw Michael in the hospital. I can't explain it. It was like I was two places at the same time."

"Can you drive?"

"Yes, I'm fine now. I'll be back this evening."

As I was driving to Seattle my mind was running a mile a minute. Why was he getting worse after I worked on him? Where did the heat come from? Why did my palms turn red and stay red for three days? Why? Why? Why? My brain was tired. I turned on the radio to distract my mind. An announcer was speaking the last few words of an advertisement. He said, "And yes, the children do need our help," echoing the words from the woman in the hospital. Startled, I turned off the radio and concentrated on my driving.

At the hospital, I parked and sat still for a few minutes thinking, if it didn't help Michael last time, why would it help him this time?" I went in; David was waiting for me.

"Daryl, the nurse is in with Michael right now. When she's finished, we can go in."

"What happened?"

"We don't know. He had some type of relapse."

The nurse came out and asked, "Are you Mr. Harrison?"

"Yes."

"Just between you and me, I want you to know Michael was improving after you saw him a few days ago. I told the doctors they needed to reduce his medication, but they didn't agree. I think he had a relapse because he improved but the drugs were too strong for him. I hope you can help him, Mr. Harrison."

She walked away. David looked at me and asked, "Are you ready?"

We walked into the room. The same odor was there as before. Michael was tossing back and forth on his bed. The sheet was already pulled down to his waist. I again heard this voice say, "Place your left hand on his chest and your right hand on his stomach."

As soon as my hands made contact, heat started flowing. Sweat again flowed from my forehead. I continued to hold my hands in place until the heat decreased. "That is it," I said.

"Look at you! Your shirt is dripping wet. Where is all that heat coming from?" David asked, amazed.

"You're asking the wrong person."

"Can we get together in a couple of days? Some of my colleagues would like to meet you and talk to Kitesa," David asked quietly.

"Let me think about it. I need to understand some more of what is occurring myself."

"I'll call you in a few days, Daryl, and see how you're doing."

I left for home. As soon as I walked in, Wanda said, "Don called and wants to get together with you."

Now what do I do? I felt as if I was living in two different worlds. Then she said, "Your mom and dad also want to come over to visit."

I now knew who my parents were, but my feelings of them had not returned. Except for Wanda and our children, my family members were emotional strangers to me.

When my parents came over to visit that evening, we had a pleasant but awkward visit. I could remember past events, or at least the events I had been told over the last few months, but deep inside I didn't know them, and I knew they didn't know me.

Just before I fell asleep that evening, I heard the loud popping in my brain. I felt myself flying at a high rate of speed. The next thing I remembered was waking up in the morning. I got up to get a cup of coffee and Wanda was sitting there drinking her tea looking out at the lake. I heard myself say, "Wanda, I think we need to open up a place of some kind to help children."

I could not believe I said that. Wanda looked surprised. "Why did you say that?"

"I don't know. I wasn't even thinking about it."

"I had a dream of such a place," Wanda said. "It was in the mountains."

"You had a dream?"

"Yes, I was just sitting here thinking about the dream when you walked in and said we should open up a place for children."

Just then the phone rang. It was David. "Daryl, wonderful news. Michael has made a turnaround. They decreased the drugs yesterday after you left. He's going to make it."

I almost dropped the phone. "Wanda, Michael's going to make it!"

I forgot David was still talking. "Daryl, can you make it up here this Saturday to meet with my colleagues? We can visit with Michael as well."

"Yes, I can make it."

"Can you be here at noon?"

"Yes, I'll be there." I looked over at Wanda and said, "David wants me to meet his colleagues. Do you want to go with me?"

"I don't think so. I want to hear about what happens, but I'm not ready to see someone speak through you," Wanda said nervously.

Surprised at her reluctance, I said, "But I think you need to go. We need to find out more about what is occurring here."

Another phone call interrupted us; someone from our bank asked me to come to the special services department to resolve a problem with a check. I told her we would be there shortly and hung up, looking perplexed.

"Who was it? What's wrong?" Wanda asked.

"It was the bank. They think someone is forging my signature."

That afternoon we drove over to our bank. We went into the special services section and I introduced myself to the woman who had called. She showed us the check and my signature card. "The signatures aren't even close," she stated.

"That's my signature. I remember writing this check."

Obviously upset, she sighed with exasperation. "You need to sign another signature card before we can process any more checks, Mr. Harrison. I also need to look at your driver's license."

I showed her my driver's license. "This is not the same signature you have now," she said suspiciously.

"I don't know about that." I pointed at the check. "This is my signature now."

"Well, sign this new signature card."

Wanda looked over my shoulder at both signatures. "They are different," she said. "When did that change?"

I took a deep breath and said, "Let's go."

I called Don and met him for lunch the next day. "Daryl, are you ready to get back to work?" he asked as soon as I sat down.

"I don't know what I'm ready for," I answered truthfully.

I shared with Don my experiences with Michael. "Daryl, you are starting to scare me. This is strange shit. Look, let's just go back to building apartments. Can't we just forget all this has happened?"

"How can I forget it? My life is strange when I'm awake and strange when I'm asleep. I'm meeting with David's colleagues this Saturday. Then maybe I can answer when my life will get back to normal."

"Shit, Daryl, you can't meet with this group. Word will get out about you. The more people that know, the more damage it will do. You know I saw Tim and Judy yesterday. She said she saw you at the bank. She said the hypnosis is not working on your weight. Judy is getting suspicious about why you're continuing to see David. Come on, Daryl; let's just get back to work. Drop this stuff. It will ruin you." That evening, I felt I was being pulled apart. People wanted the old me, but I could not find the old me. I was not even sure if I liked the old me.

After Wanda and the kids went to bed, I went into the formal living room and sat on the couch. I began running through all of the events of the last couple of months. I felt something in the air, and the hair on my arms began to stand up. Everything became very still, as if I was frozen in time. I found myself staring at our five-post lamp across the room. On top of each post was a round glass globe forming a spiral, each globe higher than the next. All five globes were lit up. Frustrated, I asked out loud, "Kitesa, if you are real, make the third bulb burn out."

A booming voice came from all corners of the room: "At this time we shall demonstrate unto you. Do not ask again. It is our purpose to assist you, not to prove to you." Immediately, the third bulb burned out. I felt shocked and then comforted.

I said, "Kitesa, if that is you, I want to meet someone like me, or at least someone who has someone speaking through him."

The same voice said, "In three days you shall know of one. Now go rest, beloved."

"Three days," I thought to myself. "That's when I meet with David and his colleagues." Then the energy of the room cleared, and. I felt like I was sitting in a hollow space.

I got up and walked to our bedroom. As I reached for the door, it opened by itself. It felt like all the air was sucked out of my lungs. I walked into the bedroom to Wanda's side of the bed to see if she was asleep. She was. Turning to face the door, I saw it close on its own. I quickly got undressed and slid under the covers, pulling them up to my neck. I lay there thinking about everything that had occurred in the last hour. I felt the covers being pulled down. I grabbed them and pulled them back up. They were pulled down again. This time it awakened Wanda.

"What are you doing?"

"Nothing. Someone is pulling down the covers." I was shaking.

She quickly sat up to see the covers again being pulled down. Then the corner of the bed by her feet went down.

She curled up her legs underneath her, staring. "Someone's sitting on the bed. Who is here?" she asked nervously.

"I think it is Kitesa."

I told Wanda about the light and the three-day message. "I don't know if I'm ready for this," Wanda said. At that moment the corner of the bed rose back up. The presence in the room was gone.

When I walked into David's office the following Saturday, I was surprised at the number of people there. David's colleagues were psychiatrists and psychologists. I sat in the recliner. David talked to the group about the series of events that had occurred, including Michael's healing. I noticed one man sitting in the corner of the room. I knew I had met him somewhere, but I could not place him. He refused to look at me, which I thought was strange. When David finished speaking, he asked, "Daryl, is there anything you want to ask before we ask Kitesa to come and speak to us?"

"Yes." I looked over at the man in the corner and said, "I have met you somewhere."

He jumped up and said, "God damn it, this is scaring the shit out of me."

David, with a surprised look spoke up and said, "What is going on here?"

The man replied, "I've been having Daryl in my dreams for the last couple of weeks. And I know I've never met him before."

"That's it! You were in my dreams, too."

"Look, David," said the man, "this is really scaring the shit out of me."

"Calm down, Mark," David said.

"Mark, that's the name," I said.

"What do you mean?" David asked.

"That's the name he told me in my dream," I answered, smiling.

Mark turned his faced down, refusing to look at me. I glanced around the room and saw that everyone looked surprised.

"Can we get started now, Daryl?" David asked me.

David started counting down and within a few seconds Kitesa entered into my body. He looked around the room and started talking to each person. He spoke of their fears and their clients' issues for about an hour; then he left. When I regained consciousness, I began visiting with David's colleagues. Toward the end of our meeting, a woman named Kathy looked at me and said, "Daryl, for the last three days I've been feeling I need to give you the name and phone number of a woman I know. I think she can help you understand what is occurring with you."

I knew that was the person Kitesa said I would meet. I glanced at Mark, but he still would not look at me. David then told the group we had to go to the hospital and see Michael. Everyone quickly got up and left. I never encountered Mark again to discuss any significance to our meeting in the dream state.

Michael was still in the hospital recovering from his illness. This time the elevator took us to the fourth floor without any detours. Margie hugged me and said, "Michael is going to live. He's doing much better. His doctor is in there with him now."

When the doctor came out, he asked me, "Are you Mr. Harrison?" he asked.

"Yes," I replied.

"Listen, Mr. Harrison, I don't know what you have done, and I don't want to know, but keep doing it; it's working. Thank you for helping." Then he quickly turned and walked away.

David and I walked into the Michael's room as he was sitting up to watch TV. His color was normal, and he had a big smile on his face. Michael said, "I told my dad how you worked on me and how your hands got hot. My dad tried to make heat come out of his hands, but nothing happened. I felt better when the heat came out of your hands. Will you work on me again?"

"Yes," I said. "Lie down." Again the heat came out of my hands but not with the same intensity as before. A few days later, Michael was released from the hospital.

On the way home, I reached into my pocket and looked at the name that Kathy had given me—Sharon White. I wondered if she could really help me. I told Wanda about it and she asked, "Are you going to see this Sharon?"

"I think I will. Do you want to go with me?"

"No, I don't think I'm ready just yet," Wanda replied.

I wasn't sure if I was ready. It was one thing to have a spirit speak through me but another to go speak to one. The following night I had the popping sound in my brain; when I awakened, I knew I had to call Sharon White. I called her after breakfast.

"Hello," I said, "Kathy gave me your name. I've been seeing David Calof."

Almost before I could finish the sentence, she said, "Yes, Kathy told me all about you. Would you like to come over today and visit?"

"Yes, I would like that."

She lived about an hour from our home. I told Wanda I was going to see Sharon and asked her again if she wanted to come.

"No, I have to go to work today," answered Wanda, looking relieved.

I arrived at Sharon's house and knocked on the door. A woman with dark curly hair and piercing brown eyes answered. She was wearing a long flowing muumuu with bright colors swirling all around. Her voice was deep and raspy. "Hi, Daryl. Welcome. Do you want some coffee or wine?"

Thinking it was much too early for wine, I opted for coffee.

We sat down and she told me how the entity works that comes through her. She then explained how to operate her tape recorder. "Are you ready?" she asked.

"I think so," I replied, not quite knowing what to expect.

Sharon sat down in her rocking chair; her body stiffened and another voice came out of her mouth. "Greetings, you wish to speak with us?"

"Yes, can you tell me about Kitesa?"

"Indeed!" the voice said. "Kitesa is one of three who shall assist you; then one evolved beyond eons of time in the essence of love shall come forth. You shall travel the earth with this one who shall speak to many. Be not fearful, for you are loved and you have come to this earth to fulfill this work. Allow it to be, for it shall be a work of strong love."

"Strong love? What is that?" I asked.

"Strong love is a work that tells souls what they need to hear, not what they want to hear. Many come only to hear what they want to hear, not what they need to hear."

"What do I need to hear?" I asked.

"You shall be moving soon from your domicile; it is not yours. It would be of mental and emotional benefit to move to Vashon Island; you need to be completely surrounded by water."

"What?" I never expected to hear something about moving.

"Good-bye," the voice said, and Sharon returned.

"Well, that was short and sweet," she said. "Do you want some more coffee?"

"Yes, no, maybe I will have wine instead," I stammered, trying to make sense of what I had just experienced.

As I drove home, I slowly realized that the thought of moving to an island appealed to me. Everyone had told me that I was living in my dream house, but it felt like the home of someone else. When I walked into the kitchen, Wanda was preparing dinner. She turned and asked, "What happened?"

"How would you like to move to an island?" I blurted out.

"What? An island? What are you talking about?"

"You can listen to the tape," I said, handing her a recording of my session.

Wanda listened to the tape after dinner. "I think I'm ready to talk to Kitesa. I want to find out what he thinks about all of this."

"Do you want to do it now?" I felt relieved that she wanted to become more involved.

"Can you do it on your own?"

"Well, if I just relax and count backward, maybe he will come and speak to you. Let's wait until Jason and Tami go to bed," I suggested.

Later that night we went up to the recreation room and sat in our round orange chairs. Wanda got a tape recorder and we sat there looking at each other. "Well, what happens now?" Wanda asked.

"I don't know; maybe I need to call him in my mind."

As soon as I said that I could feel the sensation of the beach ball on my lap. Kitesa came and greeted Wanda, "Greetings, little one."

"Can you help us understand what this is all about? Why are you speaking through Daryl, and are we to move to an island?" Wanda spoke quickly, her hands tightly grasping the arms of her chair.

Kitesa said, "Your child is standing in the corner behind us. He has a question for you."

Wanda turned around and there was Jason. Kitesa then said, "Little child, the candy you have hidden behind you is not good for you."

Wanda asked Jason, "Do you have candy?"

"Yes, Mommy. Can I have this?" He held out a candy bar.

"No, honey you need to go back to bed," answered Wanda.

"How did Daddy know I had candy when his eyes are closed?" Jason asked.

"That is not daddy; that is Kitesa," Wanda attempted to explain.

"What?" Jason said even more confused now.

"Go to bed. I'll explain it to you in the morning," Wanda gently said.

Jason left.

"Now to your questions," Kitesa said. "I will be here for a short time and then another will come for a time and then another will come for a time before the one of strong love shall arrive. Yes, it would be beneficial at this time to move. Your energy does not work well with this house. Yes, indeed it is of goodness to move to Vashon Island. You will be surrounded by water."

"But we live on a lake," Wanda said, not understanding the difference.

"Yes, but you are not surrounded by water, indeed salt water. Then you shall move to the mountains. The water will assist you to grow in spirit. The mountains will assist you to grow in consciousness. All of this shall be made clear, little one. It is always your choice; spirit will never force you to move. But indeed, you shall begin to find difficulties in your house because of your energy shift. Dreams shall come unto you when you are ready. Go now, little one, and rest."

I felt as if I woke up out of a deep sleep. "What did he have to say?" Wanda filled me in on what occurred during that long twenty minutes, including the interaction with Jason.

The next day David called and asked to get together next Saturday. I told him about Kitesa coming through. He thought it was wonderful I could control when he came through without hypnosis.

We met on Saturday and talked about the experience of Kitesa. He then told me about an unusual jogging experience. The afternoon after we last went to see Michael at the hospital, David decided to go jogging by Lake Washington. As he was running, he was trying to fit into his mind everything that had occurred. He then asked Kitesa, "If you are real, will you show yourself to me?"

David then heard footsteps of someone jogging behind him. He turned to see who it was so he could make room on the running path. "No one was there," he told me. "But I could hear the footsteps and then I felt this energy move into my body. I felt this powerful surge as if I could run for miles. I think that was Kitesa."

Despite the excitement from his interaction with Kitesa, I noticed he seemed down. I asked him if anything was wrong.

"I got a call this morning from my mother. She just found out she has cancer. The doctors have only given her a few months to live. I am so thankful for the information earlier. I've been able to reconnect with her. But now that I have reconnected with her, she is dying, so it's very painful. I want to thank Kitesa for his help today when I talk with him."

I sat back and asked Kitesa to come. Instead as I laid back and closed my eyes, I found myself standing in front of a building. However, I could still talk to David.

"What do you see?" David asked.

"I am standing in front of a large building four stories high. The building looks like it is made out of a pearl-like substance. Each floor has windows with a different colored light. There is a large opening like doorway I am now standing in front of."

I could hear David asking me questions, but I could not see David, only the building. "Can you see inside a window?"

"I will try," I answered.

I felt myself floating up to a fourth story window and looking in. "All I can see is a room filled with gold light," I explained to David.

"What does the area look like around the building?" David questioned me.

"It is rolling hills with green grass and patches of flowers."

"Go to the opening you saw," David directed.

I felt myself floating down to the ground, landing in front of the opening. "Can you walk in?" David asked me.

"I will try."

As I walked up to the opening, two sliding doors slammed shut with a loud bang. The doors looked like black onyx with a large eye in the center filling up three quarters of the doors. "What happened?" I heard David ask.

"The doors slammed shut. There is an eye ball in the door."

"What does the eye look like?"

"It is a bright flaming blue eye, and it's starting to move," I answered.

"The doors are moving?"

"No, the eye is moving. Like someone moving his eye, looking at something." I felt myself snapping back into my body. "What was that about?" I asked.

"I don't know. Do you have any feeling about it?" David asked.

"No, I've never seen anything like it before."

David and I discussed the vision. We were not able to come up with any particular reason for what I was seeing.

"Daryl, I feel like our time together is coming to an end. You can call on Kitesa now on your own. But first I would like you to come back and allow Kitesa to talk to my colleagues again. They would like another opportunity to speak with him. How do you feel about that?"

"Is Mark going to be there?" I asked David. "I would like to discuss the dream he mentioned."

"I don't know. I did talk with him about our last group and his dreams with you. He is still unsettled about the whole experience, but I will ask him. We can set up next Saturday for a group session with Kitesa, if you are willing."

The next Saturday arrived, and I knew this would be our last time together. I still was not sure what I wanted to do. I didn't feel any connection to being a contractor, yet that is how I made my income. Even if I moved to Vashon, I didn't know what I would do.

David's office was filled with people waiting for me, but Mark was not there.

"Daryl," David said, "come and sit down. Would you like to explore the experience we had last Saturday with the pearl-colored building? I've been sharing our last experience with the group, and we would like to learn more."

"Yes," I said. "Maybe this time I can go inside." David began the count down to hypnotize me.

I felt myself floating out of my body. I was again standing in front of the same building. "The doors are open," I said.

"Slowly walk up to them," David suggested.

I walked toward the doors, expecting them to close in my face. This time they did not close. "Can you see in?" David asked.

"Yes, it looks like long hallways with giant pillars. The inside doesn't look like the outside," I explained.

"Are the doors still open?"

"Yes, they are."

"Can you see anyone?"

"No, just long hallways."

I began to walk through the doorway, but as soon as I entered the building, I collapsed, falling over onto the arm of the chair. Then David and the others were standing around my chair looking at me, shaking my shoulders and trying to bring me out of the trance. As I opened my eyes, David held my gaze. "Are you all right, Daryl?" he asked, concerned.

"What happened?"

"The last thing you said was, you were going to walk into the building; then you collapsed. Do you remember anything?" David explained.

"No, nothing," I lied.

In truth, I did have a strong feeling, but I wanted to keep it to myself. I felt as if I had explored my history of where I came from, although even that feeling did not make sense to me.

"Are you up to allowing Kitesa to speak with us?" David asked.

"Yes, I guess so."

David automatically started his usual count down. As soon as he said one, Kitesa appeared. He talked about forty-five minutes to the group, answering most of their questions. He would not address what occurred when I entered the strange building. When I came out of the trance, I knew this phase of my life with David was over. I didn't know why I felt that it was over, but the feeling had been growing inside me. David, his colleagues, and I had learned what we needed to learn.

Chapter 7
Seeing the World Through New Eyes

Driving home from Seattle, I knew that the door to my past was closing, and soon I would be walking through a new door leading to new pathways. I had very little emotional connection to my life before the accident. I didn't have the knowledge or memory to run my business nor did I have the desire, but still I couldn't quite let go. My past was a mystery, but the future was even more uncertain. Even though my intuition was leading me forward, I wasn't quite ready to take that leap of faith.

Maybe if I spent more time with Don, my desire and memory would return and I could leave this reality and settle into the more normal life that I had been living successfully for years. The next morning I called Don and asked if he wanted to go to lunch.

"Hell, yes! Let's get back to work. It's just you, isn't it?" Don asked cautiously.

"What do you mean?"

"You aren't going to bring any of your ghost friends with you?"

"No, Don, just me." I answered a wearily.

We sat for hours talking about our past, our future, and our prospects for becoming millionaires in a few years. But the more we talked, the more I realized that money didn't have the meaning it used to. Don picked up on my indifferent attitude toward wealth and quickly counteracted with a comment about Wanda and the kids.

He leaned over the table, looked directly at me, and said, "What about your family? Don't you want to make money for them?" It was his last ditch effort to rope me back into the life I lived before, the life that included making us both millionaires. Don had much to lose if I chose not to go back to my prior way of life.

I felt hooked. "Of course I want them to have a comfortable life. But what about my life, or what's left of it?" I asked. "I was told it would be best to move to Vashon Island."

"What in the hell are you talking about, Daryl? You just built your dream house. Drop everything and go live with a ghost? Get real, Daryl. Look, I have to go and sell a house. Let's get together tomorrow for lunch and finish our talk."

That evening I talked with Wanda about my lunch with Don.

"Daryl, why don't we talk with Kitesa? Let's see what he has to say. I feel all of this is happening for a reason," Wanda said calmly.

"Maybe later," I said. "I just want to be able to feel what I want to do."

"Well, while you're feeling, you need to go down to JC Penney and buy some new pants. Your old pants are too big and worn out," Wanda told me.

"Do they look that bad? "I asked. "My life is changing at a drastic rate, and all of a sudden you're concerned about my wardrobe?"

"Yes, go get some new clothes tomorrow," Wanda stated.

The next morning I drove to Penney's at the Mall in Olympia, but I was too early. I sat inside the mall on a bench waiting for Penney's to open. I thought about what Don had said the day before, that maybe I was crazy to think about moving to Vashon. I owned a beautiful house, I had a business, and here I was thinking about dropping everything and moving to some island.

As I was thinking, I looked down the long empty walkway in the mall. The only person I saw was an elderly lady about a 100 feet from me. I could see bright colors of blue and gold surrounding her. She walked closer, and I could see her silver hair and how well she was dressed. While I was watching her, I noticed she was watching me. She was looking straight at me without blinking an eye. I knew I had never seen this woman before, yet the color around her looked very familiar.

When she was within a couple of feet of me, she stopped and just stared at me. I looked up at her from the bench and watched her blue eyes stare straight into mine. I was about to say something when she said, "Well Daryl, I guess you are choosing to go in the opposite direction." She shook her head and walked past me. I turned around to see where she was going and she was gone. No stores were open she could have gone into. She simply vanished into thin air. I was so shaken I got up and left, forgetting I was there to buy some new pants.

When I arrived home, I was still shaking. I went out on the deck and looked at the lake. With all the strange events that have occurred in my life since December 17, I wondered why this event upset me so much.

Then I realized it was not that the woman knew my name and disappeared into thin air. It was her message about me going in the opposite direction. I decided I did want to talk with Kitesa when Wanda came home from work. I knew I needed some answers.

After Jason and Tami went to bed, Wanda and I went upstairs to sit in our orange chairs. I heard a voice telling me to place my hands on my forehead and relax. I followed my feelings; the next thing I knew, Wanda was sitting there finishing her notes on what Kitesa had said.

"Well," Wanda said, "Kitesa feels we need to move to Vashon. Your work as a contractor is over. He also said we needed to go on a vacation to get away from family and friends and just be by ourselves. I asked Kitesa if this vacation would be enjoyable, and he said that it would be. Then when we return our house would sell. Then he said that after a time, we would be moving to the mountains."

"The mountains? What mountains?" I asked thinking each answer brought with it another question.

"I didn't ask. I was in shock when he said your work as a contractor is over," Wanda stated honestly.

"Then what? What do we do after we move to Vashon?" I asked thinking of the dwindling savings account.

"Kitesa said we are not to do any advertising. We are to move and rest for 30 days. People will start calling, seeking advice and healing," Wanda continued reading from her notes.

"How are they going to know about me?"

"He said we don't need to worry. We just need to move and rest and the people will come. I don't know how, Daryl. Kitesa seems to think it is the best thing to do and everything will work out." Wanda seemed too calm, in my opinion.

"It's a slow market for selling large houses. How are we ever going to sell it? Don said the bottom has fallen out of the market. People are only investing in income property like the apartment buildings I built—or used to build." My head was starting to spin.

"All we can do is try. By the way, you should make a second attempt to get those pants," Wanda said, sounding hopeful.

The next day, I knew that I needed to call Don and tell him of our plans. I really didn't want to do this. My hands felt clammy holding the receiver. I could already hear Don's scolding voice warning me of impending doom and financial failure. I took a deep breath and told him everything.

"Daryl, you are making the biggest mistake of your life if you do this! You know that, don't you?" Don sounded defeated.

"I don't think so, Don. It feels right."

"Yeah, right my ass. You'll come crawling back here in a few months wanting everything back. You know in this market you're going to lose your ass on selling your house," said Don. The anger in his voice increased with each word.

"Look, just list it and see what happens. We're going on a vacation in a couple of weeks, so I want to list it now."

"Vacation! What the hell is wrong with you? Your savings are almost gone. You are going to lose your ass on selling the house, and you want to move to Vashon Island. I told you not to go to that chicken shit doctor in Seattle, didn't I? Now look at yourself. You're ruining your life!"

"I don't think so. Can you come over and bring the listing papers this afternoon?"

"No, I want to wait until tomorrow and see if you come to your senses,"

Don said more quietly.

"Fine, I will see you tomorrow." I felt just as frustrated with him as he was with me.

The next day he arrived about noon. I had never seen him so depressed. "Here are the papers, Daryl. Have Wanda sign them and bring them to my office."

He turned around and walked away. Halfway to his car, he turned around and asked, "By the way, do you know a woman named Karen Whitman?"

"No, why?" I asked.

"Well, her son committed suicide last week. She said you came to her in her dreams and brought her son to her. She said you helped her with her grief."

"What?" Had I heard him correctly?

"Nothing, Daryl, just some more of this crazy shit. Can you at least wait until I sell your house before you go on vacation?"

"I'll think about it."

Don said good-bye with a tone in his voice that said, "This is it. Have a nice life."

It sounded wise to wait until the house sold before we went on vacation. We could put all of our furniture in storage, go on vacation, and find a house when we returned. We could save some money doing it that way. I convinced myself that was the way to go.

When Wanda returned home she asked if Don had brought over the listing papers to sell the house. "Yes," I said and told her about Karen Whitman and her son. Wanda agreed to wait on the vacation until the house sold, but she wasn't happy about it.

The next morning, Wanda had a call from her aunt and uncle in Pennsylvania. "They haven't seen me since my mother died. They want the kids and me to come for a visit. School is out in a couple of weeks. I was thinking of taking the kids and flying back to see them."

"That sounds like a good idea. I can stay here and keep the house and yard up while they show it," I said.

The next couple of weeks passed and no one looked at the house. Wanda and our children were flying to Pennsylvania the next day, and I hoped the house would sell while they were gone. But I was worried; my intuition told me we were going about this wrong. The drive to Sea Tac airport was quiet. For Wanda, going back to Pennsylvania to see her aunt and uncle brought up many memories of her mother who died just a few years ago. Her Uncle Don had just gone through a heart transplant and was not doing well. Another uncle, Russ, had died of a heart attack in his late thirties when Wanda was a child. Most of her mother's family seemed to die young of heart attacks.

Wanda called to let me know they had arrived safely. She asked about the house, I told her no one had even looked at the house.

Late the next evening when I was reading the newspaper in the formal living room, I felt a strange energy come over me. It felt similar to going into a trance with Kitesa, but a little different. I was still conscious, although it did not feel like me. It was as if someone else was using my body, though I knew that wasn't true.

I felt this strange desire to go for a drive. I walked out the front door and got into Wanda's car. I drove through the large iron gates and down the county road. I noticed a man standing on the side of the road wearing a flamboyant, short-sleeved Hawaiian shirt. As I passed, he lifted his arm, smiled, and waved. It didn't seem odd to me that someone would be walking around late at night wearing that type of shirt.

I was still in a trance yet completely conscious of what I was doing. After hours of driving, I found myself out in the country. I remember looking at the clock in the radio and seeing 1:00 a.m. When I glanced down again, it was 3:00 a.m. I felt wide awake and out of the trance. I made a U-turn at the next intersection in the middle of nowhere. "Why did I do this?" I asked myself. I remembered making the choices, but none of the choices made any sense to me. I drove home and went to bed.

The next morning, the sound of someone knocking loudly at the front door woke me up. I stumbled to the door cursing whoever would be dense enough to wake me up from a sound sleep, especially after last night's adventures. I was exhausted.

I went to the front door. It was Tim. I opened the door and before I could even ask him what the hell he was doing, Tim blurted out, "Have you read the paper this morning?"

"No, I was sleeping. You woke me up to ask me if I read the paper?"

"Well, not really. I couldn't get you out of my mind last night. I called but no one answered. So I came over to check on you."

"So why did you ask if I read the paper?" I asked, confused.

"Where is it? I'll show you."

"I guess it's still outside in the box," I said.

Tim walked to the paper box next to my driveway. He came back into the house as I was putting on a pot of coffee. "Daryl, look what happened last night."

He opened the paper and showed me an article on the front page. "UFO seen over Thurston County." The article described different people reporting a large UFO over the same intersection where I came out of my semi-trance and made a U-turn.

"I was there last night." I said.

"Where?"

"At that intersection at three this morning. That's why I didn't answer the phone. I wasn't home." I sipped my coffee.

"Why were you driving around at three in the morning?"

"I don't know. I just felt a strong urge to drive last night, and that's where I ended up."

"Did you see it?"

"No, I didn't see anything. I made a U-turn at the intersection and drove home and went to bed."

"What is this all about, Daryl?"

"You're asking me? I don't even believe in UFO's."

"Yeah, and you didn't believe in a spirit world either. Now look at you.

You're involved up to your neck!"

That evening Wanda called from Pennsylvania asking how everything was going. I told her about the semi-trance I went into, the drive out into the country, and the UFO report. All she could say is, "What? Oh no, oh, oh boy. I can't talk right now; you can fill me in when I return in a few days."

I joked and said, "Well, I hope I'm here when you return."

"Don't play with my mind. You had better stay put," she said.

The next day I received a phone call from a doctor I had never met. "Mr. Harrison," he said, "I have heard you do healing work; is this so?"

"Well, I have worked on a few people. Why do you ask?"

"Look, Mr. Harrison, this must be kept confidential. No one is to know I've called you. Do you agree with this?" he said sternly.

"Yes, but what is this about?" I asked, wondering how he knew me.

"My son has a tumor in his stomach. Next week he's scheduled to go into surgery to have it removed, along with part of his stomach. Can I bring him to see you?" He sounded desperate.

"Yes, I'm free this afternoon. How old is your son?"

"He is ten," his voice was cracking with emotion.

I gave him the directions to my house and told him I would see him at 4:00 p.m. When I hung up the phone, I realized I didn't even get his name.

At four, I opened the door and there stood a red-headed boy with big blue eyes filled with fear and distress. His father held out his hand and said, "I'm the one who called you. Please, Mr. Harrison, you must keep this in complete confidence. I prefer not to give you my name. Is this all right?"

"Yes, but why the secrecy?"

"As I told you on the phone, I'm a doctor. If word gets out I brought my son to a faith healer, I would be ruined."

"First of all, I'm not a faith healer. I don't know what I am, but it has nothing to do with faith."

"I heard you did a miracle on that boy in Seattle."

"I don't know what I did or even if I did it. It certainly was not faith because I had no faith it would work. I'll see what I can do for your son, if anything." I wondered if I would receive directions like last time.

I asked the boy to lie down on the couch while his father pulled up a chair to watch. I moved my hand over his body and felt an ice-cold spot over his stomach area. "I can feel it," I said.

The voice did come to me and I sighed with relief. The voice told me to use my finger to place pressure on different parts of his stomach and chest, then put my right hand on his stomach and my left hand on his forehead. Intense heat began moving out of my hands into the boy's body.

"Why are you sweating?" the father asked.

"I get hot. Don't talk to me now."

The father sat back in his chair with his eyes glued to my hands. I kept my hands there for about ten minutes until the heat ended. I turned to his father and said, "That's all I can do."

"Thank you, Mr. Harrison, for your help."

He took his son's hand and helped him off the couch. They slowly walked out the front door. I thought I would never hear from him again, but the next Monday he called and said, "Mr. Harrison, I just wanted to let you know they did another X-ray on my son. The tumor has shrunk from the size of an orange to the size of a pea. Surgery has been canceled. Thank you so much, but please remember—I never saw you."

"You're welcome. I'm happy for your son," I said, grateful to hear of the outcome.

After the phone call, I went out onto the deck and thought about the entire experience of working on the boy. Why was the father so afraid? What if everyone was open to all types of healing? Maybe there wouldn't be so much suffering in this world. The phone rang, interrupting my thoughts. A woman asked, "Is this Mr. Harrison?"

"Yes, who is this?"

"I can't tell you. I have a daughter who has a brain injury. Can you help her?"

"I don't know. Who are you?" I asked again.

"I can't tell you. My husband is very well known in the political world. He doesn't know I'm calling you. Can you help my daughter?"

"I don't know. All I can do is try."

"Can I come to your house tonight and have you look at her?" she asked softly.

"I guess." I began giving her directions when I heard a click on the phone.

A man's voice said, "Who are you talking to?" There was another click and a dial tone. I never heard from her again.

The next day I drove to Seattle to pick up Wanda and the kids. It was good to see them again. "What is this about a UFO?" she asked as she stepped off the plane.

I told her what I knew and what I'd been doing, including working on the red-headed boy and the woman who called and never showed up. "I don't know, Daryl. What is this all about?"

"Yeah, as if I know what's going on!"

That evening I was out in the garage looking for something when Jason came out to watch. Lying across the concrete floor was an old extension cord I had plugged into the wall. Jason walked across the garage floor in his socks and stepped on the cord. All of a sudden there was a loud snapping sound with a spark of electricity and then darkness. I could hear Jason screaming; I picked him up and ran into the house. The lights were still on in the house and I asked him if he was hurt. When he calmed down, he showed me his foot. A large hole had burned through his sock, but his foot was untouched.

"What happened?" I asked, relieved.

"I stepped on the cord and the lights went out."

I went to the circuit breaker box and flipped the switch back on. I saw where the cord had burned in half and left a black spot on the concrete floor. Wanda came out and asked what had happened after Jason described what had occurred.

"I don't know. Look at this." I pointed to the floor and what was left of the extension cord.

"He could have been electrocuted!"

"I know; he must have been protected." I was still shaking.

"I want to talk with Kitesa again," Wanda said. "I want to ask about this, the boy you worked on, and about the house selling."

I agreed. "Let's go upstairs."

* * * *

"Greetings little one. You have questions, yes?"

"Yes, Kitesa. What happened to Jason with the extension cord?" Wanda asked.

"The cord was damaged, but your child was protected from harm."

"How or who?" Wanda asked.

"By spirit."

"What is this about a UFO? They don't really exist, do they?" Wanda continued.

"Little one," Kitesa said, "why is it that human minds think they are the only ones in the universe? Indeed, they exist."

"Well, what was Daryl doing out there when it appeared?"

"This shall be understood later."

"When is the house going to sell? No one has even looked at it."

"Was it not stated it would sell after you returned from your vacation? Have you gone on your vacation? Indeed, you have not. Little one, when you return it shall sell." With that Kitesa left.

After reviewing Wanda's notes, I shook my head in disbelief. "I don't think I believe in UFO's."

"Well, I guess Kitesa does. So we need to go on a vacation before the house can sell. That's what Kitesa said, and it seems right to me. I don't know why it feels right, it just does. You agreed to this before you had lunch with Don, remember?"

The next day we started planning our vacation. It was time to leave the past behind, and with it, the people who were trying to keep us from moving forward. I finally allowed the door to my past life as a contractor to close completely and walked without fear through the door that leads to our future.

Chapter 8
Messages

We decided to drive north into Canada to see Victoria, head east, and then go down into Yellowstone. I believed the farther away we could get from Olympia, the better it would be. No hypnotherapist, entities, UFO's, or dying children. I wanted a vacation from what my life had become. I wanted to become anonymous, mixing in with all the other tourists as we toured the beautiful gardens of Victoria or enjoyed the natural beauty of the wilderness in Yellowstone. We could just be a normal family, or so we thought.

The last week in July we packed our suitcases, loaded the Lincoln, and headed for Victoria. When we arrived, we spent the day walking through the gardens. By the end of the day, my back was quite painful, which was a surprise since it had been improving since the drowning.

That night while I was sleeping, a vibration in my body awakened me. I sat up, put my feet on the floor, and realized my back was pain free. Turning around, I noticed my body was still on the bed. In shock, I looked at what appeared to be my dead body. Slowly, I walked over to the mirror on the wall and stood in front of it. There was no reflection. Looking down at my arms, I noticed I was a transparent, milky white color. I began to rise upward. I tried to push myself back down with my arms, but they just moved through the wall. I continued to float up through the ceiling and into the room above.

I looked at the beds and saw someone sleeping. Now I'm a Peeping Tom, I thought, as I floated above the stranger's bed. I continued to rise rapidly, passing through the roof of the hotel. I could see the lights of Victoria. I kept moving higher and higher until the lights of the city appeared the size of a quarter. I began to slow down. Ahead was a flat, circular, glowing object. As soon as I entered into the object, I felt a sudden impact. The next thing I knew, I was back in my body, wide-awake in bed. The pain was gone! I looked at Wanda, ready to share the good news, and realized that while I was hovering above the city, she lay peacefully asleep.

"I thought this was going to be a normal vacation, Daryl. But I don't know what normal is anymore. Last night you spoke in your sleep again," Wanda informed me after I had told her what happened.

"What did I say this time?"

"Just before you began speaking, I woke up. I grabbed my pen and note pad and wrote down what you said."

I was amazed at her organizational skills. Obviously, I had married the right woman, even though I don't remember marrying her. She read the notes aloud.

"Ala Katuse beausa Katutatae, the energy of peace be with all. Setting of moon rising of sun, Wataska prevails over all. Anakuta Anakuto. The day of the rising sun has begun, sun of energy, peace, and love. Love and awareness from Wataska, bringer of peace, joy, truth, light, and honor among workers of the work. That which prevails shall never end. Escalate into powers that be, the powers that hold the universe together, the power of love. Universal power of that is all that will be, that can ever exist, truth, light, power of love. Time and oneness, return of the city of unity, peace, simplicity, crystal jewel, city of eternity. Energy of force, force of energy, the I Am energy of one. That is, was, and shall be. Rising moon of Wataska shall prevail to the rising of the sun, to prepare the mind for the universal mind of all that is, shall be, all that is seen. To return home is to be the completion of love and work, return of peace, and tranquility."

We stared at each other. Neither of us knew what it meant or what we could even do about it, so we finished our breakfast and headed out of Victoria.

We drove east, enjoying the beautiful Canadian countryside. When we found a point of interest we would stop to rest and let Jason and Tami run off some of their energy. As evening approached, we began looking for a place to spend the night. Wanda got out the map and found a town about a half hour up the road. "Good, we can stay there tonight," I decided.

The town had only one motel; we noticed cars parked all across the front.

"I hope they still have a room left; the next town is two hours from here," Wanda said in a tired voice.

The lobby was empty. I rang the bell and an elderly man came out of a door behind the desk.

"Yes, can I help you?"

"We would like a room for tonight," I stated hopefully.

"I'm so sorry. We filled our last room about an hour ago."

"Are there any other motels nearby?"

The desk clerk confirmed what Wanda had said. I could already hear the kids complaining about driving two more hours. As I opened the door to leave the lobby, the office phone rang.

"Just a minute sir," said the elderly man.

I returned to the desk. "Yes, I understand. No problem," the man was saying into the phone. He hung up and said, "Well, I guess I do have a room after all. These people called two days ago asking me to hold a specific room for them. They just cancelled. You can have this room if you like."

"Yes," I said, pulling out my credit card.

I walked out to the car and told Wanda about the room. We parked in front. As I was unloading the trunk, Wanda unlocked the room.

"Daryl," she shouted, "You won't believe what's in this room."

"What?" I asked, almost afraid to hear the answer.

"A small quilt with a picture of a setting moon and a rising sun. That's what you spoke of last night in your sleep," Wanda said excitedly.

"Well, I guess this is where we are supposed to stay for tonight."

"Let's go eat," Wanda suggested. "There's only one restaurant in town, so the choice is simple."

When we entered the restaurant, everyone stopped talking and just looked at us as if we had dropped in from some other planet. A waitress said, "Here, you sit at this table. It will be good for you." She treated us like family. The food we had for dinner was the best food of the entire trip.

Later that night, I spoke in my sleep again.

"The flame of eternity never goes out. Laughter from the soul keeps the flame burning. The three-point river is but a door to eternity. You will find the doorway in many different forms. We all walk through a doorway. Choose the right door to follow the correct pathway of the soul, to the brighter light and vibrant crystal speaking through the air. The jeweled crystal city of eternity has many mansions, many rooms, and many jobs as described in the physical. To return would be but the honor. Speak from the heart, speak from love, speak with truth, life and light even in honor. That which we speak is eternal love, light, and truth, love of the heart does not change. When it has reached its highest point, perfection, union of the whole mind, soul mind, Christ center of soul is. To be led by, taught by, to be given light by the God center is in truth the eternal spirit of youth, spring of happiness. Transparency of the jeweled city of eternity. Mark my words, return of union of the family to the jeweled city of crystals would be but a feast of the hope of the lightness that creates all, that was and is all."

The next day we left the little town without truly understanding what all happened. We never figured out why the people at the restaurant stared at us or why the waitress said what she did. I think in some way we were becoming accustomed to the strangeness that had engulfed our lives. We drove south into Montana through Glacier National Park. When I saw the beautiful mountains, I felt at one with them. I knew then that some day I would live in the mountains. We continued our journey into Yellowstone National Park. We found a small cabin in the northern section of Roosevelt and rented it for the night.

That evening both Wanda and I were awakened in the middle of the night. We sat up and found our little cabin was full of Indians. Fifteen or twenty Indians hovered around our bed. They were adorned in animal skins with beads and feathers. We could not believe our eyes as we sat there frozen. One Indian stepped forward and began to speak. Wanda grabbed the notebook she had learned to keep next to the bed.

"My dear brother and sister. It is given here I have well awareness of that in the conscious mind. It is the same negativity that I worked with in the freeing of my people from the white government of your country. There is one race. I am here to help you in your destiny. It is the same as mine. Ask and it will be given; we are brothers. We are brothers of the universe. We are in harmony with that which is. I perceive all men as one. I have chosen, as your souls choose, to work in harmony. To defend ourselves from the intense negativity of the earth plane, this has existed in my many life times on the earth. Ask and you shall receive. Speak and it will be known. As the eagle flies to freedom, so must our spirit. Give it freedom as the wind blows in freedom, so must our spirit flow in freedom. Be aware of the negative influence on earth. Be not part of the negative influences of the earth. I am in harmony with that which is, as you are. Bring forth to the conscious mind freedom of the wind and flight of the eagle. For we are that which is I, there is no separation in us. I am called Chief Joseph."

Then all of the Indians disappeared at once. I looked over at Wanda as she finished writing. "What just happened?" I asked, regaining full consciousness.

She just sat there and looked at me, then over at Jason and Tami who were both sound asleep. Being unable to talk about what just happened, we lay back down. We must have fallen asleep immediately because the next thing we remembered was opening our eyes to find it was morning. We both looked at each other again and asked, "Was that a dream last night?"

Wanda grabbed her notebook and looked at what she had written. "If it was, I was writing in my sleep, and we both remembered the same dream."

We loaded the car and checked the cabin to make sure we had everything. We found a feather on the floor at the end of our bed. We both looked at each other with the same thought: it must have been real. We just smiled remembering the loving energy of the message we had received the night before.

Driving south toward the center of Yellowstone, I became very dizzy and had to pull over at the next turnout. I got out of the car to walk around, trying to focus my eyes and noticed a monument.

"Are you going to be OK? What are you looking at?" Wanda asked from the car window.

"You are not going to believe this; it's a monument about Chief Joseph."

I could hear her sighing from the car; then she said, "Of course."

We spent the rest of the day driving through the park and stopping to look at the wild moose, elk, and bear. That evening we decided to stay in the lodge at Old Faithful. After dinner, Jason and Tami went to bed, so Wanda and I decided to go down to the lounge and have a drink and reflect on where our life was going. We took our drinks to a booth and sat down to talk about our experiences during the last nine months. I looked up and saw an image standing there next to our table. I could not make it out, but I could see a shape taking form in front of me.

"What are you looking at, Daryl?" Wanda asked. She felt a presence but couldn't see the visitor.

"Someone is standing there at the end of the table," I said.

"Who is it?"

"I don't know—Oh my God!" I shouted as I recognized the figure.

"What?"

"It's your mother."

"My mother!"

"Yes, Phyllis is here."

Phyllis said, "Well, move over; I want to talk to you."

"What is she doing?" Wanda asked.

"She wants me to move over so she can talk to us." I moved over and she sat down, making an impression on the bench seat. "Listen, you two have begun a journey that shall be the greatest journey of your lives. You will be tempted to give up on this journey; don't do it. You have come to complete and return home. I love you both and I will always be there. Remember, don't give up." Then she vanished.

I looked at Wanda and said, "I think I need another drink, maybe two."

"Me too," Wanda said, looking at the space where her mom had been sitting.

We left the next morning for our drive back to Olympia. For the rest of the trip, we were by ourselves.

We arrived home on Long Lake hoping there would be a message from Don that our house had sold. There wasn't. I called Don and asked him how the house was doing.

"I told you, Daryl, the market is in a down turn. No one wants to buy a large house at this time. Maybe this is a sign you should stay where you are. Who knows, maybe this Kitesa will leave you alone and you won't have to move," said Don.

I knew then if the house was going to sell, it was not going to be at the hands of Don. I would have to look for someone else.

As soon as I hung up the phone, Sharon White, the medium I had met before our vacation, called. "Daryl, my brother was just in a horrible motorcycle accident. He has severe head injuries. Can you come to the hospital and work on him?"

"Yes, I guess I could," I answered hesitantly.

"I mean right now; I don't know if he will make it through the night."

I could hear the fear and panic in her voice. "Yes, I will come now," I assured her.

"He's in the Tacoma hospital. I'll meet you at the front door; please hurry," Sharon pleaded.

I told Wanda about the phone call concerning Sharon's brother.

"Go see if you can help him. I'll keep dinner warm for you," Wanda immediately replied.

I walked out to the garage, opened the car door, and said, "What am I getting into here? He's in good hands at the hospital."

Then I heard a voice say, "Get in the car, we are ready."

I looked around and didn't see anyone. I turned and faced the car seat and saw the seat go down; I heard the sound that a leather seat makes when someone sits on it. The voice said, "Get in, it is time to go." I sat down as instructed and drove to Tacoma.

Sharon met me at the front door to the hospital. "Daryl, I'm so glad to see you. He's in a coma; follow me," she said anxiously.

At the door of the intensive care unit Sharon asked, "Do you want me to come in with you?"

"Yes, but I'm not sure what I can do," I confided.

We walked in and I saw his bandaged head. I went to the side of the bed; Sharon sat down in a corner of the room. I observed him until I heard this voice say, "Put your hands up in the air over his body."

"Who are you?" I asked, referring to the voice.

Sharon replied, "His name is Ken."

Obviously, she couldn't hear the voice. It spoke again.

"I shall make myself known at a later time. Now put your hands over his body and do not touch him," the voice instructed.

I raised my hands and put them over his body about two feet in the air. The room filled with a green cloud. Even Sharon could see it.

"Who is it?" she asked me quietly.

"I don't know, but I think it is going to help him."

The cloud remained in the room for about ten minutes and then dissipated. I put down my hands looked at Sharon and said, "That's all I can do."

She thanked me and I drove back home to Olympia. By the time I arrived home Sharon had called and talked with Wanda. She said her brother's condition had improved and he was going to make it. I shared with Wanda what the voice had said about knowing it at a later time.

"Is it Kitesa?" she asked.

"No, I don't think so. The voice is high-pitched and speaks in broken

English. It's very stern but very loving at the same time," I answered.

That evening Don called again to talk me out of selling the house. I told Don I thought the house wasn't selling because he wanted us to stay there and that I wanted to list it with someone else.

"Go ahead, stab me in the heart and destroy our friendship. You're screwing up your life, and I don't want to be a part of it. Your listing ends in two days. Go ahead and find someone else. It's not going to sell, Daryl!" He hung up.

The next day, I listed the house with another realtor I knew; within two weeks, the house sold. The buyers wanted to close in two months, which meant we would be moving just before Thanksgiving to Vashon Island. Our journey was just beginning.

Chapter 9
Alakanata Arrives

After selling the house, we decided to sell our high-end Lincoln and buy a car we could afford. We were no longer the same people who built the sprawling lakeside house or bought the luxury Lincoln. We had changed. Piece by piece, we were letting go of our old life without truly knowing or understanding what lay ahead of us.

I went to the dealer where I bought the Lincoln Mark IV. He had heard about my "experience," as it was now being called in Olympia. Out of pity or maybe sheer awe, he gave us a good price on the Lincoln Mark IV and sold us the Mercury station wagon. His knowledge of my business affairs made it all the more apparent to me that we needed to move on.

During the next couple of weeks, Wanda and I visited Vashon Island looking for a house to rent, but there weren't any available. Many houses had a waiting list. We decided to ask Kitesa if it was still a benefit to move to Vashon Island.

"Yes, stop looking; you have already made your contacts. Wait and you will be offered a house," Kitesa assured us.

I didn't know it at the time, but that would be the last time Kitesa would speak through me for many years. The day after Kitesa told us about the house being offered, I felt as if someone had died, but I didn't know who. I decided to ask Kitesa if someone I loved was about to die.

Instead of Kitesa, a different voice came through. "Greetings, this is Alakanata."

"Where is Kitesa?" asked Wanda.

"The Kitesa has fulfilled his work at this time; he shall be with you for eternity. I shall assist you in your work to teach others for a time; then, as you were told, another will come before the strong teacher comes."

"Daryl felt like someone died? Is someone we know going to die?" Wanda asked.

"The feeling Daryl has felt is the departure of the Kitesa. No one in the physical is to depart the physical."

It took me nearly two months to get over Kitesa leaving. I hadn't realized how attached I had become to him. During the transition time, I also became attached to Alakanata. He spoke in a very heavy southern accent that was difficult for people to understand. Someone asked him why he had such a thick southern accent. His reply was, "We rather enjoy it."

A few weeks later, we received a phone call from Roger, a man we had met with his wife Pam on Vashon. Roger explained that they needed to move but still had six months left on their lease; he wondered if we would take over the lease for the remaining time. I remembered what Kitesa had said about contacts already being made and told them we would love to take the house.

The day before we moved, Alakanata came through and reminded us what Kitesa had said. "Go to Vashon and rest for 30 days. The ones who need to speak with us will contact you. At the end of 30 days, this shall be your work till the end of your days."

Moving day came on November 26, 1982, and people we knew on Vashon Island helped us unload our furniture. It was midnight by the time everything had been moved into our new house. The old life was gone; our big house on the lake was gone. We had wall-to-wall furniture since this house was half the size of the one we left behind.

That evening I looked out at the trees with the stars shining brightly through the branches. Surrounded by furniture and boxes, I thought about how far we had come in such a short period of time. I thought about Kitesa and Alakanata and their messages for us, but mostly I thought about our future.

We still had one week before our house on the lake was to close. Fears began dominating my mind: "What if the deal falls through? What if no one calls in 30 days? What if Don was right, and I've made the biggest mistake of my life!"

That Sunday I decided to drive back to Olympia and see our house for the last time. I drove up the curved driveway and parked in front of the garage. I couldn't feel any life energy at the house. I had never felt it like this. I went inside. The house seemed so empty, so large. There were no sounds; even the air was still. I felt like I was looking at a picture of the house, not standing in the house. I walked through each room, thinking, "What have I done?" Suddenly, the house filled with electricity. My hair was standing on end. I became dizzy and had to sit down on the floor. The walls seemed to rotate around me. Then everything stopped and I heard a loud voice, a voice I had not heard before. The voice seemed to come from nowhere and everywhere.

"My son," the voice said, "be calm and look not back to that which was but rather look to where ye are going. This is but a building; your home shall always be with ye. The comfort of your home shall come unto ye again, in the mountains, now go. Ye have no place here; now go spend time at the lighthouse."

The energy and voice left simultaneously, and my fears about making a wrong choice left as well. I stood up, looked around the room, and knew it was time to go.

I knew there was an old lighthouse on the shore of Vashon Island, but I hadn't visited the site. After I returned to Vashon Island, I decided to drive over to the lighthouse before going back to our new home. Walking along the rocky beach, I felt a sense of peace and knew everything would be all right.

At home I shared with Wanda my experience at our house in Olympia and my visit to the lighthouse.

"The lighthouse? I remember Kitesa talking about the lighthouse and how we should go on walks there. I had forgotten about it. Let's go there tomorrow after we sign the kids up for school."

The next 28 days were very relaxing. Wanda and I, sometimes with Jason and Tami, would go for walks at the lighthouse. It became our favorite part of the island.

On the thirty-first day, the phone rang. Wanda answered and a man said, "Hello, I heard about Daryl a few months ago. When I woke up this morning I felt it was time to come and see you." Wanda asked his name and gave him directions to our home.

As soon as Wanda put the phone down, it rang again and again and again. Each caller had heard about me and knew it was time to see me. We had prepared the room downstairs with a couch and couple of chairs.

People continued to call wanting to make an appointment to speak with Alakanata or an appointment to have me assist them with energy. I began to see the world with new eyes and understanding. People in deep pain and suffering were finding a way to heal. People would explain to me, when they arrived, why they had been sent by their therapist, counselor, psychologist, or medical doctor to see me.

One woman who called had been in an accident and lost her right leg. She said the pain was worse in the leg that was amputated than it was before she lost it. I told her I would be willing to work on her, but I didn't know if I could help. I had never worked on a part of the body that was not there.

She came a few days later with three of her female friends. They told me they were all in their mid eighties. We set up a table downstairs with a small pillow and several blankets as a cushion. Her friends helped her up onto the table and then sat down on the couch to watch. Looking at her, I heard this high-pitched voice say, "Work on her leg as if it were there, for it is still there."

I asked silently, "Her leg is still there? Where?"

I heard again with laughter, "Work on her leg as if it were still there."

I placed my hands on the area where her leg would have been and felt intense heat from my hands. I looked up at the old woman's wrinkled face to see if she felt anything, but her eyes were closed. I continued for about twenty minutes and then told her I was done. She did not reply. I spoke louder and she still did not reply. The second time I told her I was finished, her three friends walked over to her. Her body was so still I thought maybe she had died.

As if reading my thoughts, I heard one of her friends exclaim, "She's dead, you killed her!" They shook her but she didn't respond. I felt the panic rise in me. What if I had killed her? What if I did something wrong?

I replied nervously, "All I did was work on her leg."

"She doesn't have that leg!" her friend responded angrily. She shook her friend again and this time the woman opened her eyes.

"Thank God!" I said to myself.

"What are you doing?" she asked her friend. "I haven't felt this good since I was thirty years old. Can't you just leave me alone? I'm enjoying myself; the pain is gone."

About an hour later she said, "I'm ready to go." Her three friends thanked me for helping her. I never heard from them again.

That evening I told Wanda about the experience and hearing this high-pitched voice. "Let's talk to Alakanata tonight. I'm sure he will tell us who this is now."

When Alakanata came through, Wanda asked, "What or who is this high- pitched voice Daryl keeps hearing when he works on someone?"

"This is a Chinese Master Healer," Alakanata replied. "But the Chinese Master has never referred to himself as a Master; he only considers himself a humble teacher.

"Where is he from?"

"He is physical but not of your dimension. He will begin teaching the one you call Daryl in a short time. He will teach about healing from the ancient dynasties of China. He will take the one you call Daryl into his dimension and bring an understanding of healing."

"Is this the one we were told about who would come later?"

"No, this one will never talk to the public. In time this one will talk to you and will teach the one you call Daryl, but never the public."

"Why won't he talk to the public?" Wanda was intrigued by this difference.

"This is not his purpose. He shall explain in a later time."

After Alakanata left I listened to the tape over and over, asking myself, "What's a dimension?"

The next day a young woman, Susan, was scheduled to come and speak with Alakanata. We were surprised when she brought a friend with her. As he came through the door, I saw a dark gray, nearly black energy field around him. He wore mostly dark colored clothes. Even his fingernails were painted black. Susan sat down next to him and said, "He wouldn't give me permission to come and see you unless he could come. If this isn't all right, I can leave. Is it all right?"

I could see that the dark stranger made Wanda nervous. Just then, Roger knocked on the door. We had become good friends with him and his wife; they both supported our work. Wanda told him about the man who arrived unexpectedly.

Roger asked, "Would you like me to sit in on the session with you?"

"Yes," replied Wanda with great relief.

While I felt myself leaving, as Alakanata was coming into my body, I saw what looked like three light beings standing between the man with the dark energy field and myself. Instead of speaking to Susan, Alakanata spoke directly to the man. Alakanata told him about his use of black magic and how he used it to control women sexually. He added that he had done this in many life times.

"You have made your choice to use the dark energies. The one next to you has not made this choice at this time." Alakanata then looked at Susan and said just before he left, "Accept the light; this is your choice for this life."

When I came back into my body, the man said, "Alakanata was right. I am a black wizard and I am proud of it, but he was wrong about Susan. She is my slave."

I could not believe what I was hearing. A black wizard? Slave? In 1982? Then Susan spoke up and said, "No, Alakanata is right. I'm not going to choose the dark again. I have had enough pain. I want to choose the light."

The man then said, "You cannot defy me." He stood up, towering over her.

"Watch!" Susan also stood up and shoved her way past him. He followed her out the door.

A year later, Susan called to thank Alakanata and me for giving her hope and the assistance to make changes in her life.

Our six-month lease was about up. We were guided to look for another house on the island and checked the only weekly newspaper on the island each week. No rentals were available. We asked Alakanata for advice and he said, "Give notice to move; a place for your physical bodies shall be discovered a week before you are to move."

When Wanda shared the information with me I replied, "A week? I think we should keep looking just to be safe."

Wanda laughed at me and said, "Go ahead, but I don't think you're going to find anything."

The next week and the week following, the newspaper listed no rentals. With one week to go before we had to move out of our house, we decided to go down to the printers and pick up the paper as soon as it was available. We drove to the small town of Vashon in the middle of the island at six in the morning and waited. As soon as they put the paper on the stand, we jumped out of the car and grabbed it. Sure enough, one rental was listed. "Three bedrooms, two baths with a den, perfect," I said to Wanda. "It has bedrooms for Jason and Tami and a place to do my sessions."

We decided to eat breakfast in town; then at seven in the morning, we called the number listed. "We would like to rent your house," I said to the man who answered the phone.

"Well, I'm showing the house to two different people today and someone else tomorrow. If you want, you can come tomorrow afternoon. Be there at three."

"I will."

I went back to the table where Wanda was sitting and said, "There are three people in front of us. Maybe we should have called at six instead of waiting an hour."

"Listen, Daryl, Alakanata said we would find a house. I'm sure we will get it. Let's go back home and finish packing."

That evening I had the loud popping sound come from the center of my brain. I remembered flying over the country side and landing on the ground in front of a large gray house. I heard a voice say, "Ye shall be here for a while."

I shared my experience with Wanda and she said, "If the house is painted gray, I guess that will be the one."

As soon as I finished breakfast, I decided to drive by the house using the directions I had received. I didn't want to wait until three that afternoon to see if that was the house I saw while I was out of body. The house was on the other side of the island about twenty minutes away. I stopped along the side of the road and looked. The house looked like the house I had seen last night except it was not gray but green. I thought out loud, "Maybe I mistook the color. It was dark when I was looking at it."

I drove back to our house and helped finish packing. "Is the house gray?" asked Wanda.

"No, it's green, but it looks like the same house. I don't know what to think."

When three o'clock arrived we drove into the driveway. A man greeted us. "Hi, I'm Jack. I spoke with you yesterday. Would you like to see the house?"

"Yes," we replied.

Wanda and I looked at each other as he took us on a tour. There was light in every room and the den was perfect for our sessions. Jack then took us out on the deck. We could see Puget Sound and Seattle beyond. Jack stopped and asked, "If I rent the house to you, would you mind if my painters come next week to finish painting?"

He pointed up toward the eaves of the roof. I looked up and saw the house had been gray; he was in the process of painting it green. Wanda simply smiled.

"No, that wouldn't be a problem at all."

Jack said, "I am not sure whom to choose. Four different couples want the house. I will think about it tonight and give you a call first thing in the morning. I need to get back to work."

On the drive back to our house we both knew we would get the house. We finished our packing and waited for the phone call.

At six in the morning, Jack called and said, "I would like you two to have the house. Can you meet me this afternoon to sign a lease?"

"Thank you. Yes, what time?" I joyfully asked.

We decided to go out to dinner and celebrate. The house was perfect for our family and work. The den was full of light and had a small bathroom off of it. It proved to come in handy when people came for a session; they always asked to use the restroom before leaving for the ferry.

Chapter 10
Alunastar Arrives

We decided to do the first session in our new home for ourselves and thank Alakanata for his help. When I sat down to do the session, my body felt different, as if my skull and spine were shifting shape. A new voice came through. "Greetings, we are the Alunastar. We shall be with ye for one year and then the strong teacher shall arrive. Many changes and contacts ye shall have this of your year; be at peace with them. Ye shall not understand all that occurs at first, but ye shall. Enjoy your evening." Then he left.

"Guess what?" Wanda said when I returned. "The third one has arrived. His name is Alunastar."

"I think he took my brain out and did something to it. It feels like my skull turned to jelly and my spine is not so stiff. Hmm, in fact, it feels a lot better."

Wanda continued sharing with me what Alunastar had said. "What is this strong teacher stuff?" I asked.

"I don't know, but Alunastar is quite strong himself," Wanda replied.

Soon after we moved to Vashon, my parents decided to move from Olympia to Flagstaff, Arizona. It was a place they fell in love with long ago, and they wanted to return. They were hoping the dry air would help with my mother's arthritis.

They needed someone to drive the U-Haul truck loaded with their furniture. I felt it was a good time to take a break from doing sessions, so I volunteered to drive the truck. Wanda decided to stay home and finish unpacking boxes. It was a pleasant drive to Flagstaff. After we arrived and unloaded the truck I decided to lie down on the couch to rest. As I was lying down, Alunastar came through and said, "It would be of benefit for the vehicle (Daryl) and the father to go on a journey."

My father asked Alunastar where the journey would take us.

Alunastar then began giving directions, naming roads and telling us how many miles to drive even to the tenth of a mile. He said, "Turn left on the third gravel road and drive thirteen and two tenths miles. Stop and get out of your vehicle and walk thirty yards north." Alunastar left without saying why or what would be there.

We got out the maps and started searching the area. It appeared to be in the middle of an Indian reservation. "This should be an interesting trip," I said.

My father and I decided to drive to the location the next day. We followed the directions exactly. The directions led us to the middle of the desert. The colors were magnificent. Orange, red, and yellow danced around the landscape. The area was barren except for a few rock formations and rolling sagebrushes. We got out of the car, walked thirty yards north, and found there was a large bowl-shaped indention in the ground. We admired the desert for a while. Nothing happened; no one spoke to us, so we drove home.

It was not until a year later I found out it was an ancient Kiva, used by Native Americans thousands of years ago for spiritual purposes. Later I found I would be returning there many times with Wanda to receive information over the years and to receive a special gift from my unseen friends. At the time I thought it was an interesting journey and was amazed at how accurate Alunastar's directions were. The following day, I flew back to Washington to resume my sessions.

My experiences with Alunastar continued. Each time I did a session with him my skull and spine felt like jelly being molded into a different shape. I could feel and see a light coming into my heart each time Alunastar arrived and I left my body.

People continued to come and see us for assistance. It became a very pleasant experience to work with all the different people and personalities. However, I soon learned that Alunastar was different; he wouldn't put up with any games people wanted to play.

For example, a young man named Randy arrived one day. When Alunastar came through, Randy leaned forward, ready for a challenge, and said, "I want you to tell me something about myself. Something I know Daryl doesn't know."

"Well," Alunastar stated in a loud voice, "ye are a sexual lover of men and ye carry blisters on your penis. Why do ye search for strangers of men and tell them not of your blisters?"

"Shit, Alunastar do you have to say that in front of Wanda?" Randy replied, as the color drained from his face.

"Ask and ye shall receive," replied Alunastar. "Now, do ye have questions of the heart, or shall we leave?"

"No, no, don't leave. I have questions."

After Randy left, Wanda commented, "I can't believe Alunastar said that. I can't believe how strong he is with people, but that guy asked for it."

A few days later, a man named Elliot, about 40, came for a session. Alunastar came through and said as usual, "Greetings."

"I have trouble in my mind from the war in Vietnam. Can you help me?" asked Elliot.

Alunastar said loudly, "Ye were never in this war, but ye are in a war with your mother. If ye choose to speak of this, then do so, or we shall leave."

Word began to spread about how Alunastar worked with people. The ones wanting to play games stopped coming, but the ones in need continued. The phone never stopped ringing. Wanda found it amazing how he worked with people, how loving and insightful he was to those who were searching for awareness and trying to heal.

One young woman who came to Alunastar was looking for a way to heal her intense fear of being controlled by evil. She brought a Teddy bear with her, believing it would protect her from evil. Just before the session was to begin, she placed the Teddy bear on the floor between herself and where I was sitting. She said, "I don't think Alunastar is evil, but I can't take any chances."

I said, "That's fine. I don't have a problem with it."

During the session our family dog Sammy, a ten-year-old white miniature toy poodle, came into the den while Alunastar was speaking. He immediately went to the Teddy bear, grabbed it, and tried to escape the room. The young woman watched in horror then leaped toward Sammy, retrieving her Teddy bear. At the time, Alunastar was speaking to her about how she placed power outside of herself and was using the Teddy bear as a crutch. She didn't seem to hear what Alunastar was saying, and she placed the Teddy bear back on the floor between her and Alunastar. A few minutes later Sammy came in again; this time he urinated on the Teddy bear. The young woman went into such shock, she could not continue the session. To this day, I don't know if she ever got the message, but it seemed Sammy did.

Our bedroom had a glass wall, floor to ceiling, looking out over the back of the property. We would lie there each night looking up at the stars as we fell asleep. One night about a month after we moved in, I was in a deep sleep when I felt someone take my hand. I was jarred awake. I opened my eyes and saw a person standing next to my side of the bed.

Just as I was ready to jump out of bed, I felt energy flow through my hand and into my heart. I immediately felt at peace. I lay there looking at him. He stood about five feet tall with golden blond hair. He had bright blue eyes and hair down to his shoulders covering his ears. I heard him speak in my mind, "Be at peace my friend. I have come to bring peace to your heart."

He let go of my hand and turned around, with the back of his head toward me. He lifted up his hands and parted his long golden blond hair. Two gold eyes appeared on the back of his head. I felt my body freeze. He turned around and faced me, "We are of the eternal light of God. We do not always look the same, but we are the same in the light of God."

He took my hand and lifted me out of bed. We walked over to the glass wall. I turned to look at Wanda and saw she was sound asleep. I saw my body lying in the bed, also sound asleep. Having had experience with this before, I felt more relaxed knowing it wasn't my dead body I was looking at. I was out of my body in a different realm, something I would experience many times throughout my life.

He asked me to look in the field behind the house. About a hundred yards away from the house, I saw a small disk-shaped craft. I couldn't believe it. The being explained to me telepathically, "I travel through many universes; this is my tool. Shall ye come and explore it?"

I replied with an astounding yes and was ready to run out to the field; however, the next thing I knew I was standing on the ground in front of the craft with the being still holding my hand.

"Your mind has had difficulty in understanding our existence. It is our love for you to share this experience," the being said as we began walking into this craft.

I had to duck my head to enter. Once inside I was able to stand up. "This is the control panel," the being stated.

I turned to look at where he was pointing. It was a panel with rounded shapes of different colored lights. A soft glow of light flowed between the top and the bottom ridges. Each ridge had a different color of light. He said, "I place my hand in the light to control the movement of the ship; each color creates a different movement."

"Can we go for a ride?" I asked.

"No, ye must remain grounded to preserve your body in the physical."

"I really want to go for a ride." I stated again, like a little boy at Disneyland.

The next thing I knew I was standing by myself out in the middle of the field. The being and the craft were gone. I thought, "How am I going to get back in bed?"

There was a flash of light and I felt myself crash land into my body. I sat up, got out of bed, and walked over to the glass wall. I turned around to make sure I took my body with me this time. I looked out at the field; nothing was there.

"Was this a dream, or was this real?" I said out loud, surprising myself.

I went over to Wanda's side of the bed to awaken her for a reality check. She was sound asleep and would not wake up. I went back to bed and fell into a deep, restful sleep. When I awoke, I told Wanda about the experience.

"Let's go down to where you saw the craft, after I show you the surprise I found this morning," she said.

"What are you talking about?"

"This morning when I came down to fix breakfast for the kids, I found a gold cat sitting in the sun room. It must have come in through the open window. He is the biggest cat I've ever seen and the most gentle. Isn't he beautiful?"

Sitting in the kitchen was an unusual looking cat, completely gold with wonderful eyes. He looked at me, blinked, then came up and rubbed against my leg.

"I guess he adopted us." I said, looking down at our new family member. We decided to name him Star.

We walked down to the spot and found three round holes in the ground. They were the same distance apart as the three legs that had supported the craft.

I turned to Wanda and said, "I think this calls for a session with Alunastar, tonight."

That evening we spoke with Alunastar and asked him what the experience was about. He stated, "This was not a dream but an experience beyond your plane of understanding. In time ye shall come to know who this one is. The cat was attracted to your energy. He desires to live with your family. That is all that is to be spoken at this time."

As soon as the session ended, the phone rang. It was a close friend of ours we had met on Vashon Island. She asked if I could do a session for her sister-in-law. "What is wrong?" I asked.

"She has an intense fear of snakes. Today she was babysitting her grandson who is four-years-old. He wandered out the back door of their house and went into the woods. She is so terrified of snakes, she would not go out to look for him. By the time she called someone, he was lost, and they needed a search party to find him. After this experience, I think she is ready to get some help. Her husband is willing to bring her to you. Can you see her tomorrow? I know it's Sunday, but she really needs the help."

I agreed to see her the next day. When she arrived she was already in denial, adamant that she did not have a problem with snakes. But her husband admitted she could not even look at a picture or drawing of a snake without having a severe reaction.

Alunastar came through and spoke to her of a past life where she was thrown into a snake pit and died from many bites. He gave her directions on what she could do to heal this past life. After the session was over she walked up to me and again said, "I really don't have a problem with snakes, but thanks for your time."

She walked out the back door and down the steps toward her car; a few seconds later, I heard a deadly scream and stepped out onto the deck. I saw her running toward me with a terrified look on her face. She ran up the stairs onto the deck, then jumped on me, digging her one-inch nails into my shoulders. Her body was as rigid as stone. She accused me of manifesting a snake that came out of the bushes and slithered over her feet. A few seconds later her husband ran up the steps and pulled her off of me, one fingernail at a time. He carried her into the family room and laid her on the couch. The woman immediately curled up into a fetal position, whimpering like a lost child. He apologized for his wife's actions. About ten minutes later, he picked her up and carried her to the car. It took more than a week for the puncture wounds to heal on my shoulders.

Chapter 11
Jonah Arrives

That evening, after the snake incident, we had a group of friends over for cake and coffee. Sharon, the first medium I met, was present. Because of our similar occupations, we had become close friends. I told her about my experience with the snake lady.

She looked at me with a sly smile. "You think she was something. Wait until your appointment arrives tomorrow." Her reply startled me.

"What do you mean?"

"I don't know, but it's going to be something. I hope they are small," she replied, still smiling. I thought perhaps she was enjoying this a little too much.

I immediately went and looked in my appointment book to see if it was someone I knew. I looked down at the names Bill and Janette Dean. I had never heard of them. I hoped they both wouldn't go crazy on me, and I wondered what Sharon meant about hoping they were small.

All evening, my concern grew. Maybe if I ask for a dream, I will have some understanding in the morning. The next morning I didn't remember any dreams when I awakened. Perhaps Sharon was just playing with me. She does have an unusual sense of humor.

Ten o'clock arrived and I heard a car pull into our driveway. I walked over to the window, hoping it was an older frail couple. The doors opened and I saw what looked like a giant of a man get out the car. "Good Lord, Wanda, come and look at this man."

She walked over to the window and said, "Oh my!"

Bill and Janette walked up the steps and knocked on the door. I opened it, and he said cheerfully, "Hi, I'm Bill, and this is my wife Janette."

They seemed friendly, and I felt relieved. "Come in."

I couldn't help but notice he had to bend his head down to walk through the doorway. "Come this way," I said, leading them into the den.

After a few minutes of visiting, Alunastar came through. He told them their entire life would be changing. They would be moving from the Seattle area and Janette would begin channeling in a few years. They would move to the four corners area of the United States. At the time, they didn't know that meant the area of Colorado, Arizona, Utah, or New Mexico; they thought it was the actual spot of the four corners. After the session they were both in a daze from what was said. To me, they seemed to be very gentle and loving people, but there was something there, something I could not put my finger on. When they left I said to myself, "Sharon must have been making a joke last night." A couple of years later, I knew the full meaning of her insight.

Bill would call from time to time, wanting to bring different friends to speak with Alunastar. On one such occasion, in early spring of 1984, Bill brought a friend he had known for years. We sat and talked for a few minutes before Alunastar came through. Alunastar began describing certain mental and emotional conditions this man has had since childhood. The man continued to reply, "I don't understand."

Then Alunastar stated, "Would you like another to come forth and bring this understanding to ye?"

The man answered, "Yes," not realizing what Alunastar had asked.

It was as if a bolt of lightning came into the room. The new voice said very directly, "For goodness sakes, this is your issue; only when ye stop denying it shall ye heal it." This voice continued telling him about his childhood of abuse and denial. The voice ended his strong comments with, "Good day."

The energy almost blew the man off his seat. When I returned, I felt like my body was going to explode, a sensation I had never felt before. Bill leaned over and asked, "Are you all right? That was sure a change of energy. Was that Alunastar?"

I answered, "I don't know. I've never experienced anything like this before."

Bill's friend stood up and walked unsteadily toward the door. I asked Wanda what she experienced after they left and she said, "A bright light came into the room and my head felt like it was swirling in circles. Do you think this is the strong teacher they have been telling us about?"

"I don't know, but I think we will find out real soon."

The next evening at seven o'clock, I had an appointment with an astrologer named Jake. I had met him a few days earlier on Vashon Island. He lived in a small, old house down by the beach. I rushed around to make it on time since I was unsure about the location. I arrived at seven and knocked on the door. Jake opened the door in his bathrobe and looked at me asking, "Can I help you?"

"Yes, I'm Daryl. I had an appointment tonight for an astrology reading."

"Come in." He sounded tired.

I walked in and noticed an old table and a couple of very old couches. "Have a seat," he instructed me.

"Were you expecting me?" I felt uncomfortable.

"Yeah, it's all right. I can do a reading for you. Sit down on the couch," he suggested again.

I sat down and felt a broken spring protruding through the cushion. I kept moving around trying to keep it from snagging my clothes. "Don't be nervous," he said, thinking that was the reason I was squirming.

"Did I wake you?" I asked.

"No, no, I can do your reading"

He sat down on the other couch across from me as his eyes glazed over. I saw a bright gold blue light come into the room and surround his head. His eyes began to shine. He told me about my past and my future, how astrology works, and how my signs interact with my life. This continued for about thirty minutes when suddenly the light moved out of his body and left the room. Jake looked up at me and said in a harsh voice, "I think it is time you should go!"

I stood up and walked out to my car thinking about what a strange visit it was. I wondered who or what that was about. It seemed like good information, though.

When I drove into our driveway, I noticed a couple of cars. It was Ellen and some other friends of ours who lived on the island. I decided to wait until they left before telling Wanda about the astrology reading. I walked into the dining room where they were all sitting at the table. Sharon looked up at me and said, "Well, did you enjoy your astrology reading?"

"Yes," I said, wondering how much to say.

"Did you enjoy the blue and gold light?" Sharon asked.

"Yes, how did you know about that?" The evening was becoming stranger by the moment.

I looked into Sharon's eyes and noticed it was not Sharon talking to me. "That new energy that came through you yesterday is Jonah, and that was Jonah tonight giving you information. Pay attention to this information."

"Jonah was sure strong with that man yesterday," I said.

Then the voice began booming from Sharon saying, "Jonah is only strong with those who choose to remain in denial of their heart. This one will teach you; pay attention. When are you going to release that name, Daryl? That is not you, it is not your vibration."

Then Sharon closed her eyes for a few seconds, looked back at me, and said, "Hi, Daryl, how did your astrology reading go?"

That evening after everyone left, Wanda and I stayed up most of the night piecing everything together. "Have you thought of changing your name?"

"I haven't said anything about it, but I have been having dreams with this gold and blue being. He keeps coming to me and calling me Hossca."

"Hossca? What kind of name is that?"

"I don't know, but I feel very attracted to the name."

"You know, I like that name. It fits you a lot better than Daryl."

The next day I called to find out the procedure to change my name. I was told it entailed filling out some paper work and then appearing before a judge to make the name change legal. When that was completed, I would have to notify Social Security, credit card companies, and the state motor vehicle department for a new driver's license.

A couple of days later I drove to the Seattle Court House. I filled out the proper paper work and handed it in. I was told to wait in another room until the judge had time to see me. "He will ask you some questions and sign your paper," the court clerk explained.

I waited for about twenty minutes and a lady came out and said, "The judge is ready to see you, Mr. Harrison."

I walked into his office. The judge was sitting behind a large desk. When I entered, he stood up, spread open his arms, and said, "Hossca, I have been waiting for you. It's wonderful to see you. All I have to do is sign my name on this little line, and you will be the Hossca."

I wondered if he did this to everyone who changes his or her name. He signed the paper and handed it to me, saying, "Hossca, go do your work and have a good day."

I took the paper and walked away. In the doorway, I turned around and looked back at he judge. He was sitting at his desk, deeply involved in reading paperwork. He seemed unaware of my presence. When I arrived home I said, "Wanda, it's getting really strange out there."

"What do you mean?"

I shared with her the experience with the judge. "Our whole life is strange, Daryl—I mean, Hossca. I don't think we will ever experience normal again."

"Did something happen to you today?" I asked.

"In the middle of the afternoon, I became so tired I had to lie down. About ten minutes later, I thought I heard someone in the house. I got out of bed to see who it was. A little boy about eight-years-old walked into the bedroom. He was dressed in a Cub Scout uniform. I asked him, 'Who are you and what are you doing here?' He would only say, 'I can play now.' Then I felt a shock go through my body and I woke up. I had been dreaming the whole thing, but it seemed so real."

I asked Wanda, "What did he look like?"

After she told me I said, "Wait here a minute. I want to show you the newspaper I bought in Seattle."

I went out to the car, brought it in, and showed her a picture of a boy who had just died. "He lived in a plastic bubble because of his immune system."

Wanda looked at the picture and said, "Yes, that's him. He was dressed in a Cub Scout uniform. I guess I understand why he said he could play now. He is no longer stuck in that bubble. Perhaps he was saying good-bye, but why to me? Why not to his family?"

"I don't know. Who knows anything anymore?" I said, shaking my head.

"That's what I mean. I don't think we will ever be normal again," said Wanda.

The following week our friends came over to celebrate my name change. Sharon, being Sharon, asked Wanda, "Well, are you going to change your name?"

"Yes, I'm changing it to Rebecca."

"What! You've never said anything about changing your name. Where did Rebecca come from?" I asked.

"I don't know. I didn't know I was going to change my name until I heard myself say it." Wanda looked surprised.

Sharon then said, "Rebecca, it fits you, Wanda. That's a good name. Your role in life has changed. Yes, Rebecca is the name you need."

A few weeks later we went back to the Seattle Court House. Wanda filled out the paperwork and waited for the judge. I was hoping she would have the same judge I had. I was interested to see if he would react to her as he did me, but she had a different judge.

That next morning I was standing in front of the bathroom mirror getting ready to shave, when the reflection of my face disappeared. A second later my image returned in the mirror with a full beard. I stood there for what seemed like ten minutes, looking at myself in the mirror with a full beard. Eventually it disappeared and my normal face returned. I had never been able to grow a full beard. Then I heard a voice say, "Let your beard grow. It is who ye are."

From that day forward near the end of March 1984, I have not shaved my face, except to trim my beard. I was amazed I was able to grow a full beard.

The next week after school, we made plans to go into Tacoma and shop for new clothes for Jason and Tami. While we were shopping, a powerful storm came in with heavy rain, thunder, lightening, and strong winds. We decided to cut our trip short for concern they might stop the ferry going from Tacoma to Vashon Island. We made it on the last ferry to the island. The waves were pushing up the ferry and letting it crash down on to the water. We were forced to stay in our car with the seat belts on. It was dark by the time we arrived home.

The next day we received a call from a friend who lived a mile below us. "Were you home last night?"

"We got home just before ten o'clock; why?"

"The storm blew the power out all over the island for a couple hours last night. I went outside to find Pete. He was out running around with the other dogs. I looked up your way and there was a light on. It seemed to come from the room you do your sessions in. I didn't know if you had a bunch of candles on or not. If you did, I want to get some of those. They really light up a room."

"No, we were gone when that happened, and we didn't leave any candles burning."

After the phone call, I went into the den where we did sessions and noticed the electric clock had the correct time. Then I noticed the other clocks in the house were close to two hours off. When Wanda, now Rebecca, heard what had happened she said, "I told you so; we will never be normal again."

Jonah was now doing all the sessions. Our house seemed to fill with electric energy. Everything we touched would shock us. His key words were always, "For goodness sakes," and he would begin and end each session with, "Good day."

Whatever Jonah would be teaching to someone, we would begin to experience. One such episode occurred the following weekend. We had a group of friends over again visiting in the family room. All of us began to hear a faint sound coming from the living room. It sounded like a group of people talking in the distance. Sharon, always up for a new adventure, asked me to walk with her to the living room to investigate. As soon as we walked into the living room, the electric charge was so strong our hair stood on end. We could hear the faint sound of many different people talking all around us in a different language. "This feels like a bleed through from another dimension," Sharon said.

"That's what Jonah has been talking about this week to different people."

"Well, there you go."

"What do you mean, 'there you go'?"

"They teach and you experience. You know, Hossca, you are going to be in for the ride of your life with Jonah. I just feel it. Jonah has many different levels. Each level may sound a little different than another, but do remember they are all Jonah. Your vibration will increase as Jonah continues to speak through you. This will also change your voice vibration. It will become easier for you to allow Jonah to come through you over time, which means the accent will not be as strong. It will be easier for people to understand him."

We had two more months left on our lease, and we both knew we would not be renewing it. It was time to move to the mountains. Rebecca and I began having dreams of Colorado, but we had no idea what part of the state to choose. We knew we would be moving there sight unseen because we didn't have enough money to go check it out. We saved enough to move and cover expenses for about two months—enough time to get settled.

Jonah wanted us to find it ourselves. He would not give us a hint, except to verify it was Colorado. Sharon had suggested we lay out a map, put our hands over it, and ask for direction. She explained how some people could do that and have heat come out of their palms over the area they needed to look at. One evening we tried it and were surprised to find that both of us had heat come out of our hands over the area of Boulder. We had never heard of Boulder before, except for the "Mork and Mindy" show with Robin Williams. We found a TV station that was playing old reruns of the show. We thought maybe seeing parts of Boulder would give us a better idea about the town. It didn't. When we made a commitment to move to Boulder, Jonah gave us verification it was the most positive place to for us to live.

One night, about a month before we were to move, I was sound asleep and a strong vibration awakened me. I thought we were having an earthquake. Then I noticed I was not in bed but rather in a type of cave. Light seemed to be coming from everywhere yet nowhere. I looked down at myself. I saw I was wearing a white robe with gold lettering on the front that I couldn't understand. I looked around the cave and noticed embedded in the stone walls different shapes and sizes of books. I could not make out the lettering on the books, either, but it resembled the letters on my robe. I heard some sounds coming from another part of the cave. I called out, "Is anyone there?"

"Wait, sit down. You be here for a while," someone said in a high-pitched voice.

I know that voice, I thought. That's the voice I hear when I work on people. "Who are you?"

"Wait!" replied the voice.

I sat on the floor since there were no chairs or benches. It seemed like an hour later when I saw this little old Chinese man walk up to me.

He said, "Why you sit on floor, chair not good enough for you?"

"There is no chair here."

"What this illusion?" He pointed behind me.

147

I turned around and saw a chair that had not been there before. The chair looked ancient, made of wood with the same type of letters carved into it.

"Sit, you be here for time."

I walked over and sat down. When I looked back, he was gone. I became very tired and closed my eyes. The next thing I knew it was morning and I was in bed. It seemed so real I knew it was not a dream, but I could not understand why he did not come back and talk with me.

The next evening, I was hoping I would journey back to the cave with the old Chinese man. Nothing. The next evening came and went and again nothing. About a week later as I was lying in bed, I heard his voice say, "After you move to the mountains, I shall begin teaching your memory to remember."

"Teaching my memory to remember? What does that mean?" Thinking I was asking the old man a question, I expected an answer, but there was only total silence. I lay back on the bed and thought, "I have enough on my mind preparing for this move; maybe it would be best to wait."

Then I heard laughter and he replied, "Wait! You have already begun."

The next couple of weeks we were busy packing boxes for our move to Colorado. One day the phone rang and it was Bill. "Hossca, Janette and I have decided to take a vacation this summer and go visit the four corners. We would like to stop and see you in your new home."

"That would be nice. I'll call and give you our new phone number when we find a place."

The phone never stopped ringing. Our clients, a great many of them from the Northwest, wanted to know how they could still speak with Jonah all the way in Colorado. I explained how they could write their questions and mail them to us. Rebecca would ask their questions as written and mail them a tape of the session. Although this solution satisfied some people, a great many were disappointed that they would no longer have the ability to interact with Jonah personally. Our friends on Vashon Island were also upset about the move.

Moving day arrived. All of our friends grudgingly helped us load our boxes and furniture on the U-Haul truck, even as they tried to convince us to stay. We explained that while we enjoyed our time on Vashon, it was time to move to the mountains.

While we loaded the truck, Jason and Tami found a space for the pets. We packed the car and headed off to Colorado on May 14, 1984, ready to find our new home among the mountains. Jason recently had his 11th birthday and Tami was about to turn ten. Their only concern at the moment was how long is the drive to Colorado.

Chapter 12
Colorado, Sight Unseen

Our three-day drive was filled with excitement and anticipation. What would it be like living in Colorado? What would Boulder be like? What type of house would we find to rent? We arrived in Boulder and found a hotel that had room to park the U-Haul truck. The next day we bought a Boulder Camera Newspaper to begin our search for a new home. We were shocked to find houses renting for two to three times what we had paid on Vashon Island, and many of the available houses were much smaller than our previous house.

Each morning we would go out to the truck to visit Star. He was set up with his food, water, litter box, and blanket. Apparently, he soon tired of this arrangement. One morning we arrived at the locked truck to find the window rolled down on the driver's side and Star peacefully curled up under the truck. He seemed to prefer this arrangement until we located our new home.

After about two weeks, we found a house in Niwot, a small town about twenty minutes from Boulder. We moved into our new house May 27, and wondered what our next step would be. When we asked Jonah, he said, "Wait and be patient. Everything will work out. Ye will not be staying long in this domicile. Ye will be moving into the mountains above Boulder." In time Jonah would tell us, "Ye shall have a new domicile high in the mountains of Colorado, not Boulder, but for now Boulder."

The first evening in our new house, we were all exhausted from unloading furniture. I fell into a deep sleep; then I felt a gentle breeze on my face as I was waking up. I opened my eyes and found I was not in bed but back in the cave lying on the floor. I immediately sat up and heard the Chinese

Master say, "Sit in the chair and relax your body. It is time to remember." I stood up and turned around, seeing no one. I sat down in the same chair as before. In front of me, an image of light began to appear out of mid air, taking the form of a human. It was the Chinese Master. "Are you ready to remember?" he asked.

"Remember what?" I asked.

"Life Energy Flow."

"Life energy what?"

"Yes, we do have much work, don't we?" His voice was high-pitched. "Look at the symbols on the wall. Don't they seem familiar to you?"

"Well, yes," I said.

"These are symbols you shall translate into the mind of the culture you are in. You taught these symbols of healing during the Essenes."

"During the what?"

"The Essenes. The Jonah has talked about the Essenes, yes?"

"Yes, but I was not aware I was there and teaching healing."

"Again you shall teach this healing, but now you must remember."

"Where am I?"

"You are in a cave in the Himalayan Mountains. It is not important now just where. You are to keep silent about your journey here until it becomes time to teach. You may speak of this journey to your mate but no one else. Do you have understanding?"

"Yes, but why?"

"This too shall become known."

"Am I having an out of body experience? I don't feel like I'm out of body; it feels real."

"You are physical, but in your second body. Your other body is asleep on your sleep pad."

"Sleep pad? Oh, you mean bed. Well, how did that happen?"

"Too many questions. You must now learn Life Energy Flow. Wait here and I will return."

While waiting, I walked over to the engraving on the wall and touched the symbols with my fingers. Immediately I felt an arc of electric energy run through my body; it jarred me awake in my bed back in Niwot. I wondered if I shouldn't have touched the symbol. I was certain the Chinese Master would let me know on my next visit.

The following morning, we unpacked our boxes and wondered when our work would begin. I received a message to go back to the kiva in Arizona. We decided to make a camping trip out of it, so we drove to Arizona and stayed at the Goulding's campground. Rebecca wanted to stay at camp with our children because she felt it was important for me to visit the kiva alone.

I got up the next morning, ate breakfast, and drove to the ancient kiva, arriving about ten in the morning. There was not a person to be seen anywhere. I parked the car on the side of the road and walked over to the kiva. When I stepped into the kiva, I felt as if I was walking through an electric energy field. I sat near the edge and closed my eyes. After a few minutes I could hear and feel a buzzing sound. I opened my eyes; to my great surprise, there was a being dressed in a white robe with many different colored strips going down the side. In the center of the robe was a bright golden starburst design. I opened my mouth to speak but nothing came out.

Then I could hear him in my mind. He told me to get back in my car and drive. He gave me exact directions down to the tenth of a mile and how many feet to walk, just like Alunastar had about a year earlier. Then he vanished. The energy vanished with him and I began to feel very cold.

Back in the car, I followed the directions exactly. The instructions guided me into the middle of Monument Valley. I saw the large boulder he had described and walked toward it. The ground had a crust on it. Each time I stepped on the ground, my feet would break through the crust about two to three inches. There were no other footprints in the area. I walked around and up behind the large boulder as told. I noticed a group of flat rocks that had been stacked on top of each other about three feet high. I walked up to them and saw five small seashells lying on the top of the rocks. There was no body of water anywhere near here. The shells looked like they had been recently polished. I heard this being's voice state, "Take these; they are yours."

I picked them up. As I examined the shells, they started vibrating in my hands. I put them in my pocket and felt some change in the bottom of my pocket. I pulled the change out, two quarters and a dime. For some reason, I felt I should leave the change on the top rock where the seashells had been. About three weeks later, I received a message in a dream to return to the same site. My footprints were still in the crust. There was no indication that anyone else had been here. I walked back around the rock and saw my change on the top rock. Placed next to the change were three more shells. Again I heard the same voice, "Take these; they are yours."

A few weeks following our move into our new home, we received a phone call from Bill and Janette asking if they could come to visit. They had rented a motor home for their vacation and planned to park it in our driveway and spend a week visiting. They said, "I don't think we will be living in the four corners; it's on the Navaho Indian Reservation."

I laughed and said, "I don't think Alunastar meant on the exact spot but in the area of the four corners. The area would be considered a three hundred mile circle of the exact spot." How I knew that I'm not sure; it just came out.

By the time they arrived, they had decided to move to Boulder. I thought it would be nice having someone I knew live close by, although I realized I didn't really know them. They had come to several sessions and brought friends to sessions with Alunastar and Jonah, but I had spent very little time with them myself.

We had a pleasant visit for the week they were living in our driveway. They had decided to go back to Washington, load their furniture, and move to Boulder in August.

The day after they left, I received a phone call from someone on Whidbey Island, north of where we used to live. They had come to see Alunastar and Jonah several times. They asked me to fly to Washington and do sessions for a week in their home. They said they knew people who had not met Jonah before we left Vashon and now wanted the opportunity. Since I was not doing anything in Niwot, I agreed.

The woman who called, Juliette, was a psychotherapist. Most of the people wanting to speak with Jonah were her clients. She and her husband lived in a mobile home in the middle of a thick forest. Juliette proved to be a most gracious host. Her clients were very kind and loving people searching for spiritual understanding to their lives.

One of the people who came to see Jonah was an ex-priest named Michael from the Episcopal Church. He had a wonderful session with Jonah about religion and spirituality. When his session was complete he said, "I have a friend who is currently a priest in the Episcopal Church. In fact, she is one of the first women ordained a priest in the Pacific Northwest. I think she would love to speak with Jonah when you return to Washington."

I told Michael that I would be very happy to meet her. I thought her session with Jonah would be very interesting and wished I were able to hear the information. As a medium for Jonah, I am away from my body. When Jonah finishes the session and I return, I have no memory of what was discussed. This proves to be confusing for some of my clients because they want to discuss the session, but I have no idea what Jonah told them.

I returned home to Niwot in August a few days before Bill and Janette arrived with all their furniture. They soon found a house to rent in the foothills west of Boulder.

I was invited back to Washington for a week of sessions with Jonah. During this time Bill needed to return to Seattle and finish up some of his business. We decided to drive to Washington the last week of September and share expenses for gas and lodging. Our trip turned out to be a spiritual journey from the past with shocking results.

Chapter 13
Montana Revisited

The day before Bill and I left for our trip to Seattle, Jonah spoke with Bill and Janette. Jonah talked to Bill about a lifetime we had in the 1800's when I was a mountain man in Montana. I was a hermit who communicated with animals. Bill was the sheriff in the area. Jonah described how Bill had used his power to control people. One day while walking in the mountains, he caught his foot in a bear trap. I found him some hours later after he had lost a large amount of blood. I pulled his foot free from the bear trap, took him back to my little cabin, and nursed him back to health. Jonah then went on to describe how it changed Bill's life. Jonah's parting comment was, "Watch the right foot." Then he left.

We decided to drive to Washington through Montana and hunt for the area Jonah had spoke about. After two days on the road, we arrived in Missoula. We still had plenty of sunlight and decided to visit the ghost town named Garnet, just outside of Missoula. We drove up to what was left of the town and parked our car.

One cabin in particular caught our attention. When we walked inside, we noticed a large section of a broken mirror leaning against one wall of the cabin.

Bill and I began seeing visions of children who had died back when the town was alive. Bill began to assist the children to the light. As he was working with the children, I saw an image of a very angry woman appear in the mirror. She was furious at Bill for sending the children to the light. She had become trapped in her beliefs and had not ascended to the light. As the children had died over the years from disease, she had collected them and saw them as children in her care.

As we were working with the woman and children, I felt a change come over me. Suddenly my persona shifted from Hossca of the twenty-first century to the mountain man from nearly two hundred years ago. I no longer had any awareness of who I was in the current time frame. I looked at Bill and saw not Bill but the sheriff from our previous lifetime.

I took off up the mountain, hiking for about an hour and eventually stopping in a clearing. Bill followed. Bill could see both past and present realities and recognized the old cabin that I had lived in as a mountain man. I was sitting on the ground talking away as Hossca the mountain man, when clouds began block out the sun. The temperature started dropping and snow began to fall and swirl around us. The colder it got, the hotter I got.

Soon the ground was covered with snow. Bill was becoming concerned we would get snowed in, but he was more concerned about whether I would return as the Hossca he knew. After an hour of sitting in the snow, I shifted back into my current personality. I had no idea what I was doing sitting on a rock in the middle of the forest with snow all around me. I looked up at Bill, who was shivering. He looked at me intently and whispered, "Hossca? Is that you?"

"Yes, of course it's me. What in the world are we doing here? What happened?" I didn't remember any of the events that had occurred in the last three hours.

Bill turned several shades of red, but he said nothing and motioned for us to return to the car.

We hiked down the mountain to our car, hoping to get out before we became snow bound. When we sat in the car, I looked down at Bill's foot and saw his ankle was covered in blood. Bill grabbed a hand towel from the back seat and wiped away the blood, but more blood continued to appear, soaking the entire towel. He thought he had cut his foot without knowing because his feet were freezing. He had been walking with low cut shoes and no socks in three to four inches of snow. But when he finished wiping away the blood, he could not find a cut or scratch on his foot. Then

I remembered what Jonah had said, "Watch your right foot." I reminded Bill of Jonah's message.

"Yes, I remember. I thought maybe I would hurt it again, not have blood coming from nowhere. This is getting too strange for me, Hossca. Let's get back to Missoula and find a room."

We pulled into a hotel complex and got a room for the night. The room they gave us was on the other side of the complex, so we got back into the car and drove around to the parking area in the back. We walked into the hotel from the rear and noticed our room was the last room down a very long hallway. Bill walked about a foot ahead of me. We discussed our experiences in Garnet on the way to our room. Bill made a comment and when I did not answer, he turned around only to find that I had disappeared.

It was only a second or two since I last spoke. There was no place I could have gone. He knew I could not have walked back down the long hallway in a couple of seconds, but Bill decided to go back to the parking area and search for me. Nothing. No one in sight. He walked back around the hotel and into the lobby area, but he still found nothing. He continued searching for about twenty minutes without success. He went back to the room, hoping I would be there waiting for him.

As soon as he opened the door to our room, the phone rang. I was on the other end. According to Bill, I was very upset, telling him I had been waiting in the lounge for the last three hours for him. "Hossca, I was with you just twenty minutes ago in the hallway. You disappeared on me!"

I became even more upset and told him sternly, "If you want to visit, you better get over here. I'm tired of waiting."

In a state of shock, Bill decided to call Rebecca and ask what to do. Janette was there visiting, so Bill repeated to both of them the events of the day and asked what he should do. Rebecca said, "Hossca does this sometimes. If I were you, I would go the lounge and visit with him. I don't know who you will encounter, but I know you will learn from it."

Bill found me sitting at the bar having a drink. "How could you have been here for three hours? It hasn't been half an hour since we were in the hallway on the other side of the complex."

Overhearing the statement, the bartender said, "So you're the one he's been waiting for, for the last three hours."

"He's been here for three hours?" Bill asked, flabbergasted.

"At least," replied the bartender.

Bill's face turned pale. "Sit down," I said. "Have a drink."

After a few drinks, I leaned over and whispered, "Bill, who in this lounge looks familiar to you?"

Bill looked around and said softly, "Well, I think that man looks familiar sitting over there." He indicated a man about twenty feet away having a drink alone.

Immediately, the man got up, walked over to Bill, and said, "Hi, I'm Tutor, I would like to visit with you." The man talked to Bill for a couple of hours, telling him about his childhood pain and suffering. As it turned out, Tutor was describing Bill's childhood.

About an hour later I said, "It's time for me to go to bed. I'll see you tomorrow morning." I left Bill and Tutor alone to continue their discussion.

The next thing I remembered, it was morning. I sat up in bed and thought, I wonder what happened to Bill last night? He was lying in the other bed, wide-awake, staring intently at the ceiling.

"Where were you last night?" I asked. "I thought we were going out for dinner."

He looked at me and said, "Shit! You're asking me where I was? You're the one who disappeared and had Tutor talk to me about my childhood. And what the hell kind of name is Tutor and how the hell did he know about my childhood?"

Since I had no memory of what he was talking about, I told him I had been in the room waiting for him the whole time.

Sitting up, Bill responded in a shaky voice, "I even called Rebecca when you disappeared. She told me you do this sometimes. Look, Hossca, this is scaring the shit out of me. What in the hell is going on here?"

I thought about how many times I've been asked that question and wondered, if I truly knew what the hell was going on, would I still be here? The rest of our trip to Seattle was very silent.

Chapter 14
Going Public

The time in the Seattle area seemed to go very fast. Toward the end of my trip, Rev. Laura Fraser came to see Jonah. I was expecting to see a very hard-looking person dressed in a black robe coming to check out Jonah. I was quite surprised to see a loving, gentle woman with soft gray hair. She was dressed in a very becoming suit with a large cross over her heart.

She sat directly in front of me and quietly waited for Jonah to appear. And appear he did. The first thing Jonah started talking about was the large cross over her heart. Jonah discussed with her about the cross and its history and then continued answering her questions. After Jonah left, she thanked me and said Jonah's message helped.

I traveled to the Seattle area two more times over the next six months. The next time I met Rev. Laura Fraser she again requested to see Jonah. When she arrived I could not help but notice she was wearing a different cross over her heart, this one much smaller. When Jonah came through, he spent a few minutes talking to her about why she changed crosses. He said, "The large one was so beautiful. Why are you wearing the small one?"

The third time I traveled to Seattle, she again requested to see Jonah. I noticed Rev. Fraser was not wearing any visible cross when she arrived. Little did I know, this was the beginning of a friendship between us that would be reported on television, radio, and in magazines and newspaper headlines across the country.

Shortly after we returned from our trip, two more families that Bill and Janette knew came to visit and decided to move to Boulder. I had briefly met them when they came to see Alunastar while I was living in Washington. Within a month, we were all living in Colorado. We visited in each other's homes quite often and became well acquainted.

One evening after visiting Bill, Janette, and our new friends in the foothills above Boulder, we received an interesting lesson from Jonah. As we were driving home, Jonah came through and started driving the car down a very steep road with sharp curves. Jason and Tami were sitting in the backseat. Tami asked me a question, not realizing Jonah was in my body. Jonah turned around and looked at Tami in the back seat for several minutes as he continued driving down the curvy mountain road. Tami, Jason, and Rebecca were hoping Jonah had eyes in the back of his head because that was the part of my body facing the road. Jonah replied, "Not to worry, little ones. It is not your time to depart the physical, relax."

Driving through Boulder, Jonah waved his hand and each traffic light he approached turned green. Rebecca was thankful because she knew Jonah would not stop. When we reached the highway, Jonah was traveling about twenty miles over the speed limit. Rebecca could see a state patrol car stopped on the side of the road with the policeman holding a radar detector. "This should be fun explaining," she said. Jonah waved his hand as we passed the patrol car. The policeman did not even notice we were on the road. Jonah pulled the car into our driveway and stopped the car less then one eighth of an inch from the garage door. Later he explained that he just wanted us to know he was always around and there to assist. I had been more tired than I had thought when I got in the car to drive home. Jonah explained it would not have been safe for me to drive, besides, he enjoyed the adventure.

In November, we found a house to rent in the same subdivision as our friends and moved to the foothills. We settled in our new home, and since our friends from Washington were the only ones we knew in the Boulder area, we continued spending a lot of time together. Soon they approached me and asked if I was willing to do a public talk about my life and how Jonah had arrived. I was never much of a public speaker; in fact I would rather do just about anything than public speaking. For a week they continued working on me to give in. They said, "People need to know about Jonah and what he teaches."

I finally decided to go for it. They told me they would handle everything. All I needed to do was show up and talk about my life and Jonah. I made it clear to them it would just be me speaking. I told them if someone wanted to talk with Jonah they could make an appointment. Knowing how strong Jonah is sometimes, I didn't want to take people by surprise. I felt it would be better for me to explain to the people how Jonah works with them. When a person comes to speak with Jonah, the more prepared and clear in their intent they are, the more assistance they receive. If they chose to converse with Jonah I didn't want them coming with false assumptions of the interaction.

The evening arrived for my public talk. I was sitting there, barely able to breathe from nervous energy, waiting to be introduced. I remember talking in my mind asking Jonah to assist me. Then I noticed I had already been introduced, and a room full of people was waiting for me to walk up to the front. As soon as I stood up, I felt all the nervous energy leave. I enjoyed speaking. Everyone had questions, and the time seemed to fly by.

The next day I received a phone call from Margie McAllister, a reporter, with the **Boulder Daily Camera**. She said she had heard about my talk and wanted to do an article in the Sunday paper. She asked if I would be willing to do an interview with her. Her request took me by surprise, but I agreed and scheduled the interview at our home. When we hung up, I had second thoughts and wanted to cancel, but Rebecca convinced me to go ahead and do the interview.

The day arrived for the interview and she pulled out a list of questions. She asked, "Can I interview David Calof and speak with Jonah?"

"You can speak with Jonah, but you will need to ask David about an interview with him. I can tell you how to contact him in Seattle."

We didn't tape the session Margie had with Jonah, and Rebecca only remembered part of it. It wasn't until a few weeks later on February 10, 1985, I read the article in the **Boulder Camera**. They put my picture on the front page with the heading "Contractor is spokesman for 'Celestial'

Beings" page 1c. In the article, Margie reported what she had asked David Calof about the white cloud that appeared in his office and the young boy I assisted.

> *"I'd never seen anything like it before,"* *confirms Calof, a highly recommended* *hypnotherapist in Washington. "Here was* *this straight and narrow contractor with* *visions and physical manifestations."*

About the boy I helped, Margie wrote,

> *"Calof had a 14-year-old patient critically* *ill in the hospital with a strange, possibly* *psychosomatic, blood disease. The boy* *already had had part of his intestines* *removed. He was scheduled for an emer-* *gency operation, and his blood pressure* *was soaring at 300 over 200 according* *to the psychotherapist. Harrison put his* *hands on the boy, called on his spiritual* *guides, and the blood pressure dropped.* *The operation was canceled. Essentially* *the kid walked out of the hospital, Calof* *says.*

I sat there on that Sunday morning thinking, what have I done? I just blew my private life to hell.

The phone rang; it was Bill and Janette asking if we would like to drive up to the local ski area for a visit. We though it would be nice to get out of the house. I'm not a skier, but I enjoy sitting around in the lodge drinking cappuccinos. When we arrived at the lodge, I realized many of the people there must have read the Sunday paper. I walked in, sat down and the entire area became silent. Everyone stared; some pointed and whispered to each other. I felt very uncomfortable and soon Rebecca and I returned home where we found more than 20 messages on our answering machine. All were from strangers asking to speak with Jonah or asking for me to work on them or their children or both.

Within a couple of days, we were booked two to three months in advance. We were meeting many wonderful, loving new people whose lives were being turned around by Jonah.

Despite all the new sessions, I continued my work with the Chinese Master. One evening in early March I was again taken to the cave. This time when I arrived, he had a body lying on a table. It was an unconscious male body about sixty-years-old. "What wrong with body?" He asked in his high-pitched voice.

"I don't know. Is he dead?"

The Chinese Master rolled his eyes back and slapped his hands together, creating a sound of thunder rumbling under my feet. Again he asked, "What wrong with this body? Put hand on body."

I approached the body and felt I should put my right hand on his chest over his heart center. When my hand made contact, I could feel my own heart and chest getting tighter. The Chinese Master said very sternly, "You no take energy, you give energy."

I realized this man was having a heart attack and I was taking it on. I remembered how to reverse the flow of energy and the pain in my heart stopped. His chest started to move up and down and I could hear the voices of doctors working on him. He was in a hospital suffering a heart attack, yet his other body was here lying in front of me. The man opened his eyes, looked at me, and said, "Thank you, Hossca." Instantly he vanished from under my hand.

"How did he know who I was?" I asked.

"Soul Family," the Chinese Master answered.

"Soul family? What is that and where did he go? Where did he come from? Do I know him?"

"Too many questions. You sit; I come back," he said.

I sat down on the chair; the next thing I remembered was waking up on my back in Boulder.

The next morning I told Rebecca about my experience in the cave. "Well, how did that happen?"

"I don't know. I asked the same thing."

"What did he say?"

"He told me to sit, but then I woke up back in bed. He isn't the type of person you just sit down and have conversations with. He's very stern, but I feel a great love for him. He feels like a grandfather to me, though I know he's not my grandfather. I understand he loves me, but he isn't going to let on that he does. Just being in his presence makes my mind fill with memories of healing. He told me I would be teaching it sometime, but I think that will be another life; at least I hope so."

Later that day we had a woman scheduled to come over for me to work on her. She had severe back pain that required her to spend much time in bed. Her husband brought her. When she arrived, I had her get onto a makeshift table in the living room. Her husband sat to my side, watching. I put my hand on her lower back and began seeing pictures and hearing voices from her past. Each time I would repeat what I heard to the woman, she denied that it ever happened. I looked at her husband, and he was nodding his head, confirming it had happened, but from her position, she couldn't see her husband. I finally said, "You don't want a healing. You want to be taken care of."

Her husband nodded and said, "Yes, that's true. Even the doctors told her that."

The woman became very emotional and said, "All I want is to be taken care of." She paused and said, "No, I mean healed. I want you to heal me."

"I can't heal anyone. I can only help those who are willing to heal themselves, and you aren't ready or willing. I can't help you."

When they left, I realized that I was able to see and hear events of the past that block a person's healing. It was the same when I worked on the older man with the heart attack.

The pattern of learning began to fall into place. When I would remember an ability with the help from the Chinese Master, someone needing that ability would come to me in the next couple of days. I looked forward to going to bed at night so I could journey to the cave.

In late March we received a phone call from the Science of Mind Church in Boulder. They wanted me to come and give a talk about my experiences. I agreed, but again I had doubts about talking in public. Then I remembered how Jonah had helped me just before my last public appearance, which brought peace to my mind.

A week later, I arrived at the church to find it filled up; a long line of people wanting to come in stood at the front door. The church only had room for about a third of the people who showed up. I walked up to the front of the room and said, "Hi, I'm the burly chain smoker."

Because I had smoked three cigarettes during the three-hour interview with the newspaper reporter, she had called me a "burly chain smoker" in the article. At least the opening statement broke the ice as the crowd laughed loudly. I answered questions for about two hours. It seemed the public was very interested about my life and what had occurred since my near-death experience. The next day I received a phone call from the minister of the church asking if I would return the following month. She had received many requests from those who were not able to fit into the church. This time she wanted me to give a talk and then ask Jonah to address the group.

Our lease was about to expire on the house in the foothills of Boulder. We wanted to stay in the same area, but we wanted a house with a view. No other rentals were available. The next week I was scheduled to fly to Milwaukee to give a talk on "Atlantis, Today and Yesterday" and to have Jonah address the group. Before my trip, we decided to ask Jonah about when and where we would find the new house or if we were to stay where we were for another year. That evening when Jonah came through, Rebecca asked him many questions; the last question was about the new house.

"The Hossca shall find it in Milwaukee," he said with a big smile on his face as he left.

"Milwaukee!" I said when I came back listening to Rebecca describe the session. "What is that about? We moved here to live in the mountains of Colorado, not Milwaukee."

I hoped he was joking, but I knew Jonah did not joke. There was always truth behind all his statements. I flew to Milwaukee on a Friday. I had scheduled the workshop for Saturday and Sunday, followed by several days for doing personal sessions. On the flight I fell into a deep sleep, which I never do on a plane because the seats are far too uncomfortable. I woke up just before we landed feeling totally exhausted.

The next day during a break at the workshop, a man came up to me and said, "I understand you live in Boulder, Colorado."

"Yes."

"I also live in Boulder," he replied. "Interesting I came all the way out here to Milwaukee to meet you. What part of Boulder do you live in?"

"In the foothills above Boulder, called Pine Brook Hills."

"That's where I live," he said with amazement. "In fact, my wife and I just bought a new house in Boulder. We're looking for someone to lease our house in Pine Brook Hills. You wouldn't know of anyone who would like to rent it, would you?"

I could hear Jonah laughing in my mind. "Yes, we're looking for a house; our lease expires in a few weeks. When will your house be ready?"

"In a few weeks," he said. "When you return to Boulder, come over and look at the house and see if you want it."

"I'll be there," I said, already knowing that was the house for us to lease.

In Milwaukee, I stayed at the house of Pat, a wonderful woman who helped arrange the workshop and sessions with Jonah. Monday morning over coffee, Pat said that someone she knew wanted to talk with me. "If you are willing, she wants to take you to lunch."

"Who is this person?"

"I will let that be a surprise." I thought that was kind of strange but agreed to the meeting. When my ride arrived, I opened the door and saw a young man dressed in a tuxedo and wearing white gloves. A very long black limousine was parked at the curb. "Would you please come with me?" the young man said.

I grabbed my coat and walked out to the limousine. The young man opened the door and I saw a beautiful woman sitting in the back. "Hossca, my name is Rita. Please come in."

I stepped into the limousine and the young man shut the door behind me. "Do you like sushi?" Rita asked.

"Yes, I do."

"Wonderful. I have a table reserved for us. Charles, let's go get some sushi." On our drive to the restaurant, she told me she had been the mistress of a dictator of a third world country. She continued to talk about how a foreign government had paid her a large sum of money to arrange for this dictator to be killed. Although she was not involved in the killing, she made sure he was at the right place at the right time.

"I now live a life of luxury, but I have great guilt of what I have done. After he was killed, I started taking hard drugs and overdosed a few times. Ever since then I keep seeing things that are not there, at least physically. I also see colors around people. I feel like I am losing my mind. Can you help me?"

I tried my best to give her information about what she could do to heal. I never saw her or heard about her again.

I finished the sessions at the end of the week and went home. I told Rebecca we had found the house. "What? You found a house in Milwaukee?"

"Yes, just like Jonah said I would."

"Milwaukee?" She said, "But . . . "

I explained. The next day we drove about two miles to see the large, beautiful house on top of the mountain overlooking the Front Range. The view was wonderful, on a clear day, we could almost see Kansas. In less than a month, we were moved and settled in our new home.

Meanwhile, I spoke again at the Science of Mind church. It proved to be more interesting the second time. After the session, a man walked up to me and said, "I enjoyed this as much tonight as I did last month in Scottsdale."

"Scottsdale? I've never been in Scottsdale."

"You were," he replied. "I was there raising money for the university and someone I met invited me to your group. You sat there and told the same story tonight as you did last month, then Jonah came through and answered questions."

"What date was this?"

He pulled out his calendar and told me the date. It was the same date and time I was on the flight to Milwaukee. I remembered the unusually deep sleep I had experienced on the plane. What occurred I do not know, nor did I ever have any remembrance of the Scottsdale experience. However, I've learned to sidestep the "hows" and "whys" of my life and experiences. I smiled and said, "I'm glad you enjoyed the group," then promptly walked away before he could ask me anymore questions about an experience I didn't remember.

* * * * *

The waiting list for people wanting to see Jonah continued to grow. It seemed like all we were doing was sessions with Jonah. Many of the people who came had wonderful questions for Jonah, many that we had never thought to ask. Many wanted to know where Jonah came from. He would reply he came from a Universe of light, sound, and color. He had never been born of a physical birth, but he did manifest a body during the time of Christ, a time he calls the Essenes. He had been an Essene teacher during that time and traveled the world teaching. He maintained his body for nearly one hundred years. Later I would find out the entire experience of this time frame.

In July 1985, about a year since our last trip to Monument Valley, I received another dream to return. When we did, I found there was one more shell, making nine polished shells in all. Again I heard the voice say, "Take this shell; it is for you." Over the years, I returned to the same location. The rocks remained untouched. I never heard the voice again nor were there any more shells. In the last couple of years, the area has been closed off to the public so I have not been able to return to that exact spot again. The significance of the shells is still a mystery.

At home, we had a session with Jonah once a month. Rebecca would ask the questions and tape record the answers for me to listen to after the session. Our usual question was, "What next?" Jonah told us he wanted to start doing one-hour taped messages on certain subjects. The first tape was called "Spirituality: What Is It?" That message after all of these years continues to be one of his most popular tapes. Jonah also told us it was time to start teaching specific topics to groups locally. Our question was how? "Not to worry," was his frequent reply.

The day after Jonah told us about teaching locally, Bill and Janette came over to visit and started talking about doing what he called Jonah groups. "I've talked to a lot of people who have seen Jonah. They want Jonah to talk more about the different levels of spirituality."

We had not told him what Jonah has just shared with us. We agreed to do a group in a few weeks in Boulder. We put the word out that Jonah would do a group talk on spirituality. We thought maybe two dozen people would show up, so we rented a room that could hold fifty people. More than one hundred people showed up. It was difficult for me to leave my body and have Jonah come in while I sat in front of these people who had come for personal sessions. All I could see were all of these eyes staring directly at me.

For this particular group talk, Bill offered to do a group meditation just before Jonah came in. He thought it would direct the energy from me and on to him. I thought that would make it easier for me to leave my body.

When the group arrived, I told Bill I would wait out in the hall while he did the meditation. I stood listening through the door as Bill began the meditation. The next thing I remembered was waking up in the chair in front of all of these people. I turned to Rebecca and asked, "What happened?"

Rebecca replied, "Jonah entered into the room, sat down, and started talking. He spoke for three hours."

I looked down at my feet and noticed my shoes were not on. "Where are my shoes?"

Rebecca just took a deep breath and said, "I don't know. We'll have to look for them." After many of the people left, we found my shoes in the hallway where I had been waiting for Bill to finish his meditation.

A few days after one of the group sessions, I received a phone call from a reporter, Susan McCann, from the *Longmont Times*. She had attended the Jonah group in Boulder. She wanted to do an interview with me and ask Jonah some questions. I agreed to the interview and a few days later she arrived at our home. The interview took about two hours. She asked me questions and then asked Jonah to come through, speaking with him for a short time. The interview was published in the *Longmont Sunday Times* on March 9, 1986. She wrote a wonderful story about my life and her experiences in speaking with Jonah. At one point she asked Jonah, "And what is it I should be doing with my life?"

Jonah replied, "Moving in the direction of writing books."

"A book about what?" she asked.

"Books, my friend, for the child mind. You understand the child mind very well. You know where they escape. You can tell children never to lose their individuality and creativity, because in your culture, parents think they own their children. Do you not think you have this ability? Well, you do," Jonah replied.

Susan wrote in the article, *"I stared at him blankly. There was no way for him to know that over the past several years I had written several children's stories and thrown them in the back of my desk drawer to collect dust."* Susan also reported that Jonah would give a public talk called

"Pathway to Freedom" on March 16.

The evening before my public session with Jonah, I became very ill. My tonsils were so swollen that my throat closed up, and I had a high fever. I could not even swallow water. Every joint in my body was filled with pain. I went to bed and said to Jonah and the Chinese Master, "If you want me to do this public session tomorrow, someone is going to have to intervene. I can't even swallow water, let alone talk." I then heard footsteps coming up the stairs to our bedroom. The next thing I remember was awakening the next morning totally healed.

When the time arrived for Jonah's talk, "Pathway to Freedom," I became more and more nervous. I still had an issue with sitting in front of people and watching them stare at me, seeing them wondering what was going to happen next. I arrived about two hours before Jonah was to begin. The room began to fill; the hotel had to bring in more chairs, and then they brought in still more chairs. We had more than 200 people in attendance.

I was in another room visiting with Bill, who was very comfortable speaking in front of large groups. So, in my fear, I asked Bill if he would conduct a meditation for the group. I told him I would sit in a small room, which was actually a storage room off of the stage area, with Bill's wife Janette and allow Jonah to come in. That way, I would not have to sit in front of all those eyeballs staring at me. I was wearing a wireless microphone attached to my shirt because Jonah always liked to walk around speaking to the groups. I sat in the chair in front of Janette and could feel Jonah coming through. Jonah came into my body. He looked at Janette, looked around the small storage room, stood up, and said, "What is this? A closet! It is time to come out of the closet!"

He then threw open the door to the main room. Of course, Jonah did this with his voice coming loudly over the speaker system, right in the middle of Bill's meditation. Needless to say, we haven't tried that again.

After Jonah's talk, "Pathway to Freedom," I received a call from Carl Raschke, Professor of Religious Studies at the University of Denver. He asked if he could visit with Jonah and me. After his visit, he wrote me a letter saying, "I believe that what you are doing is quite significant, and I would greatly appreciate the opportunity to explore similar matters in future sessions."

After another visit to Seattle in September we decided it was time for a vacation. Our friends suggested we all go somewhere together, so we planned a trip to Kauai, Hawaii, an island we had not previously visited. After we landed and checked into the townhouse we had rented with the other couples, we went out to dinner. When I walked into the restaurant, the hostess looked at me and said, "Well, you had so much fun last night, you decided to come back."

"I've never been here before."

"You have, too. You sat at that table right over there and I waited on you. You were laughing all night long."

"Last night, I was giving a talk in Seattle. I couldn't have been here."

"Oh, you want to keep it a secret from your friends. Ok, you were not here last night." She gave me a strange look, then seated us at a table. She didn't talk to me or look at me the rest of the night.

It appears this was a message for me. Jonah can use my body in two different places at once. Jonah determines when there is a specific need and I am not told consciously when this will be occurring.

When we returned from Hawaii, I received a phone call from Eliot Lowey who had come to talk with Jonah once. I knew who he was but didn't know him well. Eliot wanted me to meet a friend of his named Jack Schwarz from Oregon. "He comes to Boulder with his wife Lois to do workshops several times a year. I want to invite you to hear his public talk." When I heard his name, I knew I needed to meet this man. I had not heard of him before although he had written many books on the energy system of the human body.

I went to the talk and sat in the back of the room, listening with amazement to his life story. As a young man he had lived in Europe and was part of the Dutch Resistance Group fighting the Nazis during World War

II. He described how he was captured and put into the concentration camp. During this time, he was tortured many times. He was able to bring forth the ability to block out pain and to heal his body from the injuries he received.

After his talk, Rebecca and I introduced ourselves. He and I felt a kinship with each other that turned into a deep friendship.

Jack is the only person with whom Jonah shared a workshop. Jonah knew Jack well and knew the soul. Jack was truly a master in human form. His abilities continue to confound the medical experts who studied his ability over the years.

Thankfully, I was guided to go and see him in October 2000, just before he died on November 26. Rebecca and I had a wonderful dinner with Jack and his wife Lois in Fort Bragg, California. Lois has continued his work. She is a woman of great strength and determination, and I feel will she will succeed.

A few weeks after Jack died he appeared to me in my office one evening and asked me to share with Lois his message. "Do not let the dream die." The next day I called Lois. She completely understood the message and thanked me. She is now writing a book about his amazing life.

Chapter 15
Trial for Heresy

More and more people were requesting sessions with Jonah and attending Jonah's public talks. I was increasing my ability to see the non-physical and energy fields around people. I felt very uncomfortable with some people; others I felt as if I had known for lifetimes.

During one of the sessions with Jonah, he paused and looked at Rebecca, who always sits in on the sessions. He said, "Little one, this coming week cancel all sessions. The vehicle will need this time to rest and prepare." He then turned and continued talking with the one who had come to the session.

When I returned to my body, Rebecca told me about Jonah's comment and went into the office to begin calling everyone on the appointment list for the next week. "A week off. I can use the rest," I said.

Then Rebecca replied, "He also said to prepare."

"Prepare for what?"

"I don't know. That's all he said."

"Well, maybe it is to prepare to rest for a week." I said that hopefully, though I knew full well that something was coming our way.

Early the following Monday, the phone rang. Rebecca answered it. I was sitting at the table finishing breakfast. I saw Rebecca's face turn white. Immediately, thoughts of death, illness, and catastrophe raced through my mind. When she hung up she looked at me and said, "You and Jonah are on the front page of the *Seattle Times*." Close enough.

Color finally returning to her face, Rebecca asked me, "Remember Laura Fraser?"

"Yes," I said.

"She is being put on trial by the Episcopal Church for heresy!"

"What?"

Before Rebecca could finish telling me what our friends from Seattle had said, the phone rang again. It was someone from the **Denver Post** wanting to do an interview. Throughout the day, we received calls from the **Boulder Daily Camera**, **Seattle Post**, **Seattle PI**, **Rocky Mountain News**, **UPI**, **USA Today**, **Time Magazine**, and various television and radio stations in Seattle and Denver. By the time the day ended, we were exhausted from dealing with the news media and talking with friends. I told Rebecca, "If this is Jonah's idea of a vacation, we need to have a talk."

We soon learned all the details that led to the threat of a heresy trial for Laura. She had transcribed a tape from Jonah titled "A Man Called Jesus." She was using the transcription in her Bible class at church. "A Man Called Jesus " is one of the first in a series of messages from Jonah concerning topics that are relevant in today's society. This message about Jesus Christ painted a vastly different portrait than the Bible. Jonah described Jesus with his true name as Jeshua Joseph bar Joseph, a man of great light, bringing a message of love, a message about releasing the old laws of separation and denial of the heart. Jonah went on to describe the many spiritual quests during the travels of Jesus. He also described how Jesus married and had children, indicating that his bloodline continues to this day.

The Bishop Robert Cochrane, head of the Diocese of Olympia, Washington, was not pleased. He told Laura that her introduction of the Jonah tapes was contrary to scripture and to church doctrine. Laura had told the press she had reached for something unusual, but she believed it was authentic. Jonah's teachings had changed her life. She told the bishop she did not present Jonah's words as doctrine. But she also told the bishop that as God's word was revealed through the prophets, so is his word being revealed today in various ways, as God seeks to correct man's misperceptions.

Laura believed the real issue is the right of access for any individual. One shouldn't have to flee to hidden parlors to investigate what is going on in the world today. The Bishop did not agree and gave Laura three choices: publicly repudiate the teachings of Jonah, resign from the church, or face a Court of Inquiry, a proceeding amounting to a heresy trial. Laura, not desiring to split the church, decided to resign from the church and begin her own foundation for spiritual studies. Twenty years have passed since that day. Laura and I remained very good friends, and she continued her studies with Jonah until her death a few years ago.

The following day, the Denver News team showed up with their TV cameras and asked for an interview. I found the interviewer to be very courteous with interesting questions that brought some understanding to what was occurring.

The day after I appeared on television, I received a call from Peter Boyles, a popular radio talk show host in Denver. He wanted me to appear on his radio show. I agreed to the interview without asking about his show and what type of interviews he did. When I found out, I wanted to cancel the appearance but I had made a commitment to go, regardless of the consequences. The day of the interview, I received a call from Bill. He had to take his car into the shop for repairs and asked if I was willing to drop him off on my way to Denver. He said he would enjoy going with me and on the way back home he could pick up his car. It was a very innocent trip for the both of us, I thought.

When I arrived at the radio station with Bill, Peter Boyles became very nervous. I might add, Bill is six feet seven inches tall. The interview was held in a room with glass walls; though Bill waited outside, he could see us. As the interview started, I realized Peter Boyles clearly had an agenda; he wanted to show his audience that I didn't know what I was talking about. He was not quite succeeding. During the first commercial break Peter leaned over to me and said, "You are good; you are really good."

As soon as the commercial break was over, however, he reverted to sarcasm. A few days after the interview, the press interviewed him about his conversation on air with me. He claimed I brought this "huge gorilla" with me as a bodyguard, referring to Bill. Bill, who only wanted a ride to get his car fixed, was labeled by the press as a gorilla who works as my bodyguard!

The next interview on television was with the NBC "Today" show. They wanted to come out to my house in Boulder and interview me on our deck. The woman they sent out didn't know what I did. They brought a newspaper reporter from Denver, who had previously interviewed me, with her to ask the questions on TV. Jonah agreed to appear on the NBC "Today" show, although he wouldn't agree to appear on the Peter Boyles show. When Jonah came through, it startled the woman from New York. Her high heel shoe caught in the deck; she would have fallen over if someone hadn't caught her. Friends told us later that the show was played in its entirety in Australia, although only a couple minutes aired in our country. We never saw the interview, as we were flying to another city at the time of the showing.

Following this series of interviews, I realized most reporters do not want to get to the truth, but rather they want a story that will sell. I became very disillusioned by the whole experience. My experience has been reporters emphasizing the phenomena of Jonah, rather than the reason why these events have occurred and the message of love and hope. Although I have done a few interviews in the last twenty years, for the most part I have turned them down.

My teachings from the Chinese Master were continuing. At night I could feel myself slip out of my body and reappear in the cave with the Chinese Master. Each time he would have a new person with an unusual problem he wanted me to work on. At the end of one session, he told me I would have an experience like a dream, but not a dream, of how I came to be present in Daryl's body.

He also took me on a journey into the world of viruses. He and Jonah had talked for some time about the increase of viruses affecting the human population. They told me that as many people would wait for the earth changes, moving from one location to another, it would be the viruses that would create the greatest change of all. Then the Chinese Master told me there would be a medical doctor coming to see Jonah. In time he would ask me to participate in some medical tests and that it would be appropriate for me to do so. He explained that I would learn a great deal about how my body works when Jonah is using it and what occurs with my body when I am doing energy work on people.

Chapter 16
The Foundation

One afternoon in the spring of 1986, we had a session with Jonah, and Rebecca asked questions for both of us. He confirmed what we had been feeling. It was now time to create the Foundation. I had no idea of how to go about creating it. I carried the vision of what it would be like and how it would work with children and the child within the adult, but the legal aspect was totally foreign to me.

In my conversations with Bill Dean, it became clearer we would need to hire an attorney to set up a non-profit foundation. Bill found an attorney in Denver who specialized in this area. He visited the attorney and brought back a stack of paperwork for us to fill out. I decided I did not want any surprises with the government about what I did or who I was in setting up the foundation. We made copies of all the interviews I had had with the national media and included them with the paperwork. There were five options available for a 501 (3) c organization. I decided to make the foundation a not-for-profit educational foundation.

I was still not sure what the name of the foundation would be. I continued to meditate on the name but nothing was coming to me. I knew Jonah would not give me the name because he felt it was my responsibility to discover it. Then one day while driving with some friends, one of them asked me what the name of the foundation was going to be. I answered, "It will be called the Universal Education Foundation."

Surprised, Rebecca turned and looked at me; she saw that I was also surprised. I had spoken the name without even thinking about it. Then I realized it was a name that fully describes the function of the Foundation: teaching universal understanding and bringing an educational understanding of the spiritual child, the spiritual self, and the spiritual universe.

The next week Bill, his wife Janette, his sister Pam, Rebecca, and I went to meet with the attorney. We gave him all of our completed paperwork and paid his fee. Each of us donated the money for the attorney, as the yet to be formed Foundation had no bank account or funds to even set up an account.

To everyone's surprise, six weeks after receiving our paperwork, the IRS had approved the non-profit status for the Foundation. I then went to the bank and donated a hundred dollars to set up an account in the Foundation's name. At the time we were living from month to month and a hundred dollars seemed to us like a lot of money, but we felt it was important to start the process.

Rebecca and I understood that our work with Jonah and the work of the Foundation would remain two separate organizations. Rebecca and I did not feel it was appropriate for us to use funds donated to the Foundation for our personal support. To this day, we have never taken a salary from the Foundation.

Our next step was to find some land on which to construct a building for the Foundation. I could feel a pulling southwest of Boulder, but property kept presenting itself northwest of Boulder, although every deal failed to work out. We continued our search for a year and a half. Then one afternoon Jonah gave Rebecca a message after finishing a session with someone who came for an appointment. He told Rebecca that on a date about three weeks away, we were to clear our calendar for a week. We were to go on a journey. As usual, he gave this information and left out any details.

The following day, a friend came to speak to Jonah. Just before Jonah came through, the man sitting in front of us said, "I have a townhouse I rented for a month in Crestone, a small town in southern Colorado. We can only use it for three weeks. Would your family like to use it for the one week we will not be there?"

"What week is it?" Rebecca asked, knowing it would be the same week

Jonah had told us to cancel all sessions. When he answered, we said we would love to stay in his condo in Crestone, but we had no idea where it was.

He explained, "It's southwest of Boulder, about a five-hour drive from here."

When the time came we packed up our car with Jason and Tami in tow and arrived in Crestone about five hours later. Crestone is in a high desert called the San Luis Valley. We met many wonderful and different people in the Crestone area.

One such couple was Carol and Don McDaniel. Carol was working as a psychic. She heard I was in the area visiting and asked me to do an exchange of sessions with her, which I agreed to. I spoke with her concerning the Foundation we had created and how we were looking for land. She told us she could help raise money and expressed a desire for her and Don to be on the board of the Foundation.

At that time, only Rebecca and I were on the board, and we felt we could use the help. I was to learn later she had very different motives for being on the board of the Foundation. I began to notice little signs, not realizing at the time they were actually big flashing signs, and I should have paid more attention.

Carol wanted to use the Foundation for her work with adults, not children. She felt when we found the land we should close it in our names, meaning the four of us. I told her that was not the purpose of the Foundation. When I made it clear the Foundation land would only be owned by the Foundation and in the name of the Foundation, she became quite angry and abusive. It was a short time later she and her husband resigned from the board. Later I learned that she previously had difficulties with another foundation back east.

We also connected with Alice, a hands-on healer. We told her that we were looking for land for the Foundation we had set up. "How much money does your Foundation have?" she asked.

"Forty-five dollars," I said.

"Well, I don't know what to tell you," Alice replied with a blank look on her face. "But I will keep my ears open."

About two weeks later, Alice called us after she had lunch in a local restaurant. She overheard a conversation about this man who decided to sell his property, which was the most coveted property in the valley. It was on the side of Mount Blanca, a sacred mountain to the Indians. Alice offered to contact this person for us. We accepted her offer and soon found ourselves meeting with the owner a week later. We toured the160 acres with an 100-year-old, three-bedroom cabin. We knew this was it. The owner wanted $140,000 for the land. He said he was willing to take $40,000 as a down payment, $50,000 in one year, and $50,000 in six months after the second payment. Rebecca and I looked at each other and knew if this was to be the land for the Foundation, the money would be provided to us.

We drove home and decided to write a letter to the small mailing list we had at the time, asking for donations for the down payment. If it came in, then we knew it was the right land, if it did not come in, then we would continue looking elsewhere. We sent the letter, paying for the postage ourselves since there were only forty-five dollars in the Foundation bank account. In two weeks' time, we received $40,257. We bought the land and trusted in spirit that the rest of the money would arrive in time to make the last two payments totaling $100,000.

During the fund-raising process, we had been offered a trip to Peru. Half the people going were Americans and half Australians. They wanted us to do group sessions for them throughout the trip, in return, they would pay for all of our expenses. We already knew some of the people who were going and felt very comfortable with their energy. We had one month to prepare and would be gone for two weeks. Jonah had told us we would be traveling to foreign countries, but this was our first, and we were quite excited about it. We made arrangements for the closing of the Foundation land that would occur before our return from Peru.

We departed in mid May. We had a wonderful flight to Lima where we were to spend a couple of days. I had heard of many UFO sightings in Peru, and I was excited about again having a UFO encounter. When we all arrived and assembled in Peru, I found out I was the only smoker in the entire group. However, our tour guide, a native Peruvian woman about 35-years-old, was a smoker, and we quickly became friends. We would take our cigarette breaks together, and she would share with me the little known history of Peru. I asked her if she had ever seen a UFO. She went on for hours talking about the many different sightings she had seen.

On our flight from Lima to Lake Titicaca, she arranged for me to go up and visit with the pilot. As he was showing me the different instruments, I asked him if he had ever seen a UFO. His reply was, "Is this on or off the record?"

"Off the record," I said. (Since this is off the record, I cannot name the airline or pilot.)

"Yes, about twice a month they will come and fly along side my aircraft. But the airline forbids me to talk about it on record."

"Do you ever feel threatened by them?" I asked.

"No! Of course not. They are our friends."

I did not quite understand his answer until later during the trip.

Later in the day we arrived at Lake Titicaca. That evening we had planned a group session with Jonah in a section of the hotel lobby. As we were gathering for the session, we encountered a group of scientists from Germany. They were there studying the temperatures and currents of Lake Titicaca. I was visiting with one of the scientists and the conversation turned to UFO's. I asked him if he had ever encountered one while in Peru.

"Yes," he said. "We were on an island in the middle of the lake. It was getting late in the afternoon when we heard a strange high-pitched sound. We looked up and saw a huge flying disk. We had our equipment with us and took measurements from where we were standing."

I asked him the size and he told me in metric, which I did not understand. I asked him to translate it into American measurements.

"Three point two miles in width," he said.

"How fast was it going? How high was it?" I was full of questions.

"It took 34 minutes to pass over us flying at about two hundred feet elevation."

"What did the other scientists have to say about it?"

"We were all in amazement," he said. "A couple of the men said we cannot allow our minds to believe what our eyes have seen. They have not spoken of it since."

"What other experiences have you had with UFO's?"

"That's all I've had, but I did run into a scientist from England who was studying one of the tribes on the other side of the lake. Apparently they like to keep to themselves. His jeep broke down while he was trying to reach the tribe, so he had to hike in. After a couple of days, he arrived at their village. These tribesmen said that doctors came to help the sick. They even told him the doctors could fix his jeep when they return. He asked them to tell him more about these doctors. The Indians described men in white suits that could not tear. They explained how these men would put their hands into the Indians' bodies to fix the pain. They told the English scientist they had blond hair, blue eyes, and could float in the air."

"Did he ever see them?" I asked.

"No, he said he waited a couple of days and then had to leave. It had taken him much more time to reach the tribe than he had planned because of problems with his jeep. I last talked to him a month or so ago. Say, I hear you're a medium," he said.

"Yes, I am."

"This is becoming one of the strangest scientific trips I have ever gone on. Do you mind if I sit in on it?"

"No, not at all," I said.

After the session I saw him sitting in the back of the room with another man I had not met. I went over to visit him, he had a blank look on his face. "I don't understand," he said.

"What?" I asked.

"I asked my friend if he wanted to come and sit with me. He said, 'No,

I don't understand English that well, it would mean nothing to me, so he stayed across the room. After Jonah was speaking a few moments, he came and whispered in my ear, 'You did not tell me this Jonah speaks German!' I told him 'He's not speaking German!'" explained the scientist. "But my friend insisted, 'Certainly he is; I can understand every word of German he is speaking.'"

"He isn't speaking German," I said. "He is speaking English."

"No, I hear German. I like this Jonah," replied the scientist's friend.

The scientist looked up at me and said, "I need to go to bed; nice meeting you, whoever you are."

"I am Hossca," I said. He rolled his eyes, turned around, and walked away with his friend.

A few days later we traveled to Machu – Picchu. Again we had a group session with Jonah at the hotel just outside of the ruins. Later that evening, Rebecca and I were sound asleep when an intense heat on my stomach awakened me. I opened my eyes and saw a bright yellow beam of light coming out of the sky through the window and landing on my stomach. I started to get up but fell back on the bed into a deep sleep. About two hours later I was again awakened. This time the beam of light was a brilliant blue color. Again I tried to get up and fell back onto the bed and did not awaken until morning. I told Rebecca about it as soon as I was awake and actually able to sit up and she replied, "I thought that was a dream I was having."

"No, my stomach is still sore." I pulled down the covers and there was a bright red spot about six inches in diameter. It looked like a bad sunburn. By breakfast it had disappeared along with the soreness, but my skin was peeling as if I had been sunburned. To this day, I still have periods of time when the skin on my stomach will peel off.

The next evening we met with a Bruho, much like an American Indian medicine man. Since there were about 50 of us, he said he could only answer ten or fifteen questions presented to him. He had everyone write down his or her name and put it in a hat. The names drawn out of the hat were permitted to ask their questions. The Bruho put his hand into the hat and pulled out my name. The rest of the group thought the Bruho and I had fixed it and started booing. The question on my mind, which I had not planned on asking, came out of my mouth anyway. I had wanted to know if the land next door to the Foundation land would come up for sale, so I could buy it and live there to look after the Foundation.

"Yes," he said. "You will live next door to the Foundation. Allow it to be, you need to be there."

When we returned from Peru, I inquired about the land and found out it had been in the same family for over fifty years. They were not about to sell it to anyone, at anytime, for any reason or any price. They told me never to ask again and hung up on me. I wondered what that was all about, forgetting that spirit does not always follow our time or understanding of time. Some years later, we did live next to the Foundation land, but not on the land I tried to buy, but more on that later.

I called and arranged to pick up the deed of trust, keys, and the abstract from the title company in Alamosa, a town about 50 minutes south of Crestone. Then we drove up to the land and parked in front of the cabin. We couldn't believe our eyes. There was 30 years of trash surrounding the cabin, trash we had not seen only a few weeks earlier. Yet, it was obvious this trash had been there for many years. The split rail fence surrounding the meadow in front of the cabin was not there, and never had been; the glass sliding door we had walked through in the living room of the old cabin was not there, and never had been. "What reality had we been in?" we asked each other. I knew we needed help to clean up the property. We had a picnic planned for July 4, 1988, less than a month away, to thank everyone that donated time and money to purchase this land.

Back in Boulder, we decided to send out another newsletter asking for volunteers to help us clean up the mess on the land. More than 20 people responded. We did not have enough money to pay to haul all the trash to the dump, which was a 60-mile round trip, and we needed about 40 trips with a trailer. So we decided to find a clearing on the top part of the land and create a dump for the old rusted metal, old cans, and other trash in that area. I bought a ten-foot trailer for my pickup that I used to make trips back and forth to the new dumpsite.

I knew everyone who came to the clean up party, except for one person who stood out because he was dressed in business clothes and dress shoes. He also had an unusual twitch occurring with one eyebrow. I asked him who he was; he said he was a friend of the Freeman's, whom I did know. I passed it off as a city person who just wanted to help but didn't know what to expect.

I decided I would begin cleaning out one of the very old out buildings, which had been a storage area for newspapers and magazines from the past 30 years. At the bottom of one pile, I found a tin can partially buried in the dirt floor. I opened the can and found a notebook that was not as old as the magazines I was collecting for the dump. The name on the notebook was the name of the previous owner's deceased wife. In the notebook she had written about contact with aliens from another star system. She described in great detail how they looked, what their spacecraft looked like, and where it had landed. There were even star maps written in the notes. The notes went on for pages and pages.

While I was reading with great interest, someone came in and asked me to come down to the cabin to answer some questions about where to put some of the trash. I walked down the hill into the cabin, laid the notebook on the counter top in the kitchen, and walked into the back bedroom to answer a question. I was gone about two minutes. When I came back to the kitchen, the notebook was gone, and so was the strange man with the twitching eye. I called the Freemans and asked them who this person was. They didn't know him.

I investigated. I found out the author of the notebook, Nellie, had a horse that was killed in much the same way as the animal mutilations that have been occurring around the country. The story of Nellie's horse was printed in newspapers around the world, including a description of the condition of the horse when it was found. I have been told the head of the horse is still at the college in Alamosa. I was also told that men in black came to the cabin to talk with Nellie, telling her not to give interviews about her experiences with UFO's, space aliens, or the killing of her horse.

Nellie was a very independent woman who did not want to be told what to do by anyone. As the story goes she told them what she thought of them and ordered them to leave. Nellie was found dead a short time later, supposedly a suicide. Those who knew Nellie told me she was not the suicidal type. She loved life. I was also told there were two notebooks, one hidden in her sister's candy store in Alamosa and one hidden on the Foundation land. Years ago, someone found the hiding place in the candy store and took that notebook, now someone had taken the second notebook. To this day, I regret I didn't take the time to read the entire notebook.

We soon tired of driving back and forth between Boulder and the Foundation land, so we decided to find a house in Crestone. Jonah advised us about the move and told us he would start doing sessions over the telephone. In a few weeks, we found a house for sale. We had not thought of buying a house, but the thought of owning our own home again became very appealing. We had one problem—no money for a down payment. We asked Jonah about it and he said, "If that is what you want, then create it."

We were guided to a three-bedroom house with a two-car garage in the back. One half of the garage had been turned into a large room. It would be perfect to live in this house, do our sessions, and have an office for the Foundation in the room off the garage. The owner was willing to sell the house to us on a lease/purchase agreement. One half of our rent would go toward the down payment. Since the rent was one half of what we had been paying in Boulder, we jumped at the chance.

Although most of our sessions were now being done over the telephone, we had many different people come to see us in Crestone. One such person was John Fetzer, head of the Fetzer Institute of Science and Spirituality. We had a wonderful visit before his session with Jonah. One of his main questions for Jonah was how long he had left in the physical. It is very unusual for Jonah to answer such a question, although from time to time he does. Jonah told him he had two years left. It helped John to prepare for his departure and complete his work. John Fetzer died two years later in 1991.

One day, a friend called asking if she could bring someone visiting from New York over to visit Rebecca and me. They asked if they could stop by in about two hours. We answered yes. When we opened the door, it was Laurence Rockefeller. He wanted to discuss our plans for the Universal Education Foundation. We had a wonderful visit, although we never heard from him again.

We were also introduced to a Prince of Kuwait, though Jonah chose not to talk to him. I didn't know if it was because a war was looming for Kuwait or if it was the Prince himself. We visited about his trip to the Great Sand Dunes National Park, about 45 minutes south of Crestone. The Prince said he took his daughter to the park and kept hunting for the monument. He then found out it was the sand. "You Americans," he said, "you make a monument out of sand. That must make all of Kuwait a monument."

The Foundation never received any assistance from these early contacts. We did receive assistance from our friends Frank Slavensky, as well as Diana Lynn, and Robert White of ARC International.

One month after we moved to Crestone, we began working with groups of children and teenagers on the Foundation land. During that time, strange experiences occurred. The first related to a new generator that was donated to the Foundation, as the land did not have public power to it. The generator stopped after about ten hours of use. I loaded up the generator and took it to Alamosa to be repaired. The repairman called a couple of days later and said the internal parts of the engine had rusted the valves open. "How long has it been since you used this generator?" the repairman asked.

"The day before I brought it to you. It was running great and it just stopped."

"I'm sorry, mister, but this generator has not been run in some years. The valves cannot rust open while it is running and full of oil."

He refused to believe me, and I did not have time to convince him. After we got the generator fixed and returned to the cabin, we asked Jonah about it. He told us the Indians in spirit form guarding the land did not want the noise, but I could reach some agreement with them. Jonah suggested I take some tobacco and place it on a rock in a small meadow across from the pond in front of the cabin. The next day I did this, then returned the following day to find the tobacco gone. The generator continued to work fine, but the switch in the house to turn it on stopped working. We had to go outside with flashlights to turn the generator on and off at night.

Jonah also told us that no one should walk in this special meadow at night because it was a sacred meadow. It was fine to use it during the day but never at night.

The next group of teenagers was due to arrive in a few days. When they arrived, we told them this meadow was off limits after sundown. We explained that it was a sacred meadow and the Indian spirits did not want anyone walking in the area at night. Of course, we received some looks that translated into, "Which planet are you guys from?" The first night, two of the teenagers took our warning as an invitation to explore the meadow.

The two boys walked out into the dark field. The first boy stood there and exclaimed, "Look! Nothing happened! They were just lying to us." Just at that time, an Indian with a dim glowing light around him appeared, standing a few inches behind this boy. The boy was completely unaware of the new visitor, but the other boy saw the Indian very clearly. Before he could warn his friend, the Indian put his hands on the boy's back and pushed him into the pond. He was unharmed but quite frightened. All the teenagers stayed away from the meadow for the reminder of their stay.

We asked a good friend of ours, Dennis Disrud, a child therapist, if he would begin working with us at the Foundation. He became a wonderful support and later a board member as well, and he continued working with the Foundation until his death in 1996.

One week while the teenage boys, Rebecca, Dennis, and I were sitting in the living room of the old cabin, we had an unusual experience. The boys were sitting on a couch with Dennis, while I was sitting in a chair facing the couch. The room suddenly went silent, and then the cabin shook like we had a large earthquake. The boys' and Dennis's eyes were wide open and focused on the window behind me. I quickly turned to see what they were all staring at. A small disk-like craft was floating just outside the window. As soon as I focused on it, it took off at lighting speed. The air was full of electricity; our hair was standing on end as if we had been rubbing our shoes on the carpet. We all raced outside to see which way it went, but there was nothing to see. We began searching the outside walls of the cabin for any damage. Again nothing. The electricity was still in the air with a strange smell we could not identify.

Later that night we were talking about the events of the afternoon when we noticed that strange smell increasing. I felt someone staring at me from outside the window. I turned and saw a physical being with bright red eyes staring at me. I raced outside to find it was gone. Under the tree where the being had been standing, I found a set of footprints.

I looked back at the cabin; everyone in the cabin had their noses pressed up against the window, watching me. I reentered the cabin and asked everyone to sit down. I tried to turn the conversation back to the subject matter of teens in crisis, but it didn't work. The being with the red eyes was the main topic of conversation.

Later that night, when we had all gone to bed and been asleep for some time, I found myself suddenly awakened by a bright light outside. I looked over at the bedroom window and saw it was brighter than daylight. I tried to get out of bed, but it was as if I was frozen in place. The next thing I knew, it was morning.

The strange events continued every time we went to the Foundation land. About a month later, we had another group of teenagers who came to spend a week with us at the cabin. Two of the teenagers had never been outside of the city and wanted to camp in a tent. It was their first experience camping and being out in nature. When dinner was over, we loaded up a tent that had been donated to the foundation and grabbed our sleeping bags. We hiked up the hill about a thousand feet from the cabin.

We set up the tent and laid out the sleeping bags and decided to go on a hike. The teenagers started getting nervous being out in the woods, so we went back to the tent. Soon it was pitch black due to the new moon. They could hear all the animal sounds in the woods. One of the teenagers got up and said, "I want to go back to the cabin." He unzipped the door, saw how dark it was outside, and changed his mind.

It was a hot night, so we unzipped all the windows in the tent to allow for a breeze to cool us off and soon went to sleep. In the middle of the night, I was awakened by a bright blue beam of light coming out of the sky through the window of the tent and onto my stomach. I remembered having the same experience in Peru. I lifted my arm to place my hand into the light, and the next thing I knew, I was awakening again. This time a yellow light was coming through the window and touching my stomach. I remember looking at the light; then suddenly it was sunrise.

I walked around for a while until the two teenagers woke up; then we hiked back to the cabin for breakfast. I asked Rebecca and Dennis if they saw anything last night and shared my experience with them. They said everything had been quiet, and they had all gone to bed early.

The next week we had a group of younger children spending the week at the cabin. They ranged in age from eight to twelve. The first night the blue light appeared again but this time it shined through the bedroom of the younger children. In the morning, they shared with us how the light lit up the entire bedroom in a beautiful light blue color. It did not frighten any of the children. They were hoping it would arrive again the next night, but that was the last time we had the experience of the blue light for some time.

The cabin still needed many repairs from the roof to the plumbing. Each weekend we drove over to the Foundation land to work. The cabin had been built before there was indoor plumbing. Over the years, it had been added piece by piece. The water coming into the cabin was from a gravity fed spring up the hill from the cabin. One weekend, I decided to stay there by myself to try and fix all of the leaks in the walls. Early the first night, I became quite tired and went to bed. In the middle of the night I was awakened by something. I noticed my arms were numb. As I stretched out my arms to get some feeling back into them, blue arcs began shooting out of my finger tips about four feet into the air. I laid there watching this occur and thought, perhaps this is the healing energy the Chinese Master has been teaching me about. I moved my fingertips toward myself, so the arcs of energy would enter into my body. As soon as they hit my body, I fell into a deep sleep, awakening totally refreshed in the morning.

Shortly after we were settled in our new house, a couple named Richard and Helen, whom we had met when we lived in Washington, had moved to Crestone. We renewed our friendship and spent many evenings visiting together. As our friendship developed, Richard began telling me that he felt he should be the one traveling with me and not Rebecca. I explained to him that I needed Rebecca because she helps me ground when I return to my body following Jonah's departure. Richard refused to accept my explanation and insisted it was his job to travel with me. The tension grew in our relationship. Rebecca and I wondered what it would be like to have friends who wanted to be friends because of who we are and not what I do.

One afternoon in March of 1990, we received a call from the high school our son Jason was attending. His teacher said someone had reported that Jason was suicidal. We could not believe it and did not believe it. Soon after we received that phone call, Richard stopped by. During our discussion, Richard told us he had gone to Jason's school and told the school officials that Jason was suicidal.

"You are the one who said this?" We were shocked.

"Yes," said Richard. "I told you I am the one who needs to travel with you, not Rebecca. Rebecca needs to stay home with the children."

I showed him the door and have not spoken with him since. Although

I feel I have forgiven him, his actions ended whatever relationship might have evolved.

Word of the incident spread among our friends and acquaintances. Carol McDaniel, a past director of the Foundation, claimed publicly she had a psychic vision of Jason breaking into the local grocery store because he was so depressed. The weekend the store was broken into, Jason was in California and had been there for a month visiting his cousins, but Carol didn't know that. When her story was discredited, Carol began spreading rumors about me, stating that Jonah had abandoned me and was now speaking through someone in Canada.

We turned to Jonah for answers about these disturbing incidents and why they happened. Jonah told us it was not so much about Rebecca and me, although it did affect us, instead, it was about the Foundation land. That land was one of the most coveted pieces of land in the area, and we were the ones who had it. Only a few years later would I realize how many people wanted that land and were willing to do anything to obtain it.

Jonah told us not to empower the lies and rumors being spread by Carol. The ones we are to work with are ones who will not allow their minds to be influenced by such energy. Jonah repeated a statement he had made many times: "A friend of the heart will never depart, but a friend of the mind will scatter as the wind blows." Carol would need to resolve her own karma. Later I found out she had been influenced from another life.

We still needed to raise $50,000 to pay off the balance of the loan on the Foundation land. Diana Lynn and Frank Slavensky, two prior directors of the Foundation, donated the money to pay off the loan in full. The Foundation will always be in deep gratitude for their loving support and the support of the many hundreds of people who have donated over the years to the Foundation.

Chapter 17
Medical Experiments

February of 1989, I received a phone call from a medical doctor who was the medical director of the psychophysiology laboratory at the Colorado Center for Bio-behavioral Health in Boulder. Dr. Edgar Wilson wanted to drive to Crestone and have a session with Jonah. He had also heard about the hands-on healing I had been doing for the last several years.

A couple weeks later, Dr. Wilson arrived at our home for his session with Jonah. When I opened the door, I was surprised at his appearance. I was expecting a doctor dressed in a business suit with carefully styled hair, but he looked like an old country doctor. His face was filled with lines of compassion with much light coming from his eyes. I liked him immediately. After his session with Jonah, we started talking about healing and my teacher whom I called the Chinese Master.

Dr. Wilson was in the process of studying and researching energy medicine. He asked if I would be willing to do hands-on energy work at his center, with both the patient and me hooked up to a twenty-four channel computerized EEG machine, Neurosearch-24, during a variety of a experimental tasks. The Neurosearch-24 would measure electrical potentials on the scalp while generating and analyzing a record of the electrical activity of the brain. He wanted to record the procedures on videotape as well.

I had no idea what he was talking about, so I said. "Bring that by me again, maybe a little bit slower?"

"What I am saying," he explained, "is I want you to do energy work on a patient you have not previously met. I don't want there to be any form of communication between the two of you before, during, or after the treatment. I'll have both of you hooked up to computers. I want to understand what occurs with your body and what occurs with the patient's body."

"Oh," I said, "that would be interesting. The Chinese Master has told me how I move energy and what it does for the person I'm working on. I would like to see just what happens in my body and the person I'm working on. I was told such an opportunity would be presented at some time. I guess this is it. Do you know who the patient will be?"

"No, not at this time," replied Dr. Wilson. "It's important that I know as little about the patient as possible to reduce experimenter's bias. I do know of a psychologist in the Boulder area who could recommend potential subjects."

February 27, 1989, Rebecca and I drove to Boulder to begin the process of experimentation. When I arrived at the Colorado Center for Bio-behavioral Health, I was taken into a room to wait while they were putting a skullcap on the patient's head and connecting it to a computer in an adjacent room. They only told me that the patient was a woman called LR.

I entered the room next door and saw the middle-aged woman lying on a bed with the skullcap wrapped around the top, sides, and back of her head. The wires from the skullcap fed into the computer next to the bed. I sat down on a chair placed near the bed.

As I usually do, I used my right hand opened with my palm down to scan the body, looking for the energy blockages. I found there was little energy in her second chakra, right above the pelvic bone. I began to pick up energy of severe sexual abuse when she was a child. I then found there was very dark energy coming from her left breast.

I began to work on her body with my hands. I did not talk to her and she did not talk to me: we were simply letting the computer record all the information of what was occurring in her body. As soon as I put my hands on her, the computers recorded a significant activation of theta brain waves in both the temporal lobes and the center of the brain. Theta brain waves represent a very relaxed state. The computer continued to show episodes of theta brain waves dissociating from alpha, a slightly less relaxed state. Theta brain waves were recorded moving toward the front of the head during the healing process. This form of dissociation has been observed repeatedly in other subjects who are undergoing profound, internal shifts in states of consciousness.

After the procedure, the woman's psychologist interviewed her and shared the results with the research team. Dr. Wilson analyzed the results and shared them with me. He said that LR reported a profound sense of well being and understanding during the procedure. After reviewing the data, Dr. Wilson determined that this intense emotional experience occurred as the theta brain waves formed a linear pattern from the back to the front of her head.

Her psychologist reported that even though LR could remember certain events in her early life that had previously been too painful to contemplate, she is now able to experience those events with less sensitivity. Her change in consciousness during the healing session gave her a profound sense of empowerment. LR has been able to access memories of her early childhood abuse without blocking or becoming depressed. Within two months, she had gained 12 pounds and no longer had evidence of depression. She says she feels energy moving through her body, no longer blocking in her abdomen.

At the beginning of the session, LR said that she felt a wave of motion in the second chakra. She felt the energy going into the body from my hands, creating colors she could see, beginning with red and gold and then progressing to purple, indigo, and green. At other times, it was like watching a light. She could feel the energy moving through the center of her body, but then she tended to lose contact with her body and began to experience high ringing in her ears, which left shortly after I removed my hands.

About a month later, Dr. Wilson asked me to return. This time he wanted both the patient and me to wear skullcaps. Both of us would be wired to the same computer. The process was the same as with the last person. I was not to meet this person, know her condition, or have any communication with her.

I arrived at the Center and was taken into a room to be fitted with the skullcap. I then entered the room with the woman known to me as CK. She was lying on a bed already fitted with her skullcap and connected to the computer in the room. I sat down in a chair next to the bed and waited while they connected the wires from my skullcap to the same computer. I could see CK had nerve damage in her left shoulder, arm, and hand. She had visible trembling in this part of her body. I could also see she was in deep pain from this injury. I scanned her body to make sure nothing else was occurring. I then put my hands on her body and began sending energy. After about ten minutes the trembling stopped; the pain was gone. It surprised me how quickly the healing occurred. Dr. Wilson was standing there shaking his head in amazement.

This one case, more than any other, demonstrated to me what the Chinese Master has always taught me. I can heal no one, I only supply the energy for that person to heal himself or herself. What makes this case most interesting is what followed.

CK had had this pain and trembling for several years following an accident. I was later told she was diagnosed as having Reflex Sympathetic Dystrophy, with pain extending from the shoulder down to her hand with skin changes and vasomotor alterations as well. She had undergone a significant number of treatments since her injury, which did not offer any relief from her pain. This was the first time she was without pain since that accident. She had tears streaming down her cheeks when she thanked me.

That evening she shared with her husband what had occurred and held her arm out to the side for the first time without pain. Her husband demanded to know how this occurred. She then confided in him the experience of the day at the Center. "We have to call our minister and talk to him about this," he said.

A short time later, the minister arrived at their home and she explained to him the events of the day and how I had worked on her. "This is the work of the devil!" he shouted. "You need to rebuke the devil that is in you."

She became so terrified the pain and trembling returned. The minister was quite pleased; he felt he had removed the devil from her.

After about two weeks of continued pain, she called Dr. Wilson and explained what had happened. CK wanted to return and have me work on her again. Dr. Wilson explained the situation to me. I felt a deep sorrow for this woman, for I knew how she felt and the intense fear she had programmed in her mind by this minister.

A few days later, we set up the same experiment with both of us wearing our skullcaps. I again begin to work on her. I could feel the intense fear moving through her body. I first began working on her fear energy and trying to calm her body, mind, and emotions. I then began working on her physical damage. This time it took twice as long for the energy to begin to move. Eventually, the pain and trembling stopped. She was again shedding tears of relief from the pain. I told her, "It is up to you if you want to continue to hold onto the healing energy. I cannot heal you, you are healing yourself by using the energy I am sending to you." I never heard from her again, so I don't know the end result.

This experience reminded me of a phone call I received a few years earlier from a man in Boulder. He told me his young son was dying from a blood disorder. The doctors had tried everything they could and told the father there was nothing else they could do. He had about three to five months to live. The father, Peter, asked if I would be willing to work on his son. I told Peter I was willing, but I could not guarantee any results. He said he understood that but wanted me to try anyway.

As it happened, the next day the **Boulder Camera** published an article on me about the Rev. Laura Fraser. My picture was on the front page of the newspaper. That afternoon Peter called me and said his minister had seen the article and had forbidden him to allow me to see his son. The minister told him it was better for his son to die than have me work on him, and if I was to work on him, Peter would go to hell fire. I told Peter I understood where he was coming from and I would respect his choice. I never heard from him again. I had long wondered if this minister was the same one who rebuked CK.

The next experiment Dr. Wilson wanted to try was to see what occurred with my brain when Jonah was using my body. Dr. Wilson had already taken many brain wave samples during my normal states of activities and wanted to compare what the difference would be when Jonah was in my energy field.

I entered in a room and was again fitted with a skullcap and wired to their computer. I could feel Jonah come into the room. The energy of Jonah caused some form of energy disruption, and Dr. Wilson's two hearing aids blew. He took out his hearing aids and said, "I guess I don't need to hear; I'll just watch the computer."

"Jonah told me he would not enter into my body during this experiment but would surround my body with his energy," I said to Dr. Wilson. Then I remembered he could not hear me. The results that showed up on his computer indicated there were bursts of theta, alpha, and beta activity, which Dr. Wilson noted as surrounding the head rather than penetrating deeper structures within.

After analyzing the data, Dr. Wilson shared the results with me. "There was no evidence of alpha localization in the posterior area of the brain on any consistent basis. During this period of time, there seemed to be somewhat random EEG activity in all frequencies. Toward the end, alpha began to reorganize, but the theta activity continued to manifest itself almost entirely in the frontal lobes. Beta activity, on the other hand, occupied both temporal lobes, indicating a three-way split in the frequency activity throughout the brain. A histogram of the previous data revealed very intense activity in all frequencies in the area of Fm and Fz. A small peak frequency wave of approximately 6.5 Hz is present as well as a 10 Hz peak in the alpha range."

Dr. Wilson looked up from his readout and realized I did not understand anything he was saying. He smiled, then rephrased the information in layman terms. "This activity is distinctly uncommon in EEG interpretation. As a matter of fact, I have never seen a pattern such as this. The activity has not been described in EEG literature to my knowledge. The anatomic location of the activity corresponds to the so-called "Crown Chakra" of Eastern Mystics."

Dr. Wilson later wrote me a letter saying, "The data appears to show a distinct difference in neuroelectric activity during the time Jonah was present opposed to all other tracings in this study. The amplitude of alpha, the dissociation of theta from the alpha activity, and the topographic localization of neuroelectric activity at onset and at the end of the data during the appearance process cannot be explained by the activity of previous data sets in different states of consciousness. It would appear that a distinctly different pattern of neuroelectric activity did occur during this channeling process. In other words, Hossca, you demonstrated a non-humanoid brain wave."

Chapter 18
John and Cassandra Denver

Late in the summer of 1989, we received a phone call from our friends in Aspen. "Would you be willing to come to Aspen and do a personal session for John Denver and his wife Cassandra? You can stay in our townhouse and we will pay for your transportation here and back."

"Yes," we said, "we would love to." It was on a weekend, so we didn't have any other sessions planned.

On our drive from Crestone to Aspen, Rebecca laughed and said, "Remember what Alunastar told us some years ago?"

"What?" I asked.

"He told us one day we would meet John Denver, but you didn't believe it."

"I guess I pushed it out of my mind. I still don't remember it."

A few hours later we arrived at Starwood, where John and Cassandra lived. We drove up to the security gate and told the guard our names. He replied, "They are expecting you. Please drive through."

We drove through the gate and found our way through Starwood and into his driveway. We parked and walked to the office at the end of garage area. "We are Hossca and Rebecca Harrison," I said to the assistant at the desk.

"Yes, John and Cassandra are expecting you. Go out this door and follow the walkway up to his house." We walked up the path. There was a view of the Maroon Bells, magnificent mountain peaks in the distance. What a beautiful place to live and receive inspiration. We knocked on the back door. The housekeeper opened the door and directed us into the sunroom. "Please make yourself at home. John just finished doing a commercial outside. He and Cassandra will be with you soon."

About ten minutes later, John came in and greeted us. I couldn't take my eyes off his face; his skin was bright orange! At first I thought I was seeing his energy field, but I had never seen such a color on anyone. He realized I was staring and looked in the mirror on the wall. "Oh, I forgot to take my makeup off for the commercial. Excuse me, I'll be back."

A few minutes later he and Cassandra came in and sat down across from us. We talked for a few minutes and he asked, "How do I need to address Jonah? Do I need to do anything special?"

"No," I said, "when he comes through, he will greet you and you can start asking your questions."

A few minutes later Jonah arrived and answered their questions. One of the main questions John had was about their daughter Jesse Belle. John had not been able to have children of his own with his first wife Annie, so they adopted two children. Doctors had told John he could not father a child. After he married Cassandra, she became pregnant with their daughter Jesse Belle. Jonah answered and told them they were soul mates. The power of their souls was able to bring forth a child.

This information in itself was very unusual; Jonah has only told a handful of people they are soul mates. Most couples are heart mates, not soul mates, a phrase that has become very popular in the new age movement. If people truly knew what it meant to be soul mates, they would opt for being heart mates. Soul mates are two halves of the same soul, therefore all the issues the soul brings into a lifetime are magnified within the relationship rather than balanced. Granted, soul mate relationships can be filled with passion, but unless the two soul mates are prepared for the intensity of the relationship, soul mate unions often burn themselves out rather quickly. However, I decided not to share this with John and Cassandra. I assumed they would figure it out on their own.

When I came out of the session, both John and Cassandra had tears on their cheeks. They both hugged us and thanked us for coming to work with them. After visiting and sharing with them how I became a medium, it was time for us to drive back down the hill into Aspen to the townhouse where we were staying.

January of 1991, Cassandra again called and asked if we would be willing to come and work with them and have Jonah do a full day workshop for their friends in their home. "Yes," we said, "but the pass is closed and it will take us a full day just to drive there."

"I'll buy you tickets to fly to Aspen," she said. "John and I would love for you to come. You can stay at our place again. John wants to cook a special dinner for everyone after the workshop."

"That would be wonderful," we said. "Thank you for your generosity."

That evening I had a very powerful dream. In the dream we were staying at John's guesthouse a few feet away from the main house. We were sitting in the living room when John and Cassandra walked in. In the dream Cassandra hugged me and said, "I love your bear hugs, Hossca."

Then John walked in and hugged me and said, "I love your bear hugs, Hossca." On the coffee table was a large box, gift-wrapped. "This is for you, Hossca," John said. "This is my gift to you."

I sat down and opened the box and pulled out a beautiful crystal bowl. I turned to John and said, "Thank you." At the same time, I could feel a surge of emotion. Then I awakened from a deep sleep. It was three-thirty in the morning.

We arrived at the Aspen airport a couple of days later, rented a car, and again drove up to Starwood. John and Cassandra spoke with Jonah and then John took us on a tour of his house. He took us into his studio and asked us if we would like to listen to his newest song, "The Flower That Shattered the Stone." I was overwhelmed by the song's beauty and message. Then he asked if we would like to watch a video he had made of another song, "Raven's Child," which was about the Exxon oil tanker *Valdez* spilling its oil in Prince William Sound, Alaska. The video showed the chairman of Exxon in between pictures of children being sold crack.

"What do you think of this, Hossca?" he asked.

"I think it's a very powerful message of the mental condition of this world."

"Do you know that SOB doesn't even want to take responsibility for cleaning up the damage his ship did to Prince William Sound?"

"I'm not surprised," I said. "Money seems to be the motivating factor, not concern for the environment."

In a somber voice, John said, "The public won't be seeing this video." I looked at him, astonished, because I thought it was a powerful message about the consciousness of the world today. Reading my expression, John explained that his corporate sponsors wouldn't allow this video to be played unless he took out the pictures of the Chairman of Exxon. I shook my head in disgust, but I wasn't the least bit surprised. We left the studio still feeling all the emotions the video had evoked. John's guests would be arriving soon.

Rebecca and I, with John, Cassandra, and their guests, went into the living room to prepare for the workshop. Jonah came through and spoke for several hours and then answered questions for about an hour. After Jonah completed his message, we walked down to the kitchen and sat at the kitchen bar and watched John fix a wonderful East Indian dinner. I was amazed at his skills. I would have thought that someone who could so easily afford a chef wouldn't bother cooking himself; however, John was quite the cook. After dinner, we spent the rest of the evening visiting with John and Cassandra. John shared with us his different projects, mostly concerning the environment, and Cassandra shared songs she had written. She has since come out with her own CD's. Her latest CD album is titled "Give It Up To Love."

The next morning John and Cassandra walked down to the guesthouse. Rebecca and I were sitting on the couch. We stood up, and Cassandra hugged me and said, "You give such wonderful bear hugs." Then I remembered the dream I had.

John hugged me and said the same thing. I turned and looked at the coffee table to make sure there was not a present waiting there for me. There wasn't. While Rebecca and Cassandra were visiting, John picked up his twelve-string two neck guitar and sat down in front of me.

"Hossca, you and Jonah have meant so much to me. I wrote this song, but I was not sure whom I was writing it for. Now I feel I was writing it for you."

He started playing his guitar and looked up at me and said, "This gift is for you. I call it, 'The Gift You Are'."

John looked me in the eyes and began to sing. The harmony laced with intense emotions swirled around me. I was in such a state of astonishment, I couldn't focus on the words of the song. Some time later, when his CD came out with this song, I was able to read the lyrics. The lyrics mention carrying your dreams in a crystal jar. When I read that, it completed the meaning of the dream for me. To this day, it remains one of my most precious moments. Whenever I get tired of working with people, I put in his CD and listen to John's song to me.

We continued to see John and Cassandra in Aspen. When we heard the news of John's death, I felt we — the world — had lost a true artist and environmentalist who was there to remind us of the fragile condition of our planet. We were invited to John's memorial service and had the chance to meet his mother and visit with Cassandra whom we still consider a dear friend. It was a very sad day, but I knew John was all right and was still singing.

Chapter 19
Closure

In late autumn of 1989, we were invited to work with a group of people in Hawaii. Jason and Tami had never been to the islands, so it offered the perfect opportunity for all four of us to go. The group was on the island of Oahu, the same island on which I had drowned, yet I did not feel any fear about returning. We made reservations at the Hilton in Honolulu on Waikiki Beach. When we arrived at the hotel, we found our room reservations had been changed. The hotel could not explain what had happened to their computer, so they upgraded us to the top of the tower in a deluxe room with a perfect view of the Pacific Ocean.

We spent most of our time at the beach after we finished working with the group in Honolulu. On the third day, we had been swimming in the ocean and returned to our room to shower and rest before going out to dinner. When I was in the shower, I felt this presence come into the bathroom. I then heard a voice say, "Finish your shower; you need to go for a walk."

"A walk!" I said. "I'm tired. I plan on taking a nap."

"You need to go for a walk," the voice said again. "You can rest later. It is of import to go for a walk."

My first thought was they wanted me to get some more exercise. I thought about it for a couple of minutes and said, "OK, I'll go for a walk." Then the presence left.

After I finished my shower and got dressed, I went outside and began walking down the sidewalk in front of the neighboring hotels. I saw an unusual hotel down the street and decided to check it out in case we were ever to come back to Oahu. The hotel did not have any doors, just an open entryway into the lobby. As I walked into the lobby, I was focused on the carpeting. It had an unusual color and design. I bumped into a man who was standing there looking up at the ceiling. Apparently, it had an interesting ceiling, too.

I raised my head to apologize, and we looked at each other in absolute shock. The man I had walked into was Don, my past business partner.

"Daryl, is that you?"

"Don, is that you?"

At the same time we both said, "What the hell are you doing here?" Six years had passed; we had not seen each other since 1983. We decided to go to the bar and visit. I soon realized that our relationship, or his relationship with Daryl, had no closure. He had been in mourning for years about losing his relationship with Daryl. As Hossca, I didn't have a relationship with him, but he was not capable of truly understanding that Daryl no longer existed. About the fifth time he called me Daryl, I told him I had changed my name to Hossca. "What did you do that for?" he asked.

"I didn't feel a connection to the name Daryl."

"Feel a connection? What the hell does that mean? What does Wanda think of you changing your name?" he asked.

"Well, she changed her name to Rebecca."

"What the hell?" he replied. He raised his arm and ordered another Scotch on the rocks. "So tell me Daryl, Hossca, whatever, did you change Jason and Tami's names, too?"

"No," I said. "They still have the same names."

"So they are connected to their names?"

I changed the subject and asked him what he was doing in Hawaii. "I've never been here before," he said. "I decided at the last minute to come. I wanted to find my girlfriend."

"What happened to your wife?"

"She left. Don't ask."

"OK," I said.

"My girlfriend Susan said she wanted to get married. I said no, and I meant, hell no! So she left and went on vacation with her parents who came here to Hawaii. She has been gone for three days and I realized how much I missed her, so when I got up this morning, I got on the first plane to Hawaii. In fact, I just got here when you ran into me. I haven't even found her yet."

We continued visiting about our lives and how they had changed. He was still in the contracting business and had earned millions of dollars building apartments and condos on the beach front in Olympia, but his personal life had been very painful. About an hour later he saw Susan and her parents walk into the lobby, and he raced out of the lounge to embrace her. He brought her over to introduce her to me, and we made arrangements to meet the next day for drinks.

The meeting provided closure for Don, but I also realized that I had no connection to Daryl or Daryl's world or to any one from my past with the exception of Rebecca, Tami, and Jason. I have since experienced a deep bonding with my sister Tina who was a child when I had my near-drowning experience. She never really knew Daryl very well because Daryl was 20 when she was born. So she didn't have difficulty letting go of Daryl and embracing me. As she became an adult, she has become a very loving part of my life.

Chapter 20
Attorney General

I believe that each person you encounter has a role to play in your life, even if it is a brief one. Often we encounter the same souls throughout our lifetimes. Your wife could have been your sister in another lifetime. Your brother in this life could have been your lover in a past life. If there is a significant amount of unresolved karma from a previous incarnation, you and the soul with which you have karma can choose to come together in this current lifetime to resolve the karma and bring peace to the soul relationship.

I knew I had known my friend Bill Dean in another life beyond the mountain man life time, but I was not sure in what relationship I knew him. This adventure called life always carries surprises, and this surprise was to be a major journey through time, and a healing beyond time. Bill, the towering man he is with a deep baritone voice, had many sides to him, as we all do. He was one of many who offered assistance to the Foundation in the beginning days of its creation, and our friendship continued to deepen. However, Bill became involved in an investment project in another state, and he began traveling often, we would hear from him less and less.

During the time we did spend together, I began having troubling dreams and felt we were drifting apart. Bill seemed to have become a different person, one I did not know. I felt he had come under the influence of other people, people with an agenda. Different people I knew began coming to me, telling me he was gathering money for his investment from several who came to Jonah. Rebecca and I have always kept our client list confidential. However, because of group sessions and presentations, people who came to Jonah privately were able to connect with others who visited Jonah.

Many lasting friendships were made this way.

It was fine for those who knew Jonah to develop friendships based on that commonality, but using those contacts to raise thousands of dollars for investments was not acceptable. I felt more and more uncomfortable about my dreams and what I was hearing about Bill's involvement with his investment and the huge sums of money being invested.

Then I heard from another friend, Jerry, a friend from Boulder. He had invested thousands dollars into this investment, then he had a family emergency and asked Bill for his money back. Bill returned the money to Jerry without incident. After hearing this, I began to doubt the dreams I was having about Bill. Perhaps this was a good investment for these people, but I realized I had only known Bill for a few years, at least in this lifetime. I thought, maybe that is the way he has always been concerning business matters, and I didn't notice it before. Maybe there wasn't a problem at all. Perhaps Bill was not the problem; perhaps it was the others involved with him in this project.

Then I received a phone call from Sharon, my close friend from Washington who was very intuitive. She warned me about Bill. Her exact words were, "Hossca, I see the shit hitting the fan with this one. This is a karmic situation you cannot do anything about. Don't stand in the way of it." With all of these messages coming to me, I knew something would happen, and I knew there was a past life connection to this series of events. I also felt some of the people involved were from the Essene time period.

We decided to ask Jonah what these events were about and if they were indeed coming from a past life. Jonah explained that the Foundation was a continuation energetically from the Essenes. There would be people drawn to participate on different levels with the Foundation. Some choices to participate would be considered positive and others negative. Ones that chose an opportunity to heal energies from the Essenes would create positive decisions. He didn't tell us at the time how varied the reactions of people can be when energies surface to create change.

We were advised not to judge the actions some people would take, but instead understand and maintain the purpose for which we created the Foundation. For three hours, Jonah spoke to us about a past life Rebecca, Bill, and I shared during the Essenes, the time of Christ. This is the story Jonah has told us.

During that time period, Jonah had created a physical body. He was not born and he did not go through the death process as we have; he simply existed. Jonah was my physical father during that time period. When I was about five, Jonah found a small boy the same age as me, wandering by himself out in the countryside, and brought him home to live with us. This young boy had been abused by his stepfather and neglected by his mother. The stepfather killed the boy's mother in a fit of rage. The boy, seeking to escape the stepfather's rage, ran away. This boy was Bill.

About a year later when Jonah was traveling, he sent a telepathic message to the family who was watching Bill and me. He told them they were to take me to England, as there was going to be an attempt on my life the next day. During the cover of night, I was taken to the sea where a boat was waiting for me. A few months later I arrived at the eastern coast of what is now England to live with a Druid family

Throughout my life, Jonah had been preparing me to continue his teachings to the Essenes and elsewhere around the world. Jonah traveled quite often to visit with me while I was living with this Druid family. The man was a Chinese healer and his wife a Druid. They had a daughter; I grew up with her and became very fond of her. In this life, she is my wife, Rebecca.

When I reached my early twenties, I returned to the Middle East, fell in love, and married a young woman I had met. She soon became pregnant and died giving birth to our daughter. It was a soul choice for her to leave the physical and there was nothing I could do to prevent it from occurring. During my grieving, my daughter and I traveled back to England seeking support from my adopted family.

During that time I realized how much I loved Rebecca, who was still living at home. *Within a year, we married and later had two children together. She raised my first child as her own.*

I had not seen Jonah physically for several years, but he always traveled out of body to teach and spend time with me. In one such experience, he told me it was time to travel back to the Middle East and continue his work with many of the Essene elders. During my stay in England, I had been taught ancient Chinese and Druid healing techniques. I was to begin teaching the different levels of Chinese healing as well as continuing Jonah's teachings. I knew it was coming time for Jonah to leave the physical by dissipating his body.

I reconnected with Bill when I returned with Rebecca and our children. Although we had not spent time together for some time, we felt a very strong connection and developed a strong brotherhood, becoming best friends.

Jonah continued telling us, during this long midnight session in Boulder, about the conflicts in personalities.

Many had become jealous of my deep connection with Jonah and the fact that I was the one who would continue his teachings. I was not aware at the time just how much conflict did exist. But after Jonah left the physical and I began teaching on different levels, the conflicts began to calm down. I began traveling often, much to Rebecca's dislike. I would travel quite often to Greece and Northern Europe. It was during these journeys away from home that trouble began brewing again.

During this time, ones were talking to Bill about how I was in the way of their plans. Bill had become a teacher in his own right, but his teaching began feeding the fears of others. Three men who studied under Bill convinced him I needed to be removed from my place of teaching in the Essenes. Bill eventually agreed but did not want any part of it. The three men caught up with me on the island of Santorini in the Aegean Sea off the coast of Greece. This was to be my last journey for a while, but my return was not to be.

These three men caught up with me, throwing me off a 500-foot cliff.

I did not think it was my time to leave, and I did not expect to leave in such a manner when it was my time. I was able to leave my body during the fall; therefore, I didn't experience the impact. The three returned to Bill in the Middle East and handed him my walking stick that had been a gift from Bill some years earlier; I was never without it. He knew by receiving my walking stick that I had been killed. A short time later, the Roman army killed Bill and many of his followers for disobedience.

After listening to the tape on Jonah's message later that night and into the early morning hours, many things began to make sense to me. What I did not know at the time was that Bill was also having dreams about that past lifetime that Jonah described. Through his dreams, Bill realized he was responsible for my death during that earlier time. He called and asked to come over to our home. He said he had a gift for me. Later that evening, as Bill arrived, he sat the gift down outside the entry door and asked me to close my eyes. When I closed my eyes I could see what was going to happen. Bill approached me; with my eyes closed, I said, "You are returning my walking stick."

Bill was shocked because he was not aware that I knew of the past events. But even with both of us knowing what happened during the Essenes, we still continued to drift apart. I knew we would come back together, but I did not know if it would be in this life.

I had not seen Bill for some time, but I had heard that his investment project was not doing well. In fact, I had heard that the attorney general of the state the investment was in was now getting involved with the project.

One day we received a phone call from that attorney general. He told us they had filed charges against Bill for fraud, and they were going to subpoena me to be a witness for the state. I told him I didn't have much information. I only knew three of the sixty-some odd investors involved with this project.

"We want to come to your house in Crestone and talk with you," he insisted.

"I don't know what, if anything, I can add, but you are welcome to come." I gave them directions.

The next morning they arrived, dressed in their business suits. The first thing they wanted to talk about was Jonah. "You will be subpoenaed by a judge in Alamosa. We want to know if Jonah will take the witness stand."

"Jonah?" I asked in a surprised voice.

"Yes, we believe Jonah has inside information that will help our case."

"Look," I said, "I have not known Jonah to give such information on people. He teaches there are no victims."

"Well, he will just have to answer our questions, won't he?" I just smiled and thought, this is going to become very interesting.

After they realized I did not have much information to offer about Bill, they leaned over the table and said, "Mr. Harrison, we have a team of lawyers working on how we can subpoena an entity speaking through you."

I interrupted and said, "You know, if Jonah does come through and speaks to the court, he is going to speak about the karma of all involved from the Essene time period." I then added, "And that was two thousand years ago. I think the statue of limitations is in effect here."

They just stared at me, speechless. After a few minutes they replied, "We don't have the answer yet, but we will be subpoenaing Jonah. We just want you to know this." I shook my head, imagining how the news media would drool over this exciting information.

A week later, I received a phone call from the attorney general's office informing me that Bill had just made a plea agreement; apparently, they knew their case was weak. The trial had been cancelled, so I didn't need to appear in court. They told me that they had dropped trying to subpoena Jonah and then promptly hung up.

Bill explained to us later he decided to make a plea agreement because he could not afford the $50,000 his attorney told him it would take to prove his innocence. He spent a few years on probation. I still don't know all the details of the case, nor do I want to. But I do know it was a karmic debt that needed to be paid by all involved in the investment project.

I do remember Jonah telling Bill in the beginning, "If this project is created from the heart, then indeed the heart will prevail."

I didn't see Bill for several years after my encounter with the attorney general. But about a year after that experience, I had a very powerful dream or out of body experience. Bill and I were driving in a white rental car out in the desert. We drove up to a square concrete building in the middle of nowhere. The building had solid concrete walls on three sides with glass windows in the front. It had the energy of a military PX. We got out of the car to go inside to buy some snacks. While we were inside, we saw many men dressed in military uniforms also buying different odds and ends. All of a sudden there was a large explosion off in the distance. The light was brighter than our sun. The shock wave from the explosion knocked me down to the floor. I opened my eyes and saw the glass windows had been blown in, and almost everything from the shelves had been scattered over the floor in disarray. I stood up and noticed all the men in the building were still lying on the floor not moving. They all had severe injuries and seemed to be dead.

I stood there thinking, where am I? What is occurring here? Then one man stood up, but his body was still lying on the floor. Then another man stood up, followed by yet another, until they were all standing up, yet their bodies were still on the floor. They formed a line in front of me, each man one at a time stood in front of me and said, "This is Carpenter Field; you must remember what has happened; this is Carpenter Field." As each made this statement, he left the building through all the broken glass. I then awakened in a deep sweat and spent the night staring at the ceiling, unable to return to sleep. The images of the dead soldiers were too vivid to forget.

Some years later, I was invited to attend a Corporate Vision Quest being hosted by a friend of mine, Robert White, who lived in Aspen. At the time, he was the CEO of ARC Worldwide. It was an all-expense paid journey to a luxury hotel in the middle of the Rockies for three days. The purpose was for CEO's of major corporations to come together and discuss how they might best use their abilities. Robert and his wife at the time, Diana Lynn, wanted me to attend to see what it was like.

The first day, we all introduced ourselves. I didn't share about being a medium, but I did share about my healing experiences. I became the subject of curiosity. One of the men attending was a General in the United States Army. He was preparing to retire in a few years and wanted to examine his abilities and discover what career would best suit him when he did retire.

When I met him, I remembered the dream about Carpenter Field and thought he might know where it is since "field" sometimes refers to an army base. So the next day, I asked about Carpenter Field but I didn't tell him about my dream. He said he hadn't heard of it but would ask someone when he called his base that night. He would let me know the next day. However, the next day, he avoided me as if I had the plague. If I walked to his side of the room, he would walk to the other side. He refused to make any eye contact with me for the remainder of the vision quest.

One of the things I did learn from this dream is that I still had a connection with Bill, and our lives would come together again in the future, in this life.

The future came to be in 1993. We had moved to Teller County just west of Colorado Springs. Soon after our move, Bill and his wife Janette called and said they had planned to move to Teller County as well.

Throughout the years our friendship continued to deepen. The healing of the Essene lifetime had come to be. Many times I can see what a person looked like in another life. I could never see Bill past a certain age in the Essene time period. Of course I found out why with our long night session with Jonah.

Chapter 21
Greece

In June 1990, we were invited to visit Greece and do two, two-day work-shops on the island of Hydra by Ioanna Golfinopoulou, a friend we knew in Boulder who was originally from Greece. She had since moved back to Greece to continue her psychotherapy work in Athens. She had arranged for us to come to Greece and work with her many clients and friends.

We decided to make a vacation out of our trip and spend a month in Greece. On our flight, I envisioned the turquoise waters and white sand beaches so commonly associated with the country. When we arrived, I was surprised at the military presence at the airport. I wasn't sure what to expect, but that was not it.

When we finally made our way out of the airport, we encountered a tank with army personnel riding on top of it. Had I actually had all my memories of Costa Rica, the experience would have reminded me of that fateful trip, but alas, it was Rebecca who made the comparison.

Ioanna and a mutual friend Alex Luisander, whom we had met in Boulder but who now lived in Athens, were there to greet us and take us to the ferry to reach Hydra. The house on Hydra was a family home of Alex's. We were told that the island did not allow motor vehicles, except for one garbage truck. It sounded like a quaint little island; we were looking forward to the visit. Since we were planning to stay in Greece for a month, we had two large and three small suitcases. Trying to fit them into the car was an adventure in and of itself.

About an hour later, we arrived at the dock to catch the ferry to Hydra. The heat and humidity were starting to get to me. Ever since my drowning experience and especially the arrival of Jonah, my body temperature was always high. The combination of high temperatures and high humidity weakens my body.

I was thankful that Ioanna, Alex, and Rebecca were able to carry the suitcases, since my energy level was so low I could hardly carry myself. A few hours later we arrived on the island of Hydra, a beautiful fishing village with restaurants and shops overlooking the water. Alex looked at me and said, "My house is on top of the island; we need to follow these steps."

Since I could hardly stand there in the heat, I wondered how I could walk up the steps. "Don't worry," Alex said. "We have donkeys that can carry the suitcases up. Perhaps you can ride one of the donkeys up the steps." I looked over at the donkeys walking toward us.

"Me, ride this donkey? Its back comes not much higher than my waist. I don't think so," I said.

"They are very strong," he replied.

"No," I said. "I can make it." They took our suitcases and tied them onto the sides of the donkeys. I thought one of them was going to collapse in front of me. Looking at the poor donkey, I thought that was all I needed right now, to get on a donkey and have it collapse under me walking up these steps. Not a nice way to start a vacation.

One-by-one, I walked up 314 steps. Forty-five minutes later, I arrived at the front door of Alex's house. I took a large drink of water and laid down.

A few hours later, I awakened. It was early evening and the temperature had cooled off some. I was now feeling much better. We had a wonderful dinner and went out onto the terrace to watch the moon reflecting on the water of the Aegean Sea. Alex was playing his flute. Looking at the water from the top of the island, seeing the many old white buildings, and listening to the flute brought back many visions of traveling to this area 2,000 years ago. It was as if I had been transported back in time to the feeling, the smell, and the sounds of the ancient Middle East.

The days that followed were wonderful. We were meeting many wonderful people who came to have personal sessions with Jonah before our two-day workshop. The Greek people are very loving and passionate. Ioanna sat in on many of the sessions to help them to understand what Jonah was saying. Many knew only a little English, so Ioanna would translate what they did not understand into Greek. Ioanna is fluent in English, Greek, Spanish and some Italian. In this case, there wasn't a need for Jonah to speak Greek, as he had German in Peru.

The following week, we held our first two-day Jonah workshop in the garden area behind the house. It had a small orchard with a stone wall surrounding it. A large square opening in the wall looked out over the Aegean Sea. It was one of the most beautiful sites in which we had ever done a workshop. The sun was bearing down and the humidity was very high. I knew that with the heat Jonah generates in my body when he comes through, it would not be wise to sit in the direct sunlight.

It reminded me of some time ago, when we were invited to do a group session for teenagers, at the home of Kent Kalb and his wife Marti in Boulder, Colorado. We decided to do the session outside, and since the temperature was mild, I didn't think I'd have a problem. They had me sit in a beautiful cherry wood chair. When the group session was over, my body had become glued to the chair. When I finally pulled myself loose, everywhere my body had touched the wood of the chair was bleached white. They tried later to stain the chair, but it was never the same.

Ioanna and Alex placed a large sheet overhead to shade the area where I would be sitting with a large fan directed at me to keep my body temperature down.

I was sitting looking out at the people and waiting for Jonah to arrive when suddenly there was a cloud of dirt flying in front of me. I couldn't believe my eyes. Two men had attacked each other and were rolling around in the dirt a few feet in front of me. I asked Ioanna, "What is this?"

Other people got up and pulled them apart and sat them back down. Ioanna looked at me and said, "They were fighting because the one wanted to sit closer to Jonah and the other wouldn't move."

"They are fighting over who gets to sit closer to Jonah?" I asked. "I can't believe this. How are they going to learn anything he has to say with this type of energy?"

Ioanna looked at me smiled and said, "What can I say? They are Greek."

I had bought a new pair of sandals for our Greek trip and decided to wear them during the session. Usually, I have to take off my shoes when Jonah is coming through to allow the heat to dissipate through my feet. Since we were outside, I thought these sandals would work. When the session was over I looked down at my feet and the brand new pair of sandals had fallen apart. They were a pile of straps lying on both sides of my feet.

Two weeks into the trip, I was hungry for American food. We decided to go into Athens, see the Acropolis, and tour the city. Ioanna had told me there was a Wendy's hamburger place in Athens, and it was air-conditioned. After we saw the sights they would drop Rebecca and me off at Wendy's while she ran some errands. It was a hot and very smoggy day, and public transportation workers were on strike. My body was again over heating, and I was looking forward to sitting in an air-conditioned building eating a hamburger or two.

I already had one experience on Hydra trying to order a hamburger. One of the food shops on the dock advertised hamburgers, but what they called a hamburger was ground ham rolled into a ball, deep-fried in olive oil, and then put between two pieces of white bread. When they handed it to me, it smelled not of food but something else. I paid them for it and put it in the trash. So Wendy's was going to be a real treat.

At last we arrived at Wendy's. Ioanna dropped us off and promised to return in an hour. When I opened the door and felt the cold air rushing across my face, I thought of heaven.

Almost as soon as we walked in, the lights and air conditioning went out. Everyone standing in line raced behind the counter and grabbed all the hamburgers sitting on the trays. The city workers who were on strike had turned off the power to the city.

There I was standing in Wendy's, no air conditioning and no hamburgers, and no one to speak English. We sat down at a table, hoping they would turn on the power, but it didn't happen.

Then I felt this sudden urge to go to the bathroom. Since no one spoke English, I couldn't ask where the bathroom was. Looking around, I saw a sign in English pointing downstairs to the basement for the bathroom. The stairs were pitch black, and the basement had no windows. Holding on to the rail, I slowly navigated my way down the stairs. I reached the bottom and felt around for the door. It was so dark I couldn't see my hand in front of my face. I felt the doorknob and opened the door to which I hoped was the bathroom. Once inside, I started feeling around for the toilet. Looking back on this, I realize it was not one of my brightest moments.

There was a burst of light in the room. Some one was sitting on the toilet and had just lit a match to light his cigarette. He looked at me as I looked at him. The light went out and the screaming started. I grabbed the doorknob and raced up the stairs to find Rebecca still sitting at the table. "Did you find the bathroom?"

"Don't ask. I don't have to go anymore." Shortly thereafter, Ioanna and Alex arrived to pick us up. "Let's go back to Hydra," I said.

My body became weaker from the heat and humidity. I decided to go for a swim in the Aegean Sea, which has a very high salt content. I came out of the water coated with salt and had no fresh water to wash off. It pulled out what little moisture was left in my body.

A few days later, we decided to take a car trip to Delphi. I was assured it was in the mountains and was cool. We would be able to stay in an air-conditioned hotel with a pool. "You can cool off and tour the sights," they promised.

It was a fascinating drive to Delphi. On the way we passed a Gypsy camp. I asked to stop so we could visit with them. Their camp looked like it had just been set up, made of plywood with blankets for doors. The children were running around wearing rags. It was a sight I was not expecting to see in Greece. When we asked them how long they had lived there, thinking they would answer a week or two, they replied they had been in that same spot for twenty years. It was interesting to see how other cultures lived and became comfortable with their own misery. It reminded me of how some of the people who came to Jonah had created their own comfort zone within the realm of their own misery.

We continued on the trip to Delphi and found our motel with a big sign advertising air conditioning. We checked in and went to our room to try and cool off. Warm air was coming out of the air vents. The room felt like it was 95 degrees. I called the management up to the room and told them the air conditioning was not working. "Of course it is working," the manager said. "Air is coming out of the vent and conditioning the room with fresh air."

"Cool air," I said. "I need some cool air."

"Ah, cool air, you want cool air. It will cool tonight," he said and walked out of the room. It reminded me of the ball of ground up ham they sold as a hamburger on Hydra.

We spent the next few days touring the area and looking at the ancient sites. I could feel the people of that time as if I were walking into that reality from long ago. It was a trip I was not soon to forget.

After three weeks my work was done and the four of us decided to go to Santorini, a Greek island not far from Turkey. I knew this was the island where I was killed during the Essene time period, and I knew it was time to go back. We shared with Ioanna about what happened here 2,000 years ago. We also knew Ioanna was my daughter during this time. It was an opportunity for deep levels of healing to occur.

The next day, we took a flight to Santorini. It was a beautiful island. We took a taxi to our motel. I was told it was a beautiful motel on a bluff overlooking the ocean. What they did not tell me is how many steps it took to get to this motel and that the motel did not have air conditioning. After seeing what the motel had to offer, I announced that I've officially had it with steps and hot, stuffy rooms and that I was going to go find a motel on the ocean with no steps, that has real air conditioning and a cool swimming pool, and there I would stay for the week.

I got back in the taxi and to my surprise, everyone else got back into the taxi with me. It took us an hour but we found a motel right on the beach with real air conditioning and a cool swimming pool. It took two days for my body temperature to cool down enough so that I felt like visiting with some of the local people.

A couple we knew there wanted me to perform a spiritual ceremony for their relationship. I agreed and told them to make all the plans, and I would be happy to do this for them. The day arrived for the ceremony. We all got into a taxi and drove for about twenty minutes. We got out, and I noticed it was the same cliff I had been thrown off of during the Essenes time period.

"What is this?" I asked.

"We want the ceremony to take place on the edge of the cliff where the sanctuary is. All we have to do is go on this trail."

I looked at the trail. It was two feet wide, loose gravel, on the edge of an 500-foot cliff. "Look, we have donkeys for you and Rebecca to ride."

"You want me to ride this little donkey on that narrow pathway with no railing. What have you been drinking? If you want me to perform this ceremony, then we will do it on the beach; end of subject." Thankfully the taxi was still there. We drove down to the beach and later that evening I preformed the ceremony.

I could not get the picture out of my mind of riding this small donkey on this very narrow rocky pathway. Perhaps I should have done it just to get it out of my system. No, I am not a fool.

That evening I had a powerful dream or out of body experience. I went back to that time. It was as if it were real. I could smell and taste the salty sea air. I had gone to a small building on the edge of the cliff, a building known as a sanctuary. I remember sitting and reviewing my life up to that point. I could remember all the ones who had come to me to learn how to use healing energy; I could see their faces and know their abilities. I could see all my children and what they looked like. I sat there observing these visions in the out of body. I remember looking down at my hands and noticing the many lines in the palms. As I was sitting there looking at my hands, I felt two people grab me from behind and lift me up. I could hear one of them saying, "Get his staff."

Although I knew they were not speaking English, it was being translated in my own mind as English. As soon as the other grabbed my staff, he said, "I have it." I felt myself flying through the air.

I could see myself falling and falling but as if it were in slow motion. I could hear myself say, "I must leave my body now." When I had that thought, I felt an explosion of light energy coming from my heart center. I stopped falling. It was as if I had become suspended in mid air. I looked down and saw my body hit the rocks below. The next thing I remember is being drawn into a long tube made of light traveling at a high rate of speed. My body came to an abrupt stop and I found myself standing in front of my father, Jonah. He wrapped his arms around my body, and I felt total peace. "Your time was complete, my son; come with me."

As he started to lead me away, I felt my body jerk. I opened my eyes and found myself sitting up in bed, back in the motel room. I could hear the air conditioner running, but in the background I could hear the most beautiful music. I sat there for a few minutes listening until it faded away. I then heard in my mind as if my soul was speaking to me, "It is now time to teach again. It is now time to continue teaching the ancient healing method to the ones I taught before."

I felt completely at peace. The Chinese Master had told me I would again teach this method of healing, but I had always resisted. This time I felt at peace with the thought of teaching again. A few days later we were back in Colorado, enjoying the cool dry air my body craved. It was again time for change.

Chapter 22
The Dream

In the June of 1990, after working with teenagers through the Foundation for two years, we felt the need to move to a larger town. Jason and Tami were getting ready to graduate from high school within one and two years and wanted a high school with more opportunities for them. We had a family meeting. We told them if they wanted to move to a town with a larger high school, it would be their choice. We had been moving them around from place to place for several years. This time, they could choose. They chose the town of Monument, north of Colorado Springs. We had been to Monument when Jason played against the Lewis Palmer High School basketball team. All of us liked the feeling of the area and the local high school

Two months later, we rented our house in Crestone and moved to Monument. Jonah had told us the house we would live in would not be ready. He said it needed a cleansing. We were not sure what he meant by that, but we found a small townhouse in Monument to rent for a few months. This allowed us to move in August, so Jason and Tami could begin attending their new high school. We continued searching for a larger house in the Monument area.

We finally found a house for rent listed at a local real estate office. "This will be a perfect house for you," the agent said. "There's only one problem. The house had a flood and is being totally remodeled. It will be ready in two months. If you would like to put a deposit on it, we'll hold it for you." We drove over to look at the house. It had three large bedrooms with a large den that was just the size we needed for the sessions. It was perfect with new carpets, a new kitchen, and new paint throughout. It was like moving into a new home.

Soon after we moved in, I again started visiting with the Chinese Master in ancient China. We went through test after test. He would take me back to my life in the Essenes. He would hold my hand and I would experience a sensation of flying through the air, not unlike a pilot would feel flying an old bi-wing aircraft with an open cockpit. When the sensation ended, I was in a different place, a different time. I could touch, smell, and experience the Essenes as if I was there physically. I could see the people and talk with them. I found myself again teaching these people the healing exercises I had learned so long ago.

During this intense training, the Essene life and my present life began to flow together. Many of the individuals that I was teaching in the Essenes, I also knew in my present life. While working with them, I would see their faces change to the face they have in this lifetime. At first, I became confused as to what time frame I was speaking to a person about. I would mention an event or conversation that took place during the Essene time frame to a person I now knew in the present and would often be met with a baffled look.

I knew the Chinese Master was doing this to encourage me to begin teaching again in this time. He continued talking to me as if it were urgent I begin teaching now. I would ask him why he was taking me to the Essene time frame and why the urgency. He would only reply, "You have choices to make."

"What choices?"

He would only repeat the same statement, "You have choices to make."

I began to have very vivid dreams of some type of event that would begin to unfold in a couple of years, but I could not seem to understand what the event was. I asked Jonah and his reply was the same, "You have choices to make."

The next time I saw the Chinese Master, I began to question him further, not just about the choices I needed to make and the Essenes, but where I came from. I felt as if I was at a closed door that I had wanted to open for a long time and someone had just handed me the key to unlock it. "You shall have a dream," the Chinese Master told me. "A dream about your past and your future, which is one and the same. You shall come to understand why you are here." He then continued to remind me that I had left the physical without completing my purpose during the Essenes.

I told him I was not planning on that in this life. He smiled his strange smile and would say, "You have choices to make." He told me, "When you have the dream, write it down. It will be a dream you shall never forget, but you need to write it down so as not to become confused about the timing of events in the dream."

The next evening both Rebecca and I were sound asleep. Rebecca heard me get up out of bed about two in the morning and walk into the living room. She could hear me speaking in another language, so she got up to investigate. Turning on the light, she saw me lying on the couch speaking, but she couldn't see anyone else present. Then Rebecca saw this white cloud begin to appear in the corner of the living room. The cloud continued to grow in size until the entire living room was filled with this cloud. It became so thick she could hardly see across the room. She could hear I was still speaking in another language. She then began to feel energy moving up and down her spine and could hear Jonah's voice in her mind. "Go back to bed little one," he said. "The Hossca is away from his body." Then the cloud began to disappear and she got up and went back to bed and fell into a deep sleep.

The next morning when I awakened I knew I had had the dream the Chinese Master had told me about, a dream so powerful it was like a physical event. I went to my computer and began writing. With my typing skills, it usually takes me about an hour to write a full page. That day I was able to write nearly 50 pages. The following is the transcript of the dream of a lifetime that takes place 1000 years in the future.

* * * * *

In my dream I returned to my spiritual home, a place I have traveled to in the future to do internal searching. My favorite location was a grassy mound covered with flowers overlooking the ocean, a place I have been to so often since a child in that life. I always traveled with my friend, a vicuna, or lama like animal who called herself Murela.

Each morning I would arise before sunrise and walk through my village on my way to the ocean. The village glistened from the rising sun lighting up each structure with different colors, as the color of a pearl when the sun shines upon it. There was always a slight breeze at this time of day but this day the breeze felt different. I could feel the breeze embracing my skin under my robe, a robe as soft as a dewdrop and as light as a feather but stronger than a rock.

As I arrived at the grassy mound, looking out over the ocean, I knew this day was going to be different, just as different as the breeze had been embracing my skin. There would be a change occurring on this day.

I came here to find answers to questions that had been troubling me, questions about strange dreams I had been having, dreams of a strange land and people with very different customs. I knew if I just lie down on my favorite spot and look up into the sky to allow the different colors to relax me, I could find the answer. The colors of the sky, lavenders mixed with pink and emerald blue, always seem to put me into a state of relaxation allowing the answers to come. This time it was different and I was not sure if I wanted to know the answer.

Yet, when I held that thought in my mind I could hear my father whom I called Jonas, also referred to as Jonah in present time, talking in my mind: "If you have a question, you must search for the answer. For to deny the answer is to deny the question which is part of the meaning of life. Life is built upon the quest of knowledge with wisdom, the eternal love of life, ones connection to God." As Jonas' voice became more pronounced in my mind, I knew I could not push away the answer.

Lying there on the grassy mound, listening to the waves splash up on the rocks, I couldn't help but remember when I was a small child. Jonas would come and walk with me, teaching me how to balance while walking on the rocks with the waves pushing against me. I had never forgotten the time I was walking with him on these same rocks and the waves were coming up to my waist. I was thinking how great I was, when suddenly I lost my balance and fell into the water. Another wave came, threatening to crush me against the rocks. I could see Jonas raising his hands; I could feel his energy levitating me up out of the water, setting me upon this grassy mound. As I looked into his eyes, I saw the love coming from him, knowing he knew why I lost my balance.

He had always told me, "Whenever one thinks he is greater or better than another, he takes on the perception of the other."

Just before I fell, I was thinking of how great I was that I could walk on the rocks. I had been sending these thoughts back to my brother of that life, my closest friend Suta who lived with us in our village. He had fallen off these same rocks the day before, and I wanted him to know I was succeeding.

I lay there, feeling the grass with my hands, enjoying the powerful aroma of flowers surrounding me; I remembered that day in childhood and so many days after that, when Jonas was teaching me the art of balance. Day after day he worked with me until I understood it was not the physical balance but the spiritual balance that I needed to learn. The more I tried to balance myself physically, the more I fell. I kept trying to keep my body rigid so the waves would not thrust me off the rocks. But as I allowed my body to flow with the waves and move with the energy of the water, I could become as one with the water and walk on the rocks without falling. It was like a dance, what I now call the dance of life.

Murela started nudging my hand sensing my frustration of not under-standing these dreams, as always Murela was there to comfort me. She always knew when I would be thinking too much, and she would give me this look that brought up the laughter from within me. I remember the day I met her, just after Jonas left the village to journey unto other dimensions. I had decided to climb the mountain that towered above our village, the highest part of our island. This was another place I would go when I wanted to be alone and reflect on the possibilities of my life and to search the choices presented to me. It was a day's journey to reach the top, so I would always plan on spending at least two to three days on the mountain.

At sunrise, the beginning of the second day on the mountain, I was lying there watching the colors of the sky change when I heard someone speaking in my mind. The voice said, "I have come to be your friend, for in our friendship I will share with you my dimension of life and you can share with me your dimension of life."

I sat up and turned around. I asked her what she would teach me. With a look that melted my heart, she said, "You are one who wants to continuously journey to the stars like your father. But you have come to Malinus, and you must learn to stay here in your body. I am here to assist you in doing this."

I did enjoy traveling to the stars and being with the many friends I had made throughout my lives. So often Jonas would tell me that I had come here to complete my initiation; therefore, I must stay here and learn to be grounded. I knew it was Jonas who had sent Murela; he had a knack for leaving no stone unturned.

I hastened down the mountain with Murela. The entire village was a family, just as the entire earth was a family of villages. All the elders of the village were like my parents, and all the children were like my brothers and sisters. Our roles were androgynous and each equal.

As I approached the village, my friend Suta came to meet us. He already knew of Murela, as did the rest of the village. Each had a deep sense of what was going on with the other. Our energy was connected on such a powerful spiritual connection we were each aware of the others thoughts but never to intrude.

I remembered that day, and then I came back to the present moment lying on the grassy mound. Murela was still nudging my hand.

I could hear Suta coming down the path toward me. I asked him to sit next to me, as I felt he wanted to talk. He told me he knew I was going somewhere soon and that I was fighting it. He looked at me straight in the eyes as he always did when he wanted to make sure I understood what he was saying. "Just because you will not be here does not mean you will be alone, for I will come and be with you in spirit. You are my heart friend, and a friend of the heart will never depart from the reality of truth. We will always be together in spirit; I want you to remember this."

Murela then spoke into my mind saying, "I will be there with you also, but you may not remember us. But you will remember our love for you."

Then I heard Jonas speaking but this time it was not in my mind; he was standing behind me. He said, "What you are feeling is a wrinkle in the dimensional wall. It is true, son; you are going on a journey and I also will come to be with you but not at first. You must make this journey on your own. This will be your season of initiation!"

I jumped up, startled by Jonas' voice, saying to him, "You did not tell me you were coming back at this time."

He just smiled and said, "Am I ever truly gone from you? Sit, I have a story I want to share with you, a story of your past, your future, and why you are having these dreams."

He started the story by asking me why my animal friend was named Murela. "Murela told me that was her name. I never thought to ask her why." I could hear Murela in my mind giggling.

Jonas smiled, and then it clicked. Of course, the name Murela means the spirit of nature from the first civilization called Mu, and the civilization that overlapped and followed called Lemuria. Both civilizations occurred on this part of the earth where Malinus is now.

The Malinus civilization is very similar to Mu and Lemuria. I asked Jonas, "Why does Murela carry the name that represents the spirit of nature and these two civilizations?"

Before I could get the entire question out of my mouth, I could hear him saying, "Murela is right here next to you; why don't you ask her?"

Immediately, I could hear Murela speaking in my mind. "The dimensional

241

wall is a condensed vibratory frequency. These walls separate different time frames. I come from the realm of nature during the time frame of Mu and Lemuria. I have come here because of the energy I carry and to bring this energy into this time frame. Many of us in different shapes and forms have come here. I have chosen to come and be with you to assist in blending the energy of the two to assist in your season of initiation. Remember when I first came, I said I would teach you of my dimension and you could teach me of your dimension."

"Yes, I do remember."

"Allow me to explain further."

"Yes."

"Your season of initiation is a completion of your journeys here on the earth school. You have been in Mu and Lemuria; you are now here in Malinus. You have also been in the third dimension twice, once in the Essene time frame and once in the time of the 1800s. In your first physical experience in the Essene time frame, you were a teacher of concepts. You were the physical son of Jonas and followed in his footsteps…almost."

"What do you mean, almost?" I questioned.

"Jonas did not die; you did."

"What happened to me?" I asked.

"You were thrown off a cliff on an island called Thera (Santorini), Greece. You carried many traumas in that lifetime. Those you thought were your friends are the ones that threw you off the cliff."

"A large cliff, I suppose?"

"Why yes," Murela said, "but you left your body before you hit the bottom. You decided to come back but you also chose not to be with humans. You came back as a mountain man in what was called Big Sky in the northern Rocky Mountains. You used your energy to communicate with the animals and nature; this was a healing lifetime for you. What is coming is a working lifetime for you. Now Jonas will tell you more about your coming journey."

Jonas looked at me, smiled, and said; "Now I will help you understand your dreams of the strange land and strange people."

"Wait!" I said. "First tell me more about this dimensional wall and how it works."

"I shall, my son; this is why I have come back to you in presence, so you can understand your dreams, for your dreams are about the dimensional wall. As you know, this is the twelfth realm of the fourth dimension. The earth has twelve dimensions and each dimension has twelve realms. The land of Mu and the beginning of Lemuria are the eleventh realm of the fourth dimension. The third dimension is the dimension you have been having your dreams about, this is where you are going."

"Which realm?" I asked.

Jonas said, "You will be working in the tenth, eleventh, and twelfth realms. You also will encounter ones from the first through the ninth. The ones you will be working with are the ones from these realms. You shall also encounter ones in the second dimension, but I shall speak with you about this later.

Now back to discussing the realms you shall journey into. Your dreams have been created because of a wrinkle in the dimensional wall. Ones in the third dimension are calling you. I will teach you about the condensed vibratory frequency, the wall that creates perceived separation of time frames.

There are many different levels of consciousness here on the earth; this is why the earth is such a wonderful and powerful school for learning. Each consciousness has its own realm of energy; the energy is contained within these walls. These walls are the condensed vibratory frequency that Murela spoke of. If one chooses because of his consciousness to participate in the third dimension and these walls were not there, it would create a shattering effect on the consciousness that would greatly inhibit the learning process of souls and could retard the soul learning."

I asked, "How does one choose the level of consciousness to enter into for learning?"

Jonas explained, "There have been ones that thought they were told and had to receive permission to which level of consciousness or dimension they could incarnate into. This is not true. Each progresses through a level of soul consciousness, which has a vibratory frequency to it. It is that vibratory frequency that determines what energy level they can enter. If you were to pour water into a small container and you had more water than what the container could hold, the excess water would spill over the rim and be absorbed into the ground. If you wanted to pour more water into the container, you would need a larger container. Water is symbolic of spirit energy and the container is symbolic of consciousness. The consciousness must grow to move onto higher levels because of the condensed vibratory frequency.

If the conscious growth does not occur, it does not allow spirit to move through it, thus creating its own block and there is not a movement through the condensed vibratory frequency. If one were to skip a level, it would create confusion and retard one's growth. For remember, my son: a soul never stops in learning; no one is running a race, although many think they are, but that comes from escapism. Each soul has all eternity to progress. This is the expansion—the essence of God."

As Jonas was sharing this information with me, I knew I had known it before. I was beginning to remember, and I knew why the dreams had been troubling me so much. I knew now what I needed to do. Jonas said, "You have not yet remembered everything. It is not time for you to go; we have much more to talk about. I will be with you, Suta, and Murela tomorrow. But for now I have another child to teach the dance on the rocks." With a smile that stretched across his face, he walked down to the beach where a child was playing in the sand.

The following morning, I was sitting on the beach watching the sunrise. I had been free from the dreams last night and felt quite rested. As usual, Murela had picked up on my thoughts and was at the beach waiting for me. Having her there was a great comfort, somehow; I always felt protected in my dreams when she was around.

I had been sitting there a few minutes when Suta arrived; I could sense his energy was different today. Just as I was about to ask him what he was feeling, he picked up on my question and said, "You know we have been brothers of the heart for eons of time. We have traveled throughout the universe together as explorers. I know you are going on a journey, but this time I will not be with you in a physical body. I shall miss our companionship."

I said, "You know that in truth, there is no time. I can go and return from this journey in the blink of an eye."

"Yes, I know, but this time will be different. I will be with you in spirit. I shall leave my body and not return to it upon the earth."

For the first time I was speechless, for some reason I had not picked this up from Suta. "You mean when I return, you will not be here?"

Suta just stood there, but I knew this was true by seeing his energy.

"But why?" I shouted. At that moment, Jonas walked up and embraced me. I was feeling something I had not known, or at least thought I had not, and I didn't understand it.

Jonas understood. "You are already beginning to tune into the third dimension. What you are feeling is sadness. It is a feeling quite prevalent in the third dimension. It is also a feeling you must master, my son. Suta will be with you in spirit when you arrive in the third dimension in the year that is called 1981. He will be with you for about six months. There will be a few more contacts after this period before he leaves the earth plane. Yes, I know your question. You will be with Suta again in the physical but in another star (school) system. I know you have many questions, but you must search these questions. It is this question burning inside you that will guide you back from your journey. Therefore, I will not give you this information at this time."

I could not help but think, why must I go where pain and sadness are beliefs?

By this time, the elders of the village had gathered around. I wondered what I had gotten myself into. Everyone there read my thoughts and smiled.

"You know, my son, everyone here had that thought at one time or another. We are all still quite alive and our love has increased. Our connection to God has increased because of the initiations we have chosen. By fulfilling this initiation, my son, you will be complete with this school."

"Why must Suta and I be separated, in the physical?"

Jonas answered, "Part of your initiation is to know in truth there is no separation. It is only in the illusion you will perceive you are separated."

He continued, "I shall tell you about the war of love. It is a war that is fought in the inner planes. It is a war that is fought between the love of God and the love of flesh, the love of spirit and the love of the material plane. This is why the war is fought in the inner planes. It is a war that brings one into his inner knowing. You, my son, are going into this war of love. It is a war that is fought not against another but within your self, for it is through this war you come to know yourself, all parts of yourself. It is through this war you shall become at one with God. Where you are going, there are many wars of brother against brother, sister against sister, parent against child, and child against parent. This is not the war of love but the war of fear, created by separation that is the abstinence of love."

Jonas paused for a moment and then said; "I know you are not hearing me at this time because of your feelings about Suta leaving. I would ask the three of you to go to the top of the mountain where you met Murela. Spend three days and three nights there and you shall have a vision. When you return, I will be here waiting for you. I shall then impart unto you your remembrance of knowledge, wisdom, and the full purpose of your journey. Then the wrinkle in the dimensional wall shall begin. Go now."

As the three of us started our journey up the mountain, all the children of the village followed us. They knew what I was feeling and they also knew how much I enjoyed having them around. They always brought such laughter to me. After a few hours, they knew it was time for them to return to the village, for we had a vision to experience.

At the top of the mountain, we found a grassy mound, the same one I came to when Murela arrived. When the sun had set, we could see millions of star systems surrounding us, as if it were a cosmic blanket being laid upon our eyes. I allowed my consciousness to remember so many beautiful and exciting cultures that existed within these star systems and the many friends I had made when they came to visit us or I them. It was such a comforting feeling, knowing that wherever I looked there were friends and memories of those friendships. Murela then spoke in my mind and said, "You know, there are ones who believe they are the only ones in the universe."

I sat up instantly and looked into her eyes, as did Suta. "What do you mean?" I asked.

Murela continued, "In the third dimension there are many who believe they are alone, that there is not life out there. There are also some who believe there is life out there, but that those beyond the stars want to control the earth. Remember, life in the third dimension is spiritually a very primitive and paranoid culture. Do you not remember? You have been there."

"Yes. I guess I just wanted to forget."

"This is why there is so much pain and disease."

I asked Murela, "What is disease?"

As soon as I asked the question I began to remember and Murela just said, "Let Jonas explain this."

I thought perhaps the vision Jonas talked about would be about this primitive and paranoid culture.

Suta and I both lay down next to Murela. Her soft fur was a wonderful pillow, and she loved the attention.

As I was entering unto a deep and restful sleep, I saw a rainbow begin to appear in the night sky. Music came from its center. It placed me in a deeper state of relaxation, and I began to feel my body lifting. At first I thought I was lifting out of my body, but then I realized my physical body was lifting off the ground. I could feel myself becoming at one with the music. My body became as light as air.

The colors of the rainbow changed and took the form of a large arch, like a doorway. The more I relaxed the more I could feel myself moving toward the multicolored doorway, a doorway into another dimension, a dimension of light, sound, and color beyond the physical. I could feel my consciousness blending with this dimension, a dimension with such power of love; it is beyond words of expression. It seemed as if a 1000 souls were singing in harmony. The more I relaxed the more exquisite the singing became. They were singing, "This is the true essence of God, for this is God. The one is God and God is all, the power of love is God." Again I heard, "The one is God and God is all."

With a sudden jolt, I felt myself landing on the ground; the rainbow rapidly dissipated. Suta and Murela were sound asleep. I wanted to awaken them but they were sleeping so peacefully. I thought I would wait until sunrise to share my experience with them. I lay back down and quickly went into a deep sleep.

I awakened about an hour before sunrise and just sat there waiting for the sun to come up and allow the morning sky to demonstrate its beautiful colors.

I was eager for Suta and Murela to awaken, so I could share my experience with them. Just as the first ray of light came up over the ocean, they awakened. I began to speak of my experience, but they interrupted and said, "We know! We saw you floating up toward the rainbow. Talk about not being grounded." Their voices held laughter. "You really over did it. We both awakened last night after you returned but we did not want to wake you up and ask of your experience. We just read your thoughts. We are still working on patience."

We all laughed and shared the love we held for each other, a love bond that will never be broken. So often I would hear Jonas say, "A friend of the heart will never depart. When a loving heart connection is created, it will last for eternity."

Then we all heard a loud booming sound, coming from nowhere and from everywhere. Suddenly, a human form began to appear out of the air directly in front of us. We could see it was the form of a child. When the form became more solidified, we could hear the sound of laughter surrounding us; then we realized it was the child that was creating the laughter. The child spoke, its voice surrounding us, as if we were sitting in the middle of twenty children all speaking the same words at the same time. The child had golden hair and almond-shaped, flaming blue eyes and olive skin. As the child spoke, the eyes would change to different colors. As the laughter stopped, the child looked at all three of us, directly into our eyes at the same time, and spoke, "My name is the name of one and I have come to fulfill your vision."

The child then said, "Murela you stay here, you will be needed to be the grounding energy for our return." The child turned to Suta and me and said, "Take my hands, for we have a vision to fulfill."

As soon as we touched the child's hands, everything around us disappeared; we saw ourselves standing on what looked like a sheet of glass overlooking the earth.

The child said, "Behold, look at what the sons and daughters of God have created."

When the child said this, it was as if our vision became magnified and we were shown the third dimension of the earth. I strained to see. "I cannot see," I said. "My vision is blurred by a gray film."

The child answered, "This is a mental virus. It is a virus that causes sleeping sickness, a spiritual sleeping sickness. When ones develop this sickness, they forget who they are and why they came to the earth. They develop a mental programming in which they think God is outside of them. When the programming takes hold, they begin to fight one another in the name of their God whom they hold a belief in. In essence, they begin to fight God and the more they fight God, the more the disease develops. They have been fighting God for so many milleniums; they are beginning to destroy the planet."

Every part of my being was beginning to shake. I shouted to the child, "Why? Why must this happen? They are destroying their home, their temple; why can't they understand what they are doing?"

The child reached over and touched my heart. I felt a peace come over me and then the child looked into my eyes and I into the child's eyes. The child said, "There are coming events to the third dimension that will begin the process of awakening the sleeping children."

I looked again at the earth; the gray film was beginning peel away. I could see the events unfolding upon the earth. The events were of such magnitude, I felt I could not breathe. I was holding my heart and crying out again, "Cannot this be averted?"

The child again took hold of me and his mouth began to form an answer and then—

The next moment, I awoke lying on the ground next to Suta and Murela. They were sound asleep; it was the middle of the night. My first thought was, how did Suta return before I did? Then I thought, this journey with the child took all day; how could this be? It seemed as though it was only an hour. I closed my eyes and soon fell asleep. I awakened as the sun rose above the ocean and the familiar colors appeared. I looked over at Suta and Murela; they were waking up.

I sat up and said to Suta, "That was one of the most powerful experiences I have had. Who do you think that child was?" I asked.

Before I finished speaking, I realized that Suta looked puzzled. He said, "What child and what experience are you talking about?"

"Yesterday morning, I was telling you about my experience of the night before, and suddenly this child appears out of nowhere."

Suta said, "I did not see any child, and I do not know of any experience you had the night before. Last night was our third night here. Today we are to go back to the village; Jonas is waiting for us."

"How could this be? Wasn't last night only our second night here?" I asked.

Suta just looked at me and said, "Last night was our third night here. You, Murela, and I have been together the entire time."

"We spent these three days walking around the mountain, sharing the experiences we have had together," said Murela.

I turned to Murela and before I could ask a question, Murela said, "Don't involve me in this." She had a special look on her face. "You are Jonas' son. You always have strange experiences that many of us do not understand." All I could do was laugh.

Well, I thought, Jonas sends us up here to have a vision and the vision I have I don't understand and you forgot you even had one. I think I'm going to have plenty of questions for Jonas.

We started our journey back down the mountain.

About half way down, we stopped near an unusual looking tree. I asked Suta, "Do you remember this tree? Isn't this the path we usually take going back to the village? I know it is!" I said, before Suta could answer.

Suta replied, "Yes, but this tree wasn't here before. Actually, I don't remember ever seeing this type of tree before anywhere on the island."

I said, "I remember; Jonas told me about these trees. They used to be on this island about a thousand years ago. It's a monkey pod tree, but what is it doing here, now?"

As soon as I said this, a child came out from behind the tree. It was the same child with the golden hair and flaming blue eyes who had shown me the earth on the sheet of glass. I just stood there speechless, and, for the first time, thoughtless too. Again I could not take my eyes off the child's eyes; they were like a magnet to my soul. I gathered myself and asked Suta, "Do you see this child? Are you sure you see this child? Tell me, do you see this child?"

Suta couldn't answer; it was as though he had been drawn into the child's eyes. He was just standing there looking overwhelmed, and his eyes were as big as Murela's.

The child spoke. "Do you not know the earth is our mother and the sky is our father? Through this union of the mother and father is the birth of flesh. I am the child of flesh, the Child of Humanity."

"Yes," I answered, "I know of this from Jonas."

"Yes," the Child replied, "and that which gives birth to the mother and the father is the grandmother and the grandfather, that which is the heavens of the universe. You must remember I am the Child of Humanity."

"Yes," I answered, "I will remember. Why did Suta not remember seeing you and taking the journey with us last night?"

The Child said, "Why do you not remember what I have shown you of events to come?"

The Child of Humanity answered for me, "Because you both blocked out the memory of the vision I gave you. Do you not know that to deny the vision I gave you is to deny the children of God? For I am the child of the union of the mother and the father, I am the Child of Humanity. Do you not know that you are in this dimension so you can return to the third dimension to bring understanding that all of God's children can be in a state of joy, a state of laughter? Do you not know why you are going on your journey as many have gone before you? You must remember; you must remember..."

I found myself waking up next to a stream. I placed my face into the cool water to awaken fully. Suddenly I thought, what am I doing here? The last thing I remember was walking down the pathway. I looked around and saw Suta sitting on a large boulder and Murela sleeping next to the large monkey pod tree. I walked over to Suta and said, "What are we doing here? I thought we were going back to the village today?"

Suta said, "Don't you remember the Child with the golden hair and blue eyes?"

I said, "Of course I remember the Child. You are the one who did not remember the Child. I was trying to tell you about the Child this morning."

"No," Suta said, "the Child that appeared from behind the monkey pod tree a few hours ago."

Then Murela awakened. I could hear her in my mind saying, "Did the both of you get a good rest?"

We both looked at her and heard her reply to our unspoken question. "The two of you said you were tired and needed a rest. I thought this was unusual, but you just lay down and went to sleep. I see you two are a little confused. You have had too much rest for a short journey."

Suta and I had the same thought: Jonas is involved in this; there could be no other answer.

The three of us took a drink from the stream and thanked the stream for its refreshing energy. We continued on our journey to the village. All the way down, Suta and I were thinking, "Jonas, we want to talk to you. Jonas, can you hear us?" There was no reply, just Suta and I hearing each other thinking, where is Jonas?

When we approached the village, we noticed the children were silent. Usually, the children loved to come up the pathway and greet us. Something was different. What was it? Only one elder met us; she had a compassionate look on her face. I read her thoughts, "Jonas is not here."

I answered, "He said he would be here when we returned from the mountain top and my journey would begin. Suta and I have been calling him all afternoon, but he has not replied. Where has he gone?"

The elder said, "Jonas said he would be waiting for you upon your return and then your journey would begin. He also said you would have a vision and he would help you to understand the vision. Was this not his statement to you, beloved?"

"Yes," I replied, "we have done this. We are now returning."

"You have not yet returned and your vision is not yet complete. When you complete your journey and vision, then Jonas will be with you."

Suta and I looked at each other. "If we have not yet returned, then why are we here in the village?" No sooner did we say this than the village disappeared and we were standing on top of the mountain with Murela sound asleep.

Suta and I asked one another, "How long have we been here?"

We looked at Murela sleeping soundly and had the same thought: let's go to sleep; perhaps we will both wake up and be on the grassy mound and be talking with Jonas, or perhaps we can both have the same vision at the same time. Then I said, "No, let's just wake up and be on the grassy hill again listening to the ocean. Maybe I never had those dreams; maybe I just dreamed that I had those dreams."

Murela jumped up and said, "Will the two of you stop all your thinking! I'm trying to get some rest. It has been a long day's journey today and I'm tired."

Suta and I said, "Did we just get here?"

We both called out Murela's name. Murela replied, "The two of you can find your own pillow tonight. I'm sleeping on the other side of the mound."

Suta and I lay down and quickly went to sleep. We awakened at the first ray of sun and asked each other, "Have we had a vision or not?"

"Where is Murela?" I asked. She wasn't on the other side of the mound where she said she would sleep. I called her name and listened in my mind for her reply, but there was nothing. Suta heard me call her and rushed over.

"Where could she be?" I questioned. "We have not been apart since we met; where could she be?"

Then I heard Jonas talking in my mind: "Do not worry about Murela. She is in the first realm of the fourth dimension."

"But why?" I asked. "Why didn't she wait until my journey to the third dimension?" With that question Jonas appeared directly in front of me with a look on his face that could melt away any worry one could ever have.

"My son, when you enter the third dimension you will enter an adult male body. This adult male body will have a mate; her name will become Rebecca. Murela is also a guardian spirit of Rebecca's. Understand, my son, that Murela is a guardian spirit capable of taking on many different forms in many different dimensions. She is choosing this role, so her energy will assist you and Rebecca to create a harmonious relationship. Rebecca is aware of your coming in her heart but not in her consciousness. Murela is a part of the soul essence of Rebecca.

"This is why I sent Murela to you, so you would become familiar with this soul. The both of you will have much work to do in the third dimension. Suta will follow you to the third dimension in a few weeks, but he will be in spirit form, and your deep connection will remain. I will share much more with you soon. When you are ready, come down to the grassy mound overlooking the ocean; I will be waiting for you."

Just as I began to ask Jonas how long we had actually been here, he replied, "You have been here for three days and three nights." With that, he dissipated into thin air, very thin air.

Suta had been standing next to me when Jonas appeared, and he had a strange look on his face. He tried to form a question. Suta then said, "When Jonas was here, I kept hearing the name Kitesa. Do you know what this name means?"

I answered, "Yes, this is your name in the third dimension." The answer astounded me. "How did I know that?"

"Where did that come from?" asked Suta.

My only reply was, "Let's go meet Jonas."

About halfway down the mountain, we saw the large monkey pod tree again. We sat next to the tree and talked about the vision we had of the child who came out from behind the tree. As soon as we began speaking of this, there was the child again. The child answered our unspoken question, "Yes, I am real. I am the Child of Humanity. The vision you saw of me was a preview of our meeting."

"What meeting?"

"This meeting," the Child answered. "Did you not have a vision of me taking you into the outer plane to see the third dimension?"

"Yes," I replied.

"You chose not to see the events coming to the earth in the third dimension. You must allow yourself to see this."

I replied, "Why didn't Suta remember this?"

"Because Suta is not going into the third dimension in physical form. He will only be there in spirit form for a short time. You, my friend, will be there for many years according to third dimensional time. Stay here with me for a short time, as I must speak with you. Suta, go on and meet with Jonas."

"But Jonas is waiting for both of us," I said.

"You are already preparing for the third dimensional time beliefs. Remember, you both will meet with Jonas at the same time. When I finish sharing with you, you will arrive at the grassy mound at the same time as Suta."

"I know. How could I have ever forgotten this? Will I also forget my home here when I arrive in the third dimension?"

"Only for nine years," the Child replied.

"Nine years," I said, "That can be within a split second, as third dimensional beings say."

"Yes," the Child replied, "but you will not think so when you are there. Everything is in slow motion there." Suta started down the mountain, and I could hear him thinking, I like this name Kitesa.

I turned around and looked at the Child. The Child reached out and took my hand, and everything around me began to dissipate. I was again on the sheet of glass in the outer planes looking at the earth. The Child said, "Take a deep breath. You must breathe deeply and hold your breath. In doing this you will not inhale the gray film called the sleeping sickness."

As I took a deep breath the gray film began to disappear. "Now we shall go closer to the earth. You are ready to remember what you shall see."

We journeyed closer; a brown haze covered the earth. I asked the Child, "What is this?"

"This is the greed of humanity."

The Child then took me to see the great rain forest. I breathed a sigh of relief and said, "Look, there is still beauty here on the earth."

The Child then said, "Look again."

I saw in rapid movement the rain forest disappearing. In its place were brown earth and brown rivers. Within the rivers were many human and animal bodies floating face down. I followed the rivers until they met the ocean and there in the ocean was smoke rising up, as if the water was on fire. I looked at the child and began to ask, "How can water burn?"

Before I could ask the question the Child said, "Humanity has sold the earth of its children to feed its greed."

"How can one sell the earth?"

"They cannot, but it is a belief system of humanity that they own the earth. Therefore, they attempt to buy and sell the earth as if they were the creator of the earth." For the first time I remembered, and I wept.

I was taken to a large city that was once next to the great rain forest. The city was full of men, women, and children who roamed the streets looking for food and selling their bodies. I saw large boats being filled with the bodies of children to be taken to the sea where they would be deposited into the water. Those who had sold the birthrights of their children were now attempting to clear the streets of their guilt.

The Child then took me to what is called the North American continent in the third dimension. There I saw large cities all covered in brown air. I asked, "Why do they breathe the brown air?"

"They have developed the sleeping sickness. They have entered the lower nature of survival and forgotten how to live. They have accepted the conscious belief that they do not have the power to change or to create change for the positive. They believe what their leaders tell them."

"Then why don't they begin to lead themselves?"

I knew the answer, but the Child replied, "They have the sleeping sickness."

Through the brown air I could see men, women, and children carrying weapons, roaming the streets in groups, seeking whom they could devour. They feared death as their parents had feared life.

The Child said, "The people of this country believe their country is the most advanced country on earth. They have even sent their weapons into space surrounding the earth. They have developed weapons that can destroy the planet; they have developed weapons to protect themselves only to have the same weapons used upon their own land. Scientists in this dimension will learn to unravel the plan of God."

The Child of Humanity saw my expression and continued, "Some scientists will alter the genetic code of human food. They will begin to use human genetics in the genetic code of plants. Many plants will become toxic to humans. Many who eat only plants will not know they are eating human and animal genetic material."

"Isn't this cannibalism?" I asked.

"They have the sleeping sickness," he replied. "Some have developed a belief Homo sapiens came from slime."

"Well, perhaps—"

"Do not become cynical," the Child interrupted.

I asked, "If this country has developed all this technology, why are there so many children living in the streets and selling their bodies? Why are there so many different diseases? Why?"

The Child simply said, "The sleeping sickness."

The Child then took me across the waters to a city and said, "Many call this the Holy City of Jerusalem."

"If this is the Holy City," I asked, "why is it surrounded by armies?"

"Each group has its own god who tells them to fight. They believe if they die fighting for their god, they will go to heaven."

"Yes, I am beginning to remember now. When I was there before, the priests who taught the most fear had the largest following. It got to be quite a game. Tell me about this heaven?"

The Child answered, "It is a belief that if you obey your god, you go there for your reward."

"And if they don't obey their god, what happens?" I asked.

"They believe they go to hell for their punishment. Many do not know this yet, but they are already in hell. Humanity has created its own punishment, its own hell."

I asked again, "If they must follow a god, why do they not choose the loving God?"

The Child answered back, "If they follow the rules, the commandments of their god, then they believe that their god is a loving God. And if they don't follow the rules, the commandments of their god," the Child answered, "then they will burn in what they call eternal hell fire."

"Are you telling me that people are following a god who will burn his children? Is this why so many adults are not concerned with the homeless children of the world, why they turn their backs on what is occurring on the dark streets of their own cities?"

"That is only part of the answer. Many Homo sapiens hold onto traditions, although they do not remember where they came from. They follow traditions that came from their parents, grandparents, and great grandparents. Many have forgotten to question authority. They have given away their inner authority."

"Has anyone come to tell them God is a loving God? That God is love—not punishment—and that their fear is their punishment?"

"Yes," the Child replied.

"And?"

"Yes, many have come. Many were persecuted because they did not fit in the mold of their traditions." Before I could ask, the Child said, "Yes, there have been ones and are ones who are now assisting people to their ascension and evolving to a higher state of consciousness. But the earth shall become Homo sapiens' greatest teacher."

With that statement I was again on the sheet of glass overlooking the earth. I began to see the land moving and smoke coming out of mountaintops. Large waves of water washed over the land, taking with it buildings, people, and much of their technology. The land in many areas moved up and down like swells upon the ocean. From the dust came many viruses that made bodies perish in a matter of days. I could hear many crying out, "My God, my God, why have you forsaken us?" The earth answered, "Why have you forsaken your mother?"

"Why have you chosen to show me such suffering in this world?" I cried.

The Child crossed his arms over his heart, bowed his head, curled into a fetal position, and said, "I am the Child of Humanity. I am waiting to be born into a world that knows hope. I am waiting to be born into a world that knows love. I am the Child of Humanity!" Then the child disappeared.

Everything around me disappeared, and the grassy mound overlooking the ocean began to appear. Standing on the grassy mound was Jonas; I saw Suta, who had just arrived.

"Suta, do you want to trade places?" I said, smiling.

Before he could answer, I said, "I know. I'm the one who needs to go in physical form. I know this is my journey, my season of initiation."

Jonas said, "My son, sit. I have much to share with you before your journey."

I sat on the grass with the flowers surrounding me, already feeling homesick. I looked out at the ocean as a pod of dolphins came to the cove, dancing on the water. I could hear their laughter and their excitement. I could hear them speaking in my mind saying, "Where you are going, we are also. We work with the healing energy of the emotional body of the earth. Whenever you are in need of us, call and we shall come to you. Even if you are not near the ocean, call. We shall come and be with you in our light bodies. We are here in service to the earth and humanity."

Jonas said, "You will find much assistance from the nature kingdom. Know, my son, if you begin to forget, go unto nature and truth shall be found."

I asked Jonas, "Are there places left in nature to go unto? The Child of Humanity took me on a journey to see the earth and what humanity has done in the third dimension."

He replied, "Yes, there are places to be found. You will find many of these places in the mountains."

I asked Jonas, "Tell me about the masters that have gone to the third dimension. What became of them?"

"Many are still there and more are yet to come. Remember my son, a master does not come to the earth and announce, 'I am a master; I have come to save you.' Many in the third dimension have made this statement. They are not masters. They are ones looking to fulfill their ego to the extent of their fear based on denial. A master will never go and order one what to do or not do, for this would interfere in free will choice. A master is there to offer assistance when true assistance is asked for. There are many different levels of consciousness in the third dimension."

"Is there, then, a level of consciousness in each realm in the third dimension?" I asked.

"Yes," Jonas replied, "and there are different masters that come to a particular realm to work with that level of consciousness. There are also ones who go to the third dimension and choose to work with all twelve realms in the third dimension. One master is not greater than another; it is always a choice. There is but one truth; there is but one law, and that is the law of love. Masters may choose different methods in teaching because of different levels of consciousness, but the basis of all teachings from the masters is teaching the law of love. This, my son, you already know. You also shall experience this when you arrive. There is much you have forgotten from your time in the third dimension, but it will come back to you."

Jonas paused and then continued. "Now about your vision. The Child of Humanity has shown you a vision of the third dimensional earth. As you know, it is in this third dimensional earth plane that your season of initiation will occur. Your initiation will be to journey to the third dimension without developing the sleeping sickness."

"How could I develop the sleeping sickness? I am already aware of spiritual truths and that of the fourth dimension. I already know I will be returning here with you when I complete."

"Yes, you are aware. But also know, when one is in the third dimension, spiritual perceptions become narrow. If you begin accepting negative emotions, you will begin to forget why you went there and where you came from. When you enter the third dimension, you will enter the body of a male who is dying physically and has left his body. Part of your initiation will be to heal the body and break through the consciousness that soul carried and developed throughout his years in the third dimension."

I was wondering how I would know Suta and Murela, and how I would remember my family who lives among the stars. Jonas gave me that special look and said, "Son, you must experience the sleeping sickness and awaken from it. It is through this experience you can assist others of your family that are there and have been infected with the sleeping sickness."

"Who is this man? Is he aware of the sleeping sickness? Does he have a family; will his family be my family? What level of consciousness does he carry?"

"Yes, as a soul he is aware but not in his consciousness. It is by his soul's permission you are allowed to assume his body. Yes, he does have a family, but his family will not be aware of the soul change for about six months. They will just think he is a little strange, different, but they will not know why for a time. Remember, his wife's spirit guide is Murela; there is a longing in her for this soul change to take place. She is not aware of this on a consciousness level, only that she feels a change coming but is not sure what that change will encompass. There will be a stronger connection with you than with the prior soul of her husband's body."

"What is this man called?" I asked.

"Daryl, is his name in the third dimension."

"Then I must look up this soul in the Akashic records."

"No!" Jonas said. "This will only pre-form your thoughts. You will know much about this one when you take over his body."

"How is this one dying?" I asked.

"He shall drown," Jonas paused, "50 feet from here."

"Fifty feet from here. How can this be?" I asked. "This island is only five hundred years old."

"Yes, in terms of being above water, but this island was an island known as Hawaii, before it sank during the earth changes."

"So I shall still live on this island?"

"No. Daryl went to this island while on vacation. It is here he shall drown."

"What is a vacation?" I asked. "I have not heard of this."

"You have not heard of a vacation because in this dimension one does not take a vacation. Taking a vacation in the third dimension is quite common. Most humans do not love the work they are doing. They try to escape it; this is called a vacation."

"Then a vacation is a glorified escape. Is that what you are saying?"

"Yes, for many, that is it in simplistic words. You are already picking up on the terminology and language they use."

"Yes," I said, "I am remembering more each day. Then Daryl must not have enjoyed his work or his vacation. Was he aware he was going to drown when he planned this vacation?"

"No, not on a conscious level. He has chosen to go to Hawaii and vacation to recuperate from an illness he contracted in the jungles of Central America. The first day of his vacation he developed gout, a disease marked by painful inflammation and swelling of the joints. Remember, Daryl did not enjoy life."

"Did not enjoy life?" I asked. "How many parts of his body are disturbed?"

Jonas looked at me with one of his looks and said, "He also has difficulties with his spine. A few years ago he had a tumor removed from this part of his body. It left scar tissue on the spinal cord that creates much pain for him. His eyesight is also deteriorating."

I said, "Is there going to be anything left of this body to use?"

"Understand," Jonas said, "that Daryl as a soul is choosing to leave his body and allow you to take it over. In truth, he is being of service to you and the work you shall do."

"This soul is being of service to me? Look at what he is leaving me. How am I ever going to heal this body?"

Jonas stood up and looked at me sternly. I knew his answer would be strong. "Have you already taken on the sleeping sickness? Have you already forgotten the healing energies you carry? Have you forgotten why you are going on this journey? Have you forgotten the souls you shall meet again and will embrace you with an open heart? Have you forgotten who you are?"

"Yes," I answered. "I had forgotten, but now I remember, and I shall not forget again. It is due to my love for you that I shall remember who I am. I am a part of God and I am the son of Jonas. I know I am going to be with a part of my family whom I love and I shall always love."

"Remember, my son, I love you as I love God, for in God ship we are not in separation. Soon you shall enter the wrinkle in the dimensional wall, and there I shall be with you. The wrinkle in the dimensional wall is not physical, but a wall between dimensions created by vibrations. It is here I shall assist you to enter your new body."

"You mean used body," I said.

"I shall not answer any more questions until you have entered the wrinkle in the dimensional wall. Go now and be with Suta. In a short time, you both shall depart."

Suta had been there the entire time, listening to our conversation. I looked at him, and we both had the same thought at the same time. We took off our robes and jumped into the ocean to play with the dolphins. Looking back toward the island, we saw Jonas dissipate his body. I then knew my journey was about to begin.

I swam up to my favorite dolphin that I called Dovies. As I reached her, she spoke into my mind and asked me to hold onto her fin, as I did so often when we swam together. She loved to take off with me holding on. She would go under the water and then come up to the surface, both of us becoming airborne. I could feel the water rush across my body. It always created such a feeling of renewal for me.

Unexpectedly, Dovies took a deep dive with me still holding on to her fin. I could feel myself holding on tightly, wondering why she was doing this. Then I could feel her fin dissipate from my grip. I felt as if I were in a whirlpool being pulled down even deeper. I tried to swim to the surface, but I was pulled down again. As I began breathing in water, I started to lose consciousness.

Suddenly, a current of water pushed me up to the surface where I saw a large man standing on the beach looking at me. I felt I was looking though the eyes of another, and I felt the fear that was impregnated in those eyes I was looking though. I heard this scream coming out of my mouth directed to this large man on the beach. "I'm drowning! Help, help me!"

Even while I was screaming and feeling this fear I thought, this is not my feeling. Abruptly, I felt the hands of another man push me farther into the current, and I was pulled down again. I could feel the thought, I am now going to die; then I thought, what is this "die"? We do not die; we just ascend when we are complete. Where are these feelings coming from, where is Jonas, where is Dovies? Jonas has always been there when I needed him, but where is he? I then felt another current of water push me up to the surface.

This time I saw the large man take off his sandals, walk across the coral, reach down, pull me up, and place me on the beach. People standing around me, dressed in the strange clothes I had seen in my dreams. I looked into the eyes of the large man who had placed me on the beach; I knew that I knew him, not his body, but his soul. He smiled, acknowledging the recognition, and turned to this woman kneeling over me and said, "He will be all right." Then he disappeared from sight without a trace.

The people standing around me said, "Let's take him up to his room."

I kept thinking, who are these people and why do they want to take me to a room? Why is it so hard to move my body and why am I seeing this gray fog? Where is Suta, where is Dovies, and where is Jonas? I felt myself being pulled up by these people and heard them making a groaning sound. Why can't I move my body? I could see a strange building; why couldn't I see through it? Where did this building come from? Where did these strange people come from? About half way up to this building I could feel my body begin to expel water from my lungs. My spine began hurting and my foot was filled with pain. Why does my body have pain? I have never had pain before. "Jonas," I cried out, "where am I?"

After I finished expelling the water from my lungs, these people continued carrying me up to this building. I could hear them continuing to groan. When we reached the building, I could see doors made of a material I could see through, so I gave the thought for them to open. They just stood there like stagnant energy.

I then knew where I was. I had made my journey into the latter part of the twentieth century. These people opened the doors with their hands and took me down a long hallway. We came to another door, one I could not see though. They opened this door and took me into a room. I saw this soft platform and I knew it was what people slept on. They called it a bed. They took me over to this bed and sat me up on the edge of it. As they did this, I saw a sheet of glass on the wall that holds one's reflection. I looked into this mirror and watched it reflect the appearance of my new, large, pale body in living color.

With that, I took a deep breath, fell backward, and stopped breathing. As I did this I held onto the thought, I'm going back home. I began to forget where I came from, who I was.

I could feel myself lifting up out of my body and watching from above. I knew then I could not leave this body. I had to stay with it, but I also knew I could not enter into the body at this time. I began to understand that the strange man standing next to me, who helped me up to this room, was Tim, Daryl's brother. Tim shouted, "My God, he's not breathing! Call the paramedics!" He shook my face.

I continued watching and thinking how strange it is in the third dimension that humans want to hold onto these bodies. They didn't look to see that I was above the body, and then I began to understand. Ones in this dimension didn't see the soul, only the body. This must be a part of the sleeping sickness.

Suddenly the door flew open and in came men dressed in white clothing pushing a small platform on wheels. They came over to my still body and put a cup over my face saying, "We must put oxygen into him. Start CPR! Call the hospital; let's take him in now. We can't wait."

The men dressed in white began trying to lift up this body and put it on the platform with wheels. They began to grunt and then grunt again. I hovered above the body thinking, if these two men cannot move this body, how am I going to move it around? Then with a third try, they lifted the body up and onto the platform. I gave a sigh of relief and thought, there is hope. They began to push the platform down the hallway and then outside where a large vehicle with flashing red lights was waiting. Again they tried to lift this platform with the body on it into the vehicle but this time it was just too much. They called over another man, dressed in dark blue with a gold and silver badge on his chest, to help them. His hand became compressed between the platform and the vehicle. All he could say was, "Shit, shit!"

I thought, this is it; they are going to drop the body right here in the street.

While watching, I had the thought that I could heal his body now and prevent the pain they were having. But I heard a voice say, "Not at this time. Allow these events to unfold."

They finally placed the platform with the body intact into the vehicle with the flashing lights and off we went to the hospital. The vehicle moved down different roadways until it came to a stop at the hospital. Here we go again, lifting this platform. This time there were more men who came running out of the hospital. They were able to lift the body without dropping it.

Down the hallways we went. We finally came to a stop in another room with tubes and hoses hanging from the walls. A man dressed in white clothing came into the room. He placed a needle with a long tube attached to it into Daryl's arm. These people in white clothing became more and more excited; they pulled out wires and placed devises onto the chest of the body, and the body jumped. How could this body jump? I am not in it; no one is.

Then I felt myself being pulled down a long tunnel. The tunnel was made of white light with the sound of music coming from its walls. The further I traveled up this tunnel, the less I could see my body laying on the platform.

As I came out of the tunnel, there was Jonas standing in brilliant light. Behind him were a group of beings, dressed in the same strange clothes as I had seen on the people who were carting this body around. I asked Jonas who they were and he said, "They are the friends and loved ones of

Daryl. You must not go beyond where I am. The energy behind me is for Daryl, not for you."

I looked at Jonas and asked, "Why didn't you tell me I was going to make this journey when I was swimming with Dovies?"

"Because my son, you needed to make this journey in a state of joy, not in a state of anxiety. When you swim with Dovies, you are in a state of great enjoyment. You are now in a wrinkle of the dimensional wall. Here, ones will know me as Jonah and I have a journey to take you on. Allow Daryl to pass. Come and journey with me, my son."

Jonah took hold of my hand as we began to move at a high rate of speed through many realms of light, lights of bright lavenders and pinks with a touch of emerald. We approached what seemed to be a physical plane, yet not physical. In front of us was a large building that gave off a light of an emerald-colored crystal. At the entrance, I saw two large doors that had the appearance of black marble. Within its center was a large eye with a pupil the color of a blue flame. Jonah looked into this eye, the eye blinked, and the doors began to open. There I stood looking into a large room filled with pillars of glowing white light. Jonah walked up to the first pillar and called a name, "Marieia," and then said, "Wanda Louise Stull Rebecca Harrison."

As he called out this name the light emanating from the pillar began taking on a form, a human form. Jonah said, "This is the one you will know as Wanda, the wife of Daryl, one you have been with often. It is this one you were told about, for whom Murela is the spirit guide. When you reenter your new body, you will know her as Wanda but soon she shall take on a new name, Rebecca. Wanda was the energy name she took on to work with Daryl. Rebecca is the energy name she will use in working with you. Rebecca will assist you in remembering your purpose. She will assist you to again teach healing, to teach the children. She carries the energy to ground you into the physical. She shall also become a teacher of children, a spiritual teacher. She has been a teacher of physical children."

Jonah held my hand and looked into my eyes with his flaming blue eyes and said, "Son, I now must show you one of your tests in this life. When you reenter your new body, you will not remember what I am showing you consciously, but this vision I shall show you will be imprinted in your soul."

I then looked back toward the pillar and a new vision began forming. Standing, as if in a long line, were souls that had denied the love of life. They had chosen to deny the light of love, the Christ consciousness. Each took a turn, trying to convince the consciousness of Rebecca. They were speaking with her about me, saying I had betrayed my love for life, my own Christ Consciousness. They were coming to Rebecca, giving messages that I had turned to the dark, which is the denial of the Christ consciousness.

Then Jonah said, "They also will say I, your father, have abandoned you. Know this well, my son; abandonment shall not exist between us, never! This is not her test but your test."

"You must love those for what they are doing. You must not judge or condemn them. Your test is to hold these souls in light, the Christ light. Your test is to know and know that you know the dark will never prevail over the light. In the third dimension, there is a belief that there is evil. In truth, there is no evil; there is only God. Those that have denied their God essence because of fear are thought to be evil. The paradox is, the ones who hold onto the belief of evil are themselves coming from a state of fear. It is the lower emotional body of humans that creates entrapment on the karmic wheel. More precisely, the fear held in the emotional body.

"These souls of denial will attempt to create fear for you. If you accept the fear, it will cause entrapment in the third dimensional karmic wheel. They can only interfere in your journey if you accept their fear. They cannot force their fear onto you. Know this, my son, where two or more are gathered in the name of the Christ consciousness, they are sealed by the protection of love of which negative forces cannot enter. This is why you and Rebecca have chosen to come together in the fulfillment of your initiation."

I asked Jonah, "Why can't I retain the memory of these events? Then I will know what to look for."

"My son," Jonah said, "the memories of these events are in your soul. It is for you to bring this memory into the consciousness of your new body. What is the purpose of soul knowing if it is not brought into the physical? In the physical it must be manifested. There are many souls in the physical who have much knowledge and wisdom. They will not allow their consciousness to bring it forward because of the many belief systems they inherited contrary to their soul knowing. Again it is the acceptance of fear in their emotional body."

Jonah took my hand and said, "Let's take a rest and return later. I have something I want to show you."

Instantly, we were standing on the side of a grassy hill overlooking a small lake. "Look across the lake," Jonah said.

Standing on the other side was a group of souls, all dressed in white robes glowing with a golden hue. They were all singing in perfect harmony. The depths of their voices created a rippling effect on the surface of the water. As the voices grew in strength, flowers began coming up out of the side of the grassy hill. All life became alive with music. I could feel my heart embracing these souls that were singing. I felt myself being drawn toward them across the water. As I came closer to the other side of the lake, I saw myself become at one with them. My light body began blending with theirs. The sound of their music was everywhere.

Suddenly, I felt a jolt of energy shoot through my heart that sent me flying backward. I found myself lying on the grassy hill next to Jonah. "What was that?" I asked Jonah.

Jonah reached down with his hand, helped me to stand, and said, "You are connected to your new body. Remember your body is in a hospital. They just placed an electric probe on your heart to try and revive you. They think you are dying. We must now return to the hall of records. I have more to show you in the pillars of light and it is soon coming time for you to awaken your body out of its coma."

Within a flash, we were again standing in the hall of records. As far as

I could see, it was pillar after pillar, each emanating a glowing light. Jonah took me to another part of the hall and said, "There are two other souls I must show you. These souls are in the form of children. They are the children of Daryl and Wanda."

As Jonah said, "Jason Russell Harrison," the pillar we were standing next to began taking on a form as the first one had.

I began to see the form of an eight-year-old male child. I saw an Oriental Master standing and speaking to this child but it was as if the child could not hear what the Oriental Master was saying.

Jonah then said, "This child called Jason is a mystical child. This will not become known until the child reaches the age of mid-thirties. Jason is a student of the Oriental Master and will become a teacher himself. He will become a teacher of discipline when this one reaches the age of forty. Your conscious mind will have many worries of this one for a time, but do not worry. This child is well protected. Remember what I said, this child is a mystical child. On one level this child will know that his original father has left the physical, yet the physical body of the father will still be there. The inner mourning will come out as anger, but this will heal. The Oriental Master will be working with him while this one sleeps. This will assist in his healing."

We walked up to the next pillar and Jonah called out the name, "Tami Arlene Harrison," and again a form began to appear.

This form took on the body of a female child at the age of seven. I could see two different female masters standing next to her. She could see these masters, but her conscious mind always wanted to argue with them. "She is one of strong will and determination. Everyone around her will know this. This will assist her in her life's calling when she is an adult, indeed with her own child. This one will become an adult when she is still a child."

I gave Jonah a puzzled look and he said, "In time, you will come to understand. She will become what the world will call a mental healer." The pillar began losing its image.

Then Jonah embraced me and said, "You must now return to your body. They want to place needles in your spine; you have enough to heal as it is. When you return and awaken the body, you will have amnesia that will last for six weeks. The purpose of this is to allow your consciousness to turn inward and work on healing the body. Through this, you will be encountering ones that will assist you in your work."

"I do not understand," I said.

"I know you do not," Jonah said, "but you will. Because of the amnesia, Suta can make contact with you. Remember in your soul, his name will be Kitesa. In two years time, I shall come and be with you, much in the same way Suta will."

"What?" I said. "I understand even less now."

"I know my son, but you will come to understand this. It is now time."

With that statement Jonah vanished and there appeared Suta and Murela. I looked at them, thinking, what a trip this is going to be; thank you for coming. With that thought, the building we were in also vanished and the hospital room appeared in its place. Suta and Murela were still standing next to me. The three of us looked at the body and each gave a large sigh. I embraced Suta and then Murela and walked over to the body to enter it. I could hear Suta saying, "In a few months, our friends from the stars will come to you."

I was in the body and opened my eyes.

* * * * *

I awakened from the dream in a deep sweat. I felt I had experienced two different levels of consciousness at once. I could feel the consciousness of my soul Hossca as I came here, and I could feel the consciousness of my physical body. There were two different experiences of my drowning in Hawaii, one from my physical conscious perspective of Daryl, and one from my soul conscious perspective of Hossca.

It had been nine years since that experience in Hawaii; now I feel complete in my understanding of what Jonah and the Chinese Master had been teaching me over the years. I came at peace with teaching Chinese Healing and sharing my experiences with others who want to learn.

Sixteen years have passed since I had that dream. The dream is still a part of my body as it was the evening I had it.

Chapter 23
England

In July of 1992, we were invited by Ioanna from Greece to visit England, where she was living and working at the time. People from England, Greece, and Scotland wanted to have personal sessions with Jonah. We also planned a workshop in Avebury and in Scotland. We had long wanted to visit England and see the crop circles occurring throughout the countryside. It seemed like a dream vacation mixed with work. We rescheduled all of our private sessions with Jonah and cleared the month of July.

Two weeks before we were to go on our journey, I was in our garage cleaning out dried mud that had collected on the garage floor. I got into our little car to back it out of the garage. I turned around and looked out the back window of the car to guide the car out of the garage and to the side of the driveway. When I put my foot on the brake to stop the car, the brake pedal went to the floor. The car surged backward and came to a sudden stop by the force of a large pine tree. The impact caused a snapping sound in my lower back. It felt like an explosion.

I got out of the car to check the damage and found there was very little damage to the rear bumper, but I couldn't bend over and had pain shooting down my legs. I very carefully walked into the house and told Rebecca what had occurred.

"Lie down," she said. "We'll put some ice on it. I thought you just took the car in to have the brakes fixed?"

"Yes, I did, last week. The dealer told me they inspected the brakes and there was nothing wrong with them."

As it turned out, they had not checked the brakes at all, even though it was still under warranty.

I laid down with an ice pack on my lower back. The pain began to subside, but my legs were turning numb. The next morning I couldn't get out of bed nor roll over. I made an appointment with a chiropractor in Colorado Springs. Rebecca had to drive since I could hardly walk. The chiropractor looked at my back and refused to work on it. He said he thought I had ruptured a disk and would not touch it without an MRI. He recommended a medical doctor he knew, so we called him up and set up an appointment for three days later.

When the medical doctor saw me he said, "You have at least one if not two ruptured disks. But I will not know for sure until you have an MRI."

"I don't want an MRI," I said. "I'm leaving for England in a week. Can't you just give me some pain medication to help me get onto the plane?"

He just looked at me and said, "What kind of fool are you? You want to travel half way around the world with this injury?"

"I am sure it will be fine," I said, "just give me a prescription for the pain."

If I had some medication, it would cut the pain enough so I could work on healing myself, although I was not going to tell him this. I picked up the prescription on the way home. When I got home, I took one of the pills the doctor prescribed for me, hoping the pain would decrease in a short while. I waited and waited and waited some more. I took another pill. Still nothing. The prescription wasn't working. "I'll try to connect with the Chinese Master tonight," I told Rebecca. "I'm sure he can help me out."

When I saw the Chinese Master, he said, "You have a choice to make."

"What choice?"

He again replied, "You have a choice to make."

Then he did something he had never done before. He gave me a strong, loving embrace. "Make a wise choice," he said. "This will be your initiation."

When it was time to leave for England, my back was still the same. I felt I had to go, even though the doctors warned me not to take the trip.

We made arrangements to drive to Denver the day before and stay at the home of our friends Mark and Nancy Duvall. They graciously offered their bedroom for me to rest before our trip the next day. Mark went out and bought a cane for me to use. It became a very helpful tool. We left our car at their home, and they drove us to the airport. When we arrived I could hardly get out of the car. After a few minutes, I was able to stand up with my new cane. I walked into the airport, found the nearest seat, and sat down while Rebecca went to check us in. "Where is your husband?" the man behind the counter asked.

"He is over their sitting down. His back is hurting him," she replied. He looked over at me and then looked at Rebecca with a very different look in his eyes. A light was shining from his eyes into Rebecca. "How would you like to fly business class?" he asked Rebecca. Before she could answer, he said, "All I have to do is poke this one button," looking down at his computer.

"Yes," she said, "we would love to."

"You will have much more room, and it will be very comfortable for you," he explained. Then he told Rebecca, "Look." As she watched him he put his finger on the button and replied, "It's done; enjoy your trip."

Rebecca came over to where I was sitting and shared with me her experience. My first thought was we made the right decision. We boarded the flight to London. Being in business class was a wonderful experience, although my back was in worse shape than before. By the time we landed in London nine hours later, I couldn't get out of my seat. The pain was so intense, I couldn't even begin to stand. The stewardess told me to wait until everyone else got off the plane and then they would have a wheelchair brought in for me. "We will take you to the Red Carpet Club and you can lie down and rest for a couple of hours," they said.

Everyone was so helpful and caring. I had never experienced this type of assistance on an airline before. They wheeled me into the Red Carpet Club, lifted me out of the wheel chair, and laid me on a couch. "Here, Mr. Harrison, rest for as long as you need," the assistant said.

We had planned to rent a car and drive to Avebury. Ioanna didn't have a car and our mutual friend Sophia was using her car to commute to her work every day as a dentist.

After about two hours, I tried to stand up. It took three tries, but I made it with the use of my cane. The airlines had already assisted us through customs in the express lane. All we had to do was find the car rental desk in the airport. When we arrived I was hunched over using my cane and leaning on the counter. They asked who was going to drive. I said, "I am."

The man behind the counter looked at me and said, "You're going to drive in your condition?" He just shook his head and said, "You Americans."

About ten minutes later, the paper work was finished. Rebecca asked, "Do you need a wheelchair to reach the parking lot where the car is?"

The man behind the counter shook his head again in disbelief. I said, "I will walk." I was trying to assure myself as much as Rebecca and the car agent.

"Are you sure you want to drive?" Rebecca asked.

"Do you want to drive?"

"I wish I had driven when we were in Australia," she replied. "I'm not sure if I can drive on the left side of the road, but you've done it before."

"I'll start out," I said, "and we'll see how it goes."

I was able to drive to Avebury. We pulled up into Ioanna and Sophia's driveway and I sat there for a few minutes, trying to get enough energy to get out of the car. I felt as if I was permanently glued to the seat. Ioanna came out to greet us. She knew about my back injury. She and Rebecca helped me into the house. I lay down on the living room floor to rest; the pain increased to the point that I couldn't even roll over. I ate dinner lying on the floor with Sophia, Rebecca, and Ioanna sitting next to me, keeping me company. "I'm sure I'll be better tomorrow," I said.

"Good," said Ioanna. "Our Greek and Scottish friends will be arriving tomorrow. Next week we are to drive to Scotland and work with some more people," she replied.

About three hours later they helped me off the floor and up the stairs into the bedroom. It was a beautiful room with a large window looking out over Ioanna's flower garden in the back yard.

That night I went into a deep sleep. It was the first night since I had injured my back I was able to sleep all night. I remembered meeting with many different people, but I couldn't remember who or why. I felt it was about my physical condition. When I awoke in the morning, my back was even worse than the day before. I couldn't get out of bed or roll over. The pain pills were useless. Eventually, I crawled on my stomach, using my elbows, to the bathroom down the hallway. It took an hour to make the trip to the bathroom and back into bed. I was as quiet as possible. I told Rebecca what had occurred while she was sleeping. Obviously, my condition was not improving as I had hoped.

Later that afternoon some of the people from Greece and Scotland began to arrive. Rebecca and Ioanna were able to help me crawl downstairs and lay down on a blanket on the grass lawn, so I was able to visit with the people. The love they expressed for me was a great healing. It was as though they could not do enough for me. I had dinner laying on my side in the back yard. The others got their plates of food and sat around me, visiting. I felt I was in a very special place with very special people. It helped heal the emotional pain I was feeling from the physical pain, although the physical pain continued to increase.

The next day our friends Kent Kalb and Marti, arrived from the United States. Before our trip to England, we had made plans for after my work in England to travel by car across Europe with Kent and Marti, but it was not meant to be. We were able to enjoy each other's company in Avebury only.

The following day I began doing sessions lying on a blanket on the grass lawn. Jonah wouldn't talk about my condition, which did not surprise me, as I knew this was my initiation. At the time, I wasn't aware how this initiation would end.

As the days went by, my condition did not improve, but I was able to make it up and down the stairs by crawling on my hands and knees with the help of Rebecca and Ioanna. We decided to do a group session at the Stones of Avebury, a place often referred to as the feminine Stonehenge. Everyone got together, helped me to the car, and drove me to the area about two miles from Ioanna's and Sophia's house.

It was evening when we chose to do the group. We arrived at the stones and they laid me down on the grass. My head was a few feet away from one of the large stones. Sheep were grazing all around us and the stars were shining brightly. Everyone sat in a circle around me, waiting for Jonah to come through and answer his or her questions. The session lasted a little more than an hour. I kept having flashbacks of the Essene time period. When I left my body and Jonah came in for that evening, I could remember returning to the time of the Essenes.

We continued to visit for another hour under the stars. Everyone helped get me back into the car. We decided to cancel our trip to Scotland the next day since I wouldn't be able to travel by car or train for any length of time. After about a week, everyone returned home.

Since we had time on our hands, Ioanna asked Jonah if he would dictate a book. She had been feeling a book that Jonah would help her with. In one session, Jonah agreed to give information about the crop circles in the form of a book called, **Prophecy of the Blue Light.** The book was published in Greece some time later. Soon after Jonah finished dictating the book, my back took a turn for the worse.

One evening my back started to twist and cramp, putting pressure on my lungs. Now it was no longer about pain but the ability to breathe. Ioanna called the local doctor who came out in his van. The country doctors, at least in the area of England we were in, would make house calls and drive a van full of medicine. The doctor couldn't believe the condition I was in. "I will give you a shot," he said. "This shot will take away all the pain."

He stuck a large syringe in my hip and said, "In a few minutes the pain will diminish."

I waited few minutes; nothing happened. I waited a few minutes more and still nothing. I told the doctor there was no decrease in the pain at all. "I don't understand," he said. "This is the most powerful pain killer I have."

"It's not working," I said.

"Perhaps it will take longer," he said. "I must go now. Let me know how you are doing tomorrow."

The next day the pain continued to increase well beyond what two ruptured disks would do.

The doctor returned and gave me another injection in the hip; he said he could do nothing more. Later that afternoon, the pain increased so much that I began slipping in and out of consciousness. During that time, an entity called David began speaking through me to Rebecca and Ioanna. He said he was an aspect of me from another dimension. David said, "I will watch over the vehicle's physical body. His emotional body from the Essenes is blending with the present emotional body. You and Ioanna are to assist the grounding of this body for half an hour. Hossca will be making the decision, now that he has completed whether to return or leave this physical plane. You will know within twenty-four hours what he has decided. I will not be speaking through this one again."

Ioanna and Rebecca worked with me as they were instructed. They then discussed the information given and meditated on it. An hour or so later they decided. Ioanna should call for an ambulance. They felt being in a hospital would assist me physically while I made my decision.

When the ambulance arrived, the paramedics realized they couldn't get the stretcher up the narrow, winding staircase. They tried to move me off the bed, but the pain was too great. They brought a bottle of nitrous oxide up for me to breathe, hoping to reduce the pain. I lay there deeply breathing the gas for about five minutes. They helped me crawl out of bed onto the floor. I passed out. One of the ambulance crew decided to give me a shot, not knowing I had just received one a few hours ago. Ioanna and Rebecca were downstairs trying to keep out of the way and didn't know about the additional shot.

I regained consciousness and crawled toward the stairs. One paramedic pulled on my arms while the other held the gas mask against my face.

They decided to have me go feet first when we reached the stairs, so the other paramedic could begin to pull on my feet. Half way down the stairs the gas bottle emptied. The paramedic pulling on my feet went to the ambulance for a new bottle. "I can't believe this," he said. "One bottle will last us four or five people. He's on his second bottle!" At last I reached the stretcher just when the second bottle emptied.

It took about 30 minutes for the ambulance to arrive at Princess Margaret Hospital in Swindon. Rebecca and Ioanna followed in our rental car. Later, Rebecca told me how she was amazed she managed to keep up with the ambulance through all the roundabouts.

They took me into the emergency room. Seeing how much pain I was in, the nurse gave me another shot in the hip. She didn't know the ambulance attendant had already given me one. So now I had three shots of very powerful pain medication in a few hours' time, including two bottles of nitrous oxide.

When Rebecca and Ioanna arrived in the emergency room they told the doctors about my auto accident three weeks ago. The head doctor ordered an x-ray. They wheeled me into the x-ray room and laid me on the table under the x-ray machine. I could hear the machine make a sound; then the technician came out and said, "I'll return in a few minutes; don't move."

In all of my pain, I was able to laugh a little at the statement, "Don't move." As if I was going to get up and walk around. Lying on the table, I realized I couldn't move my legs nor feel anything in my legs or feet.

The technician returned and said, "We have to take another x-ray. This one came out blank."

I thought maybe I had died and this was an illusion. I heard the x-ray machine make its sound and again the x-ray technician said, "Don't move." But when he returned, he said the film was blank.

Three more times, he tried to take an x-ray. All of them showed a blue glow of light on the film—no body, no bones, just a blue light. He finally said, "I can't take another x-ray."

They wheeled me into another room in the emergency section of the hospital. When they lifted me off the gurney and onto a table, the pain increased and I could hardly breathe. A different nurse gave me another shot in the hip; I said, "That's the fourth shot I've had today. It's not working."

She gasped and said; "One shot should put you out for a fortnight!" As she spoke, I felt myself leaving my body. I could hear the nurse shouting at everyone to get out of the room. "He has no blood pressure, no pulse; his eyes are dilated."

A doctor ran in; he forced Rebecca and Ioanna out and closed the door.

They both peered through a small window in the door. As they watched, Jonah took over my body. They saw my body lying there with no blood pressure and no pulse; my eyes followed the nurse. When the nurse saw my eyes moving, she ran out of the room, almost knocking Rebecca and Ioanna over. She returned a minute later with a doctor from India. He ordered everyone in the room to leave and then taped a paper over the window of the door and locked it. No one is sure what he did to me, but about fifteen minutes later, I was back in my body.

My memory was meeting my maternal grandfather, whom I had known in the Essenes. He wanted me to stay with him. "You do not need all of this pain and suffering," he said.

I then traveled to meet the Chinese Master. Again he embraced me. "You have more children coming," he said, "children and grandchildren." You have not begun to teach. Will you return or shall you stay with me? You have a choice to make. Make a wise choice. If you choose to remain here with me, you will be complete, but ones in the physical need you. You have a choice to make. Make a wise choice," he repeated.

The next thing I remember was opening my eyes and seeing the doctor from India leaning over me. He put his hand on my forehead and spoke into my ear, "You have some work to finish."

He smiled, unlocked the door and walked out. The nurse, Rebecca, and Ioanna rushed into the room. Another doctor came in and said, "We must take him to the orthopedic ward. You can come back tomorrow and visit."

The next morning I was feeling much better, but I still could not walk or turn over in bed. "We are going to put you in traction for a week," the doctor said. "Although we have a slight problem. We do not have a strap to fit around your waist."

Just when he finished saying that a nurse came in and said, "Look, this package just arrived from somewhere. I think it will fit Mr. Harrison."

"Where did that come from?" asked the doctor.

"I don't know. This package was on the counter at the nurse's station."

"Well, you're in luck, Mr. Harrison," the doctor replied. "Let's hook him up."

When they placed the weights on the end of the ropes, the pain increased and made it hard to breathe. "Give him a shot," the doctor said. "This one will not be like the one you received last night."

They gave me the injection and within minutes the pain was gone. "It worked this time!" I told the nurse.

"You amaze me, Mr. Harrison," replied the nurse.

The hospital reminded me of one in the United States during the fifties. When I wanted to raise the bed, I would call the nurse, and she would bring the crank and crank up the bed. When I wanted the bed lowered, she would have to return and use the same crank. If I wanted to make a phone call, they brought in the phone on a small hand truck and plugged it in. It was a pay phone.

Each day I was feeling better. Rebecca and Ioanna came early each morning to visit and talk about the events that led up to my second death experience.

The food wasn't appetizing. I had ordered an egg salad sandwich, which consisted of a hard-boiled egg ground up into powder and placed between two dry pieces of white bread. The English were never really known for their culinary talents, at least in the hospital; however they were delightful people to be around, and I did get plenty of tea.

The nurses were wonderful. They enjoyed having an American in their ward. They were all smokers, but I was the only one in the room of six patients who smoked. So one nurse would lift the weights and the others would push my bed out into the stair well area. We would all smoke and visit together.

On the third day, the doctor came and said he wanted to do a CAT scan. He needed to see how much damage had occurred to my spine. He said, "We only have one MRI in this part of England, but I feel it could damage your spine for you to travel the distance it would take."

That afternoon they took the CAT scan. Later the doctor arrived and said, "Mr. Harrison, we need to operate soon. Two disks ruptured, and they are placing pressure on your spine."

"I don't want an operation," I said.

The doctor became very angry. "What, you don't think the English can do as good a job as your American doctors?"

"No," I said. "If I have an operation, I want to be near my family."

In fact, I didn't want anyone to operate on my spine, English or American. I think the doctor had overhead me talking about the hospital food with Rebecca and Ioanna. But my answer seemed to appease him.

When the fifth day arrived, I told the nurses I wanted to go home in two days. "You must have the doctor's permission," they replied.

"Then tell the doctor I want to go home in two days. That will be a week of being in traction," I said.

"You don't even know if you can walk, Mr. Harrison."

"I can walk," I said.

"How do you know? You haven't even stood up since you arrived here," replied the nurse.

A few hours later the doctor came to see me. "So, Mr. Harrison, you want to go home."

"Yes, to my friend's house in Avebury."

"When are you planning on returning to America?" he asked.

"In nine days," I answered.

"Nine days? You may not be able to walk again," he said. "What type of seat do you have booked?" he asked.

"Coach class," I answered.

"No, absolutely not! If you sit in coach class you will have to be carried off the plane when it lands in America. You may never walk again. If you insist on going, I'll call United Airlines and speak with their doctor. I'll arrange for you to fly business class. They will charge you to do so."

I agreed. I was willing to agree to anything to get out of the hospital.

A few hours later, I was thinking about all the events that led up to my being in the hospital again. What a life I've had! What a life Rebecca has had with me.

All of a sudden, I could feel Jonah's presence. I looked through the large glass window into the hallway. I couldn't believe it. I could see Jonah standing in the hallway looking at me. He smiled, put up his right hand with his palm facing me, and said, "Well done, my son."

He turned around and walked through the wall on the other side of the hallway, where the fire alarm was. As he passed through the wall, the fire alarm went off. Nurses started running up and down the hallway shouting, "Get the beds; get the beds!"

They rolled the beds down the hall and onto the landing outside. "I don't think there's a fire," I said to one of the nurses.

"Hush!" she replied.

About a half hour later they returned us to our rooms. "It is now safe," they said.

I couldn't help but laugh. Jonah does have a different sense of humor.

Two days later the doctor came to see me. "Mr. Harrison, I have arranged for you to be released today. I have also called United Airlines, and they agreed to put you in business class. They are going to charge you $1,980 for you and your wife to fly back to America."

"Thank God for credit cards," I told myself. "At least I'm out of this place." An hour later the nurse came in to disconnect the weights and straps.

"There, Mr. Harrison; see if you can walk. Take your time. You're not to be released for another hour."

I lay there trying to put energy into my legs, hoping they would support me. I rolled over in bed with very little pain and sat up for the first time in the hospital. This is great. I lowered my feet to the floor. My legs collapsed and I grabbed onto the bed. The wheels of the bed were not locked and the bed started rolling across the room with me hanging on. I could hear my roommate shouting to the nurses, "Runaway bed! Runaway bed!"

I shouted, "Jonah!" The bed stopped just as I was about to lose my grip.

Just at that time Rebecca and Ioanna walked into the room. "What are you doing?" they shouted.

"I'm being released," I said, laughing at myself, half on the floor and half on the bed.

"Here, we brought your cane. I think you need to use it," said Rebecca.

The nurses arrived and helped me back onto the bed and locked the wheels. "Now, Mr. Harrison, you can't be doing things like this. You have to be very careful. The doctor is surprised you can move your legs at all."

I thanked them for all of their help and for the cigarette breaks they took with me several times a day for the week I was there. Rebecca went to the front desk and asked how much money we owed. They replied, "We will charge your insurance company directly. Don't worry about it."

Rebecca had called our auto insurance company in Colorado and told them what had happened. They said, "No problem, just have the hospital send us the bill."

The nurse arrived and gave me a prescription for enough pain pills to last me until I returned to America. "You're not a citizen," she said, "so you will have to pay full price."

Rebecca went to the hospital pharmacy and filled the prescription. The cost was six dollars. When I returned to the United States, I found the same prescription by the same manufacturer cost sixty-eight dollars.

That afternoon I returned to Ioanna and Sophia's house in Avebury. I was able to walk without pain by using the cane. The feeling had returned to my legs and feet.

"We have a surprise for you," Ioanna and Rebecca said.

"What is it?"

"There is a wonderful French restaurant down the road. We know how you disliked the food in the hospital, so we're going to take you for a treat," and a treat it was.

We returned almost every day, or went to an English pub for fish and chips, one of my favorites.

After my release from the hospital, we heard that a crop circle had appeared a few miles from Ioanna's house. The next morning we drove to the farm to see it. Using my cane, I slowly walked with Rebecca and Ioanna to the center of the crop circle. I could feel the energy coming up from the ground into my feet, up my legs, and up through the top of my head. I decided to lie down and allow the energy to flow into my back.

As I was lying there, a vehicle pulled up next to ours. Two men got out and started pulling equipment out of the trunk. They put on gas masks and gloves, and they were holding some type of equipment. They looked like aliens walking toward us. In fact, they were government scientists wanting to do tests on the new crop circle. I thought, here I am enjoying the energy coming up out of the ground into my back, while these scientists are dressed like they are exploring another planet. As they approached, I started laughing, which they perceived as an insult and walked away. We enjoyed the rest of the afternoon lying in the crop circle and feeling rejuvenated. Later we headed for the local pub to have fish and chips.

We spent the rest of the week touring the area, including Stonehenge. The day we arrived at Stonehenge, I began to feel quite strange. I was feeling the effects of all the drugs they had injected into my body during the week I was in the hospital. I was standing next to one of the large stones when I felt like my insides were going to fall out. I raced to the public restrooms, hoping there would be an empty stall. There was. My body had collected all the toxins to be expelled. In about ten minutes, my body began to feel like it did before my auto accident, although I still needed the cane to walk because my muscles were weak.

The next day, I was so full of energy that Rebecca and I decided to take a train into London. We wanted to tour the sights and ride the double-decker buses. It was a thrill to tour England at last without pain. Walking with a cane in downtown London was a rare experience for me. The English people respect disabled or injured people. There was always someone asking if I needed help. It was quite a contrast from my experiences in the United States when I returned using my cane. During our stay, the bond between Ioanna, Sophia, Rebecca and me became even stronger.

* * * * *

It was time to return to the United States. As soon as we arrived at the airport in London, we checked in with United Airlines. They verified my identity on their computer based on the information the doctor at the hospital had given them. Within a few minutes, a man arrived with a wheelchair. "Mr. Harrison, we will take you to the check-in counter to upgrade your ticket."

At the check-in counter, we were greeted with a long line. The young man told us to wait; he soon returned and wheeled me up to the front of the line. The woman behind the counter said, "Mr. Harrison, I see we are to upgrade you to business class."

"Yes," I said.

She looked down at her computer and began typing in information. She asked to see our passports. I reached for my wallet and pulled out a credit card and laid it on the counter with our passports. She looked up at the credit card and at me and said, "Mr. Harrison, there is no charge for this. Put away your card."

She handed me the new tickets and the man wheeled me away to the customs area. Again he said, "Wait one moment, Mr. Harrison." When he returned, he said, "You have been checked through customs."

He wheeled me to the gate, and a stewardess left the Boeing 747 to greet me and help me out of the wheel chair. She walked with me to the business class section of the plane and said, "Mr. and Mrs. Harrison, these are your seats. Please enjoy your flight."

A few minutes later the rest of the passengers boarded. Two women came up and said, "We think you have our seats."

The stewardess checked our tickets and their tickets. Both sets of tickets were for the same seats. "Remain seated, Mr. Harrison," said the stewardess. "I'll check out the problem."

A few minutes later she returned and said, "Mr. and Mrs. Harrison, please come with me. United has decided to up grade you to first class."

Rebecca and I looked at each other thinking, did we hear that right? But only for a second, then we were up and following her to first class. Our seats were recliners. They laid flat like a bed with a touch of a button. In front of our seats was a coffee table. I have never flown in such luxury before or since. The trip to England became a trip of a lifetime, a time that took a life and returned a life with help from spirit.

Chapter 24
Reflections

Following our return from England, we immediately began receiving calls about the rumors circulating about me having a heart attack. We corrected the misinformation, explaining what had occurred in England to all that called us directly.

My auto insurance company demanded I see a doctor to examine me and see how serious the damage was to my spine. They were very angry at the dealership for not properly fixing the breaks. They wanted the entire car examined in detail. Engineers and attorneys were hired, which included filing a product liability claim against the dealership and the car manufacturer.

The insurance paid for five years of massage and chiropractic work on my body, while the process worked through the system. They wanted me to continue seeing medical doctors, just to make sure they were not treating something else. On the advice of a neurological specialist, the insurance company wanted me to start wearing a steel leg brace. They informed me I would soon lose the ability to use my right leg because of extensive nerve damage; they were surprised that I could even use my right leg. I told them, "You will never put a brace on my leg."

When the insurance company received the bill from Princess Margaret Hospital in Swindon, it didn't include any bills for the emergency room where I had my death experience. When we questioned them, they replied, "We did not charge Mr. Harrison for his visit to the emergency room; therefore, there is no bill or paperwork from that time."

The insurance company was very happy. I know the experience was a choice presented to me on whether or not to stay in the physical.

About a year after my return to the United States, in 1993, my spine began to weaken. The doctors wanted to take another MRI to see what was going on. They found what they thought was a tumor growing on the spine due to constant irritation in the area. They decided to wait one month and take another MRI to see if there had been any changes in my condition.

When they did the second MRI, they found the tumor had almost doubled in size. The doctor decided he wanted to do a biopsy on the growth. So, we made another appointment for an additional MRI for a week later, to be followed in a few days by the biopsy. I made an appointment for the doctor after the third MRI was done, expecting to make another appointment for a biopsy.

I was shown into the doctor's office and asked to wait for about five minutes. Half an hour later the doctor arrived. His face was flushed with anger, and he was stumbling over his words. "I have just looked at the latest MRI," he said. "The doctor who read the films said you have had the growth surgically removed. Now you and I both know it was only a week ago you had the MRI, and you and I both know you have not had surgery. This is absolutely preposterous!"

I said, "Yes, that's correct. I haven't had surgery, and I said in the beginning I will not have surgery again on my spine."

"Well!" he said. "There is nothing I can do for you. I don't need to see you again." He turned and walked out of the room.

When I went to the front desk to check out, the nurse came up to me and said, "The doctor will not see you again."

The following week I asked for a report on the final MRI. I obtained a copy of the report for my files in case it went to trial with the auto manufacturer and dealership. As it turned out, it didn't go to trial.

A year later, out of curiosity, I called the office where my MRI was done and asked for a copy of the same report. The office informed me the doctor's MRI report was missing, which did not surprise me. I still have the MRI report in my files showing where the growth was removed.

Soon after, my spine began to strengthen; it is now stronger than it was before the accident.

* * * * *

After working with thousands of people around the world with Jonah, one thing has become very clear. Jonah works with people by going straight to the core of the problem and bringing it to their full consciousness to be understood. Jonah is not one to use flowery words to stroke the ego. He is always direct and to the point, which some people do not like.

Jonah is a very strong teacher with infinite patience for those who are willing to heal, whether the healing is needed in the mind, emotions, or body. Jonah makes it clear he will never heal anyone. He will give all the assistance available to people for them to heal themselves, including advice to consult a doctor, herbalist, or therapist in addition to their own research. It is the same teaching as the Chinese Master. No one ever heals another. One can assist you to heal yourself. I have never healed anyone, but I have been in the presence of many healings. Sometimes a person's energy is so low he or she doesn't have the energy to heal alone. Someone can assist to increase the person's energy level, so the person can use the energy to heal him or her. There are times when the soul choice for healing is death from this plane onto the next.

Many people have had different experiences with Jonah, whether they are in Jonah's presence or having a session over the phone.

One time, Rebecca and I had been invited to do a group session with Jonah by a group of psychics who had read about me in the newspapers. When the session was completed, many of the psychics explained they had seen four platforms being lowered, two behind and two in front of Jonah. They said it looked like some type of rope at each corner of the platforms. On each platform a person sat taking notes of what Jonah was saying. We asked Jonah about this later, but he would only reply, "It is not of import," meaning it was not important for us to know.

Another person, a physics professor at the University of Colorado, came to see Jonah in person some years ago. She wanted to set her tape recorder next to Jonah. We advised against it, explaining how a week earlier our tape recorder had broken, so we had borrowed Tami's tape recorder. We unintentionally set the tape recorder too close to Jonah. When Jonah came through, smoke started pouring out of the recorder. We bought her a new one the following week. We explained the occurrence to the professor, but she refused to listen.

She said she knew all about physics and was not worried about her tape recorder. The next day we received a phone call from her. She complained the message did not record; in fact, her tape recorder did not work and would not work again. She said the wires were fried. She then demanded, "I want you to pay for a new recorder." We reminded her about the warning we had given her. It had been her choice to ignore the warning. She needed to take responsibility for her choice. We never heard from her again.

Many people have heard a heart beat on their tapes with the message removed. In one case, a person listened to the recorded message from Jonah, but when he tried to listen to it again the next day; he heard only the sound of a heartbeat.

On another occasion, a married couple came to speak with Jonah.

At the beginning of the session, they asked Jonah to prove himself, which Jonah is not into. For whatever reason, when they asked the question, Rebecca saw their car just outside the window behind them take off. Rebecca thought someone had dropped them off and was planning on coming back when the session was over.

Following the session, the couple found their car down the hill in an empty field, just feet from going off a ledge. The car was still in gear with the emergency break on. They became quite upset that Jonah did this. We don't know if Jonah did this because of their question or if their own guides did this. In either case, they chose not to return.

On yet another occasion a couple was having a session over the telephone. They bought new batteries for their tape recorder and set it next to their speakerphone. When the session was over, they found the session with Jonah did not tape. In fact, the new batteries melted inside their tape recorder.

Such events are not common with Jonah, but they show that energy is directed to people to assist them in whatever way they need, whether they are aware of it or not. Many people have experienced events in their lives and built pictures in their minds of those events. Some of those pictures only exist in the subconscious mind. Often those pictures continue a pattern of self-abuse, depression, and or anger. Jonah will help ones discover those pictures and help them release or recreate them into positive experiences from other times. Jonah has helped thousands heal the pain and suffering that interfered with their ability to experience a joyful life.

When Jonah first began speaking through me, he gave us two warnings. The first was a warning about ones attempting to separate Rebecca and me. The second warning was that some would claim to be a medium for Jonah. Jonah told us he would only be speaking through me and would continue to speak through me until I left the physical. Jonah has stated that when the chosen time comes for me to leave the physical, his work would also be completed on the earth plane.

I walk in two different worlds, one physical and one non-physical. Both worlds are very real to me, like a transparency of one world being placed on top of the other. I hear, feel, and experience both worlds simultaneously. My sister once asked me why I had such a problem with hearing people who are talking to me; she wondered if I was losing my hearing. I explained that I continuously hear the energy vibrations from the other world, which makes it challenging to hear people in this reality.

I know that one day I shall pass from this world and go home. I feel I live in a strange land with strange people, as if I am on an extended trip but longing to go home, knowing I will go home when the time is right. I chose to remain, while in England, after I was shown my future involving children and grandchildren to be.

Many of the people and relatives Daryl knew, I do not relate to in terms of memory or emotions. Some have had a difficult time adjusting to the fact that I am not Daryl. I have never been Daryl, and I will never be Daryl. I only carry second-hand memories I have been told but have not experienced as Daryl. I have had the opportunity to meet Daryl in my journeys into the non-physical realm and thank him for allowing me to come into the physical in addition to the opportunity to teach Life Energy Flow and the opportunity to share my father, Jonah, with those who seek assistance.

We continued working with teenagers on the Foundation land in Colorado. The money seems to always be tight, but the assistance to the children continues.

One weekend we had a strong windstorm that blew off most of the roof shingles, which we had been patching over the years. We decided it was time to do something, as it took the rest of our reserves to replace the roof. We were continuing to have problems with UFO groups wanting to come onto the land without our permission. In addition, the state of Colorado was attempting to take away the water rights, which had belonged to the land for over a hundred years. With all of the signs being presented to us, we decided with the board to put the property up for sale. Within days, we had two cash offers for $220,000. Since the property was paid for, it provided a windfall for the Foundation to buy a new facility.

We chose to relocate the Foundation center to Teller County, Colorado, where most of the directors live. We looked at land with a building already on it. Spirit always seems to work in mysterious ways. We found property that had been for sale for some time. We put an offer on the land only to find the owner refused to sell it to us. Then we found another property with a building already on it, but again the owner refused to sell it to us. After the third attempt to buy property fell through, Rebecca and I decided to sit on a large rock on our land and meditate on what the block was.

A blue being appeared, standing in front of Rebecca, but the being was not on our property. It was on the property next door to us, which was undeveloped and not for sale. The next day, I contacted our real estate agent to inquire about the status on the property next door. She called us back and said she found the owner living in California. He told her he was very surprised to receive a call about the property, as he had just decided to sell it the day before. Within thirty days, we closed on the property. We soon found a contractor to build for the Foundation a five-bedroom house with two large rooms where we could do activities with the teenagers

Within one year, the entire project was complete. One day, soon after completion, I was sitting on the front deck looking out at the mountains, when I suddenly remembered what the Bruho in Peru had told me. "Yes, you will own the land next door to the Foundation."

I couldn't stop laughing. I saw how my mind had worked at developing a picture of what things would look like, when in fact it was quite different. The truth was the same; we owned property next door to the Foundation land.

The new location gave us the opportunity to work with teenagers through all seasons from the surrounding community. It gave them the opportunity to come and talk out their problems before the problems developed into external and internal behavior issues.

It has been my dream to begin working with adolescents and teenagers born with unique abilities such as strong intuitive, healing, and/or psychic abilities. They would be children who are unaware of how to use their abilities because their parents do not understand and may be as confused as they are. Many children are born with abilities but suppress them because parents and schools lack understanding. The energy often turns into deep depression and anger. These children need assistance to understand that their abilities are natural. Some simply need help to understand how to use these abilities in the light. It is the light that will set them free from their internal struggle. Jonah did a taped message about such children titled, "Children of the 21st Century." ("Children of the 21st Century Continues.") is soon to be released.

The Foundation continues to expand. I know I carry the vision of the Foundation within my soul. I can feel when it is time to create change and movement for the Foundation. For the last year, I had been receiving visions from my inner being to begin looking at selling the current land the Foundation was on. It was time again to expand what we have to offer those in need. To accommodate this growth, it was time to sell the Foundation land and move to a new facility in the Woodland Park area of Colorado.

This new center will work with all ages. We sold the property to an investor from Washington State for full price, providing sufficient funds to purchase our new facility in Woodland Park. There is space for some of my students to use Life Energy Flow, a location to continue my work with teenagers, and room to expand our work to include adults. The Universal Education Foundation Alternative Healing Center plans to offer many different healing modalities as we grow. Our goal is to offer assistance in healing the mind, body, and spirit to dysfunctional family units, military men or women returning from war with emotional or mental trauma, and abused women.

Tami has worked in the public school system for years, assisting teenagers with special needs, and she has worked with women's shelters as well. She plans to become very active in the future activities of the Foundation Center. We are looking forward to new adventures and continued growth as we move forward with the Adventure Called Life.

Chapter 25
Life Energy Flow
Tai Yi

While I have been writing this book, many have asked me to write about the Life Energy Flow Tai Yi exercises I teach. The name Life Energy Flow is the English version of Tai Yi. Tai Yi has many different meanings, but the core is Supreme Movement. It is not supreme in terms of better than, but rather supreme in terms of the full function of the human body. In a perfectly balanced body, all the energy points work together and support one another. There are more than 4,000 exercises. At this time, I have taught several hundred.

The human body is a grid of energy. Many are aware of meridians in the physical body, but many are not aware of the meridians in the mental and emotional as well as in all seven of the twelve bodies the human body carries. All of these meridians interconnect at points I call gates. These thousands of gates in, on, under, and above the surface of the skin form a complex grid system. Each exercise is specific to an imbalance a person may have.

For example, one of the exercises is titled, "Balancing the Six Emotional Energies." This exercise is for ones who are burned out mentally and emotionally. "Bonding" is an exercise to assist ones wanting to heal and families wanting to heal their family unit. "Dead Child" is an exercise for ones who have experienced extreme child abuse. "Heart and Brain" is an exercise for ones lacking stability; they don't know what they want to do with their life or where they fit in.

"Primordial War" assists ones that have been in a war and still carry war energy, which can lead to self-destructive energy. This exercise can also assist families who have been at war with other family members, such as parents and children. "Under Protection of the Mind" is an exercise for ones with low self-esteem who then act out negative actions of the parents. "Dismantling Fear Pattern" is an exercise for ones in counseling to help them find their own inner truth.

I started my first class in 1994, followed a few years later by a second class. It is my desire to begin a third class for young adults who carry a strong knowledge that healing is their soul-chosen purpose. This class will be limited to ones between the ages of 18 and 30. Each person wanting to attend this new class needs a strong commitment to learning and unlearning of old programmed thoughts.

I am very proud of my students who made the commitment to continue learning these exercises. Some have set up their own practices, assisting many hundreds of people. My students come from various backgrounds: dentists, psychologists, engineers, nurses, chiropractors, acupuncturists, massage therapists, school teachers, mothers, fathers, grandmothers, and great grandmothers. They come from all walks of life with a common purpose, a desire to assist others to heal.

I am currently working on a new book with help from Rebecca, Tami, and my faithful sister, Tina. It will offer some of the simplistic exercises and a more complete understanding of how Life Energy Flow works. I have carried this knowledge in my soul and with the help of my dear teacher, the Chinese Master, I have brought this knowledge forth. It is my desire to keep the knowledge intact in its true form, unpolluted by others. Some have wanted to change the exercises, not understanding what they were doing, not understanding they could harm others. I have asked some to leave the class. It is my purpose to keep Tai Yi in its perfect form to assist others in need.

During one session with my Chinese teacher, I asked him why I was chosen to bring Life Energy Flow Tai Yi into this age. He laughed at me and said, "You were not chosen, but rather you chose to be the one to bring it into physical knowingness during this age, a time when humanity has forgotten the many points of healing the mind, body, and spirit." He continued speaking with me about my involvement with Life Energy Flow Tai Yi. I had retired from using Tai Yi on the general public. I had felt there was not enough time with everything else I was doing. In our continued discussion he reminded me of the ability I had and I should continue using it and to look closely at an opportunity to be presented in the future.

Epilogue

In 1993, we moved to Teller County west of Colorado Springs and bought a small, two-bedroom house on five acres. Jason and Tami had completed high school and were attending college. Jonah told us in 1994, to begin searching for vacant land in the Teller county area. We used his advice and found a larger parcel of land about half an hour south of Cripple Creek.

In 1995, land values increased dramatically. It was our goal to eventually build a house on the land we purchased. In 1997, we were able to sell our two-bedroom house for a profit, enabling us to build a larger home on our land. In time, we built a house on the land and sold it a few years later, enabling us to buy a home on acreage in a different part of Teller County closer to Woodland Park. The long hours of driving required us to be away from our animals for longer periods of time than we desired.

Jonah began doing what he called Intensives three times a year, lasting from Friday evening to early Sunday evening with topics such as "Spiritual Completion," "Essence of the Soul," and "Awakening the Master Within." Jonah teaches exercises on how to heal and prepare for coming changes with the earth's environment. During each Intensive, Jonah conducts five interactive mediations leading ones to their own inner discovery.

I continue to see the Chinese Master. We visit about my present life and past lives—one as a mountain man in Montana and another with the Essenes—as well as other lives in different dimensions. He is one of the strongest teachers I have ever had, but I would never trade him for anything. He is pure love, but he does not tolerate or accept incompetence on any level.

After writing this book and rereading it, I realized how much editing was required to make this book a finished journal of my life. With much help from Frank Slavensky, who strongly believed this book needed to be published, and with assistance from my little sister who painstaking edited every page, my goal was accomplished.

Jonah teaches that often the answer is right in front of us. For several years I looked for ones I could trust to edit the book without changing the content. Then one day it dawned on me to ask Tina, my sister, a professor at a university in Oklahoma. She was born after Daryl left home, so I did not have the opportunity to get to know her as a sister. She was born weighing three and a half pounds at 28 weeks. No one expected her to live, but live she did. Through editing the book, Tina and I have been able to bond to a much deeper level. I have come to enjoy and respect her deep intellect balanced with a loving heart.

Tami gave birth to our first grandchild, Bethany Ann, in 1993. Jason gave us our first grandson, Jonathan, in 1998, with another grandson, Jeremy, born on my birthday in 2004. Having grandchildren has been a wonderful spiritual experience for both Rebecca and me.

Jason went to college to become a licensed heating and air-conditioning installer and service provider. He now works for a non-profit company assisting disadvantaged people needing heat and other comforts most people take for granted.

Tami completed college and received her BA degree and a Master's degree just as the dream I had written 16 years ago predicted. She has taught teenagers at a Colorado middle school as well as teaching at the University of Colorado in Colorado Springs. Tami is also pursuing her second master's degree in Public Administration, focusing in nonprofit management.

In early 2005, my dear friend Bill Dean started a school for troubled adolescent boys in Teller County, Colorado. He recognized the value in using Tai Yi to assist the boys emotionally, mentally, and physically. Bill and his wife Janette have been and are students of mine in the Life Energy Flow Tai Yi School of Healing. Many of the exercises the boys needed I had not taught, nor would I be teaching for some time. Bill requested numerous times, until I relented and decided to come out of retirement, that I begin using my ability on these students. I had remembered what my teacher had told me about accepting an opportunity. I felt this was it. One thing lead to another and I saw how the boys were thriving and healing. None of the boys are ever forced to have Tai Yi. They must request this assistance. Since it has been offered, every boy has requested and continues to request Life Energy Flow Tai Yi as part of their healing.

Life Energy Flow Tai Yi has brought much healing on many different levels. It has brought Bill and me much closer. We have a common goal of assisting children to heal, much the same as we did in the Essene lifetime. Eagle's Nest School for Boys is now a very active part of my life. I still continue my work with Jonah, as I will for the reminder of my life. I have realized when ones are doing what they love, they find the time to do it all. Each day I am thankful to carry this knowledge in my soul and consciousness and I am thankful for the ability to teach and use it again.

After reading and rereading what I had written, Rebecca and I read it together and look at each other in amazement. How could all of this occur in one lifetime? But through it all, Rebecca and I have continued to grow deeper into a sacred marriage beyond time.

As to the rumor concerning the "heart attack" and others over the years, Rebecca and I have learned to look at the bigger picture and do our best to empower the positive in our lives. Over the years, we have come to accept that some would rather believe an illusion in their mind than the truth. Jonah has taught us there are people with beliefs so strong, a contradicting physical event could occur within their sight and they would continue to deny it ever occurred.

We are not to judge where, when, or how one chooses his or her learning but to respect each individual's soul path. When humanity comes to understand the power of love and compassion, mankind will truly be free and at peace.

The End
For Now

Those who desire to learn more of our
work may contact us at the name and
address listed below.

Jonah Life Institute llc

**PO Box 250
Divide, Colorado 80814
719-687-7676
Hossca@aol.com
Web site
Jonahlifeinstitute.com
Or
Jonahlife.com**

ISBN 1425112097-9

9 781425 112097